The Nat Turn[...]

A Mystic Chord Resonates Today

By
Walter L. Gordon, III

6/2/11

Dr. Ouellette:

I feel I know you. Joan speaks so highly of you. Hope you enjoy the book. It so spread the word. It is available on kindle, I-pad, Amazon.com.

Nat [signature]

ISBN 1-4392-2983-X

Library of Congress Control Number: 2009901696

Dedication

To Teresa and Maya Luz

Thanks to Margaret & Quincy Troupe,
as well as Danielle Moody for the
index and print preparation

Table of Contents

Preface

*A religious prophet and his band of followers commit
a bloody massacre on American soil, beheading
victims in the process. In the aftermath most of the
band are killed or captured. Agents of the
government go after them without mercy or due
process. Eventually the courts step in and establish
the rule of law. The leader of the religious band
escapes and is a hunted fugitive for several months.
Finally he is found in a hole in the ground on a farm
near his birthplace. When interrogated after capture
he tells his inquisitors his purpose was to strike
terror in the white inhabitants.*

This scenario does not describe the tale of Saddam Hussein or
Osama Bin Laden. Actually it is a summary of the facts about
the 1831 insurrection led by Nat Turner in Southampton,
Virginia. In 2006, *The Atlantic* magazine listed Nat Turner as
one of the 100 most influential Americans of all time.[1] The
rebellion he led has continuing relevance for Americans,
especially in this age of terror.

The nation's response to the Turner insurrection has
striking parallels in post 9/11 America. The initial reaction
was vengeance, including torture and summary slayings, often
of innocents. Eventually the courts assumed control and
dispensed justice. The 1831 insurrection teaches that to deter
violence, the nation must move past vengeance and torture and
adhere to traditional values by upholding the rule of law.

I have written *The Nat Turner Insurrection Trials* to
explore these parallels. It is the first book on the 1831
insurrection to examine it as a terrorist attack and to draw
lessons from it that are applicable to post 9/11 America. It is
also the first book by a legal scholar to examine in detail the
50 Southampton insurrection trials of slaves and free blacks.
Nat Turner, a literate slave, was the only leader of an
American slave insurrection to bequeath a written record of
his thoughts and state of mind. The book extensively uses the
first person voice of Nat Turner extracted from his

Confessions.

I am a descendent of slaves and a product of the black student movement of the 60's. It was then I first read Turner's *Confessions*, and later, when I taught black politics, it became part of an analysis of African-American political thought. Soon after, I became a lawyer and have practiced, taught, and written about criminal law for many years.

After 30 years, and prior to September 11, 2001, I had reread the *Confessions* and was impressed with Turner's literacy—his ability to read and write, at a time when most whites were barely literate, if at all—as well as Turner's foresight to speak his mind, preserve his voice, so it passed down through the generations.

I have firsthand experience with today's criminal justice system that inflicts penal servitude on a disproportionate number of African-Americans. Of course, this led me to wonder what was the experience of the Turner rebels with the courts in Southampton? In what type of system were they prosecuted? Did they receive justice? I began with a bias, based on my experience, that there was no way they would have received fair trials. Like any competent criminal lawyer, first I had to visit the scene of the alleged crime.

In the late 1990's I drove through the Chesapeake Bay's tidewater region to Courtland in Southampton County. Courtland is a small community out of another age. The courthouse dominates the town. I toured the town and was shown Southern grace and hospitality by the local officials, took a tour of the courthouse, saw the jail nearby and the spot where Nat Turner was hung, the town's most famous personality.

In Nat Turner's time Courtland was named Jerusalem and county court officials dominated Southampton. The court tried slave cases in special courts of *oyer and terminer*, without juries or appeals, and also appointed the sheriff and head of the militia. Large slave owners controlled the county court.

Nat Turner was a slave on a farm about 10 miles outside the town. A black sheriff's deputy gave me directions to Barrow Road, which runs through the countryside where Turner and his band made their bloody trek to Jerusalem. I drove across the bridge over the Nottoway River, and into the countryside where the bloodiest slave rebellion in American history had occurred. The area is deserted with scattered farmhouses and fields. I drove the route the rebels took and went to the famous Cross Keys, which is a junction at the heart of the killing ground, on the way passing the crossroad called Black Head Signpost, where a slave's head was impaled in the wake of the insurrection.

The trip on the back roads reinforced my curiosity about the rebellion and its aftermath, particularly the trials of Turner and his cohorts. I began to research and write the book. Then September 11th happened, and the parallels between today and yesterday became even more compelling.

Nat Turner's trial occurred immediately after the bloodiest slave insurrection in American history. It was a blow to the "Mother of Commonwealths" in its heartland. Racial polarization was at its height and Nat Turner was a religious zealot who believed he was the second coming of Jesus Christ. The atmosphere of hate, fear, and vengeance was palpable, like it was in the aftermath of 9/11. The story also promised insight into the interplay between freedom and slavery, wealth and poverty, black and white. I wondered if the origin of the dualism in criminal law between whites and people of color had its origin in slave law?

This book explores the prosecution and execution of Turner, as well as 49 others, slave and free black, whose cases were adjudicated in the wake of the insurrection. The central issue is could an insurrectionist get a fair trial in the wake of the gravest terrorist act in the more than 200-year history of U.S. slavery? I was surprised to find fairness had occurred. A third of the slaves and free blacks were acquitted and others had their death sentences commuted by a sale out of state. The book explains why this occurred.

The 1831 insurrection was the culmination of a rising tide of insurrection in Antebellum Virginia. Likewise, the fairness in the application of the rule of law by the Virginia elite through the slave courts, intent on impartial fact finding, not vengeance, was the end product of experience in defusing an insurrectionary situation. After Nat Turner's there were no more slave insurrections in Virginia until 1859 when John Brown, born the same year as Nat Turner, raided Harper's Ferry.

Chapter 1

Southampton, Virginia 1831

(A) The Eclipse of 1831

1830-31 was a time of trans-Atlantic social upheaval and rebellion. Belgium, France, and Poland were in revolutionary ferment. In the U.S. this ferment was infused with the fundamentalist religious sentiment of the Second Great Awakening, especially among the Baptist sects. On February 12, 1831 a great eclipse transected the nation's east coast from New England to the Gulf of Mexico. In Washington D.C., where President Andrew Jackson was preparing to run for a second term, the former President John Quincy Adams wrote in his diary: "There was an eclipse of the sun of eleven and three-quarters digits; the sky perfectly clear, but the weather, for the season, was uncommonly cold... There was no darkness, but at the greatest obscuration the light of the sun was pale and sickly. The planet Venus and the star Vega were seen as they sometimes are after sunrise."[2]

The great eclipse of 1831 darkened Richmond, Virginia, where 48-year-old Governor John Floyd, owner of 12 slaves, medical doctor and veteran of the War of 1812, and a former Jackson supporter, was contemplating the future. Floyd, recently elected by the legislature, was the first Governor to serve under the revised 1830 constitution. A fierce advocate of state's rights and an ally of Calhoun in the brewing nullification movement, Floyd did not respect Andrew Jackson. He confided to his diary: "I have often said and here state that Jackson is the worst man in the Union, a scoundrel in private life, devoid of patriotism and a tyrant withal, and is only capable of using power that he may have the gratification of seeing himself obeyed by every human being."[3]

Floyd was an experienced military and political leader, having served as a Major in the militia, and as a legislator in both the Virginia House of Delegates and the House of Representatives. He left Congress to serve as Governor and was the first from the western part of the state. Despite his ownership of slaves, he believed slavery was an evil because it

9

retarded economic development and he vowed to bring legislation to gradually emancipate and deport the state's slaves.[4]

1829-30 was an important period in the political evolution of Virginia. Since 1776, Virginia had been governed by a state constitution that restricted white male suffrage and concentrated legislative power in the hands of the slave holding elite. Since the legislature selected the Governor and judges, the large slave owners dominated the three branches of government. The white population continued to grow after the Revolution, especially in the western part of the state. There was continual agitation in the decades before 1829 to hold a state wide convention to reform the constitution. Finally, the Jacksonian concept of universal white male suffrage had a triumph when a statewide vote, which voters in Southampton opposed, set a constitutional convention for 1829.

The convention, which met in Richmond from October 1829 to January 1830, was a battleground for class and regional politics, the propertied versus the property less, east versus west. The key issue was the extension of the vote to property less white males, on the basis of one man, one vote. The issue was also sectional, since the western part of the state, which subsequently became West Virginia, composed of non-slave owning white farmers, was seeking representation based on population, which would come at the expense of the slave owning east.

James Trezevant, a member of the Southampton oligarchy and a magistrate on the slave court, was one of three representatives from Southampton at the convention where he was joined by the leading lights of Virginia politics, including former Presidents James Monroe, who presided, and James Madison, as well as John Marshall, former Chief Justice of the Supreme Court. Trezevant, from the conservative Tidewater, resisted all change in the status quo, "fearing disruption of the old and established order of things".[5]

The convention ultimately reached a compromise, which preserved the power of the slave owners in the east. Even though white male suffrage was expanded, a third of the state's white males were still denied the vote. The new constitution also provided that the formula used to distribute power was fixed so that further changes in the white male population, particularly the growth in the west, would have no impact on it.[6]

Even though slavery was not explicitly raised at the convention it was evident from press coverage and political agitation leading to the convention that the future of slavery in Virginia was on the table. If majority rule prevailed, slave owners believed that western interests would undermine slavery. Slaves, through the grapevine, were aware of this reality and there were reports that slaves believed that emancipation was the hidden agenda of the convention and some slaves even believed that the convention had voted for emancipation and it was being kept secret from them. As a result, white officials had deep fear of slave unrest and insurrection.[7]

(B) Southampton County

Southampton County, in tidewater Virginia's Black Belt, lies 150 miles south of Washington D.C. and 70 miles below Richmond and roughly the same distance west of Norfolk. It was founded in 1749 and is 600 square miles in the southeast of the state, near the North Carolina border. The famed Dismal Swamp, which straddles the borders of both Virginia and North Carolina, was 25 miles away.

Jerusalem, renamed Courtland in 1888, with a population of 175 in 1831, was the county seat. Southampton was an isolated county, with no newspapers of its own. Jerusalem sat on the banks of the Nottoway River, which was the major artery for travel and moving crops. Soon after the county was created a courthouse was built. Southampton was well-known for its potent apple brandy and many homes had a still and a brandy stocked cellar.[8]

In 1830, Southampton had a population of 16,074, composed of 6,573 whites, 7,756 slaves and 1,745 free blacks. Nearly 60% of its population was African-American and its free black population was one of the largest in tidewater Virginia. The county, especially in the upper part, had a strong

Quaker abolition tradition and this resulted in manumissions that freed many blacks.[9]

Southampton in 1831 was a microcosm of the South and the nation. It had an "oligarchic social and economic structure" that was obscured by a democratic veneer, characterized by widespread white male suffrage. Wealth and power was concentrated in the elite that dominated the county. To belong to the planter elite, ownership of 20 or more slaves was typical. In 1830 only 13 percent of the county's 734 slave owners owned 20 slaves or more. Only 15 men, the aristocracy, owned 50 slaves or more and there were three men who had plantations with over 140 slaves each.[10]

Two-thirds of the white families in Southampton owned slaves. However, concentration of slave owning was a reality. Persons who owned 10 or more slaves controlled more than three-fourths of the slave labor in the county.[11] Farms that could engage in the gang system of production were the most efficient and productive. In Southampton, farms with ten or more slaves owned the best land and produced most of the cotton and peas and nearly half of the corn and pigs. Small slave holders outnumbered the large owners despite the concentration of ownership. This meant that many slaves lived on intimate terms with their owners, often working the fields together.[12]

Southampton was an agricultural county, with regional differences. The Nottoway River bisected the county into upper and lower regions. In the upper portion of Southampton the white and black populations were equal and small and middle sized farms with few or no slaves dominated. Corn and beans were the main crops. The upper part of the county was a microcosm of the upper South.

The lower portion of the county, like the lower South, had larger plantations and slave holdings; the black population outnumbered whites. The lower part of Southampton, with its larger units, produced cotton for market.

The upper and lower parts of Southampton developed different political identities in the 1830's. The upper portion supported the era's liberals, the Whigs, while the lower portion was solidly Democratic, the party of Jackson. The upper part

12

of the county was also home to the Christian evangelical movements of the era which supported abolition. By contrast, the slave owning mentality had a stronghold in lower Southampton.[13]

The type of agriculture in Southampton did not lead to the ownership of large numbers of slaves. Small slaveholders, owning 9 slaves or less, made up 25% of the population. They had similar interests to non-slaveholders who owned land and together the two groups were a majority of Southampton's residents. The elite, who owned 20 slaves or more, were likely residents of lower Southampton. The whites who owned no property or slaves, the lower class, were also more likely residents of the lower part of the county.

(C) The Great Eclipse in Southampton

The eclipse had a peculiar appearance in Southampton, a green or blue day that left citizens with the expectation that something terrible was to happen. For one resident of the county, a 30-year-old field slave, Nat Turner, born and raised in lower Southampton, literate, deeply religious, and well versed in the Bible, the eclipse was the sign from the Holy Ghost he had awaited since 1828.

Nat Turner had visions in which he talked with the Holy Spirit, and was convinced he was divinely ordained to bring a bloody end to slavery. On May 12, 1828, the Holy Spirit had told him:

> ...the Serpent was loosened, and Christ had laid down the yoke he had borne for the sins of men, and that I should take it on and fight against the Serpent, for the time was fast approaching when the first should be last and the last should be first. And by signs in the heavens that it would make know to me when I should commence the great work—and until the first sign appeared, I should conceal it from the knowledge of men—And on appearance of the sign, I should arise and prepare myself, and slay my enemies with their own weapons.[14]

Nat Turner had waited three years for the sign. The

13

eclipse of the sun was it and he sprung into action:

> *And immediately on the sign appearing in the*
> *heavens, the seal was removed from my lips, and I*
> *communicated the great work laid out for me to do,*
> *to four in whom I had the greatest confidence.*

These four—Hark, Nelson, Sam, and Henry—were also field hands.

Hark, 31 years old, owned by Joseph Travis, shared the same homestead with Nat Turner, who was owned by Travis' son-in-law, Putnam Moore, a minor. The two knew each other well, as both had been jointly owned by Thomas Moore, who had died. Hark was known for his powerful body and physical strength. One observer said, "…he was one of the most perfectly framed men he ever saw—a regular black Apollo." He was also compared to Hercules and legend has it that Hark named himself after a Muslim general whose armies conquered much of modern day Iraq and threatened Damascus in 1810.[15]

Sam, a field hand owned by Nathaniel Francis, and near the same age as Hark and Turner, lived nearby. Nathaniel Francis was the male head of a large extended family in lower Southampton. Sally, his sister was married to Joseph Travis, and the families and slaves had frequent interaction.

Nelson—known as a conjurer who could foresee the future—was owned by Jacob Williams, who had a small farm four miles from Jerusalem, the county seat, and owned six slaves. He had hired a white overseer, Caswell Worrell, to supervise the slaves on new ground he was planting.

Henry, the fourth member of the group, was owned by Jacob Porter, and lived on his plantation with 29 other slaves, 10 of whom were men. The plantation was close to the Travis farm so it was easy for Henry to communicate with the others. The five were the hard-core conspirators and were destined to all become Generals in the slave army.[16]

The five also came from a tradition of black on white violence in Southampton County. Between 1785 and 1827, 34 slaves were tried for attacking whites, 16 were convicted, while in the same period only 8 slaves were tried and convicted for attacking blacks.[17] Southampton was one of

14

three Virginia counties with the highest homicide rates for slaves killing whites between 1785 and 1830. This high murder rate was not based on the number of slaves in the population or other demographic factors. Instead, it reflected a tradition among slaves in Southampton to resort to violence to settle grievances with whites.

This tradition was a product of earlier actions by aggressive slaves. In 1799 a coffle of slaves passing through Southampton from Maryland to Georgia rose up and killed their owners. They were convicted and hanged for conspiracy and insurrection. This violent act became part of the slave culture of Southampton. This was the tradition on which the insurgents drew.[18]

Nat Turner was considered a Prophet by his fellow conspirators as well as numerous slaves in the area. One observer noted: "...in his immediate neighborhood, he had acquired the character of a prophet; like a Roman Sybil, he traced his divination in characters of blood on leaves alone in the woods." Aside from the four, the only other person Nat Turner confided in was his wife, with whom he left his papers. She was whipped before she gave them up. They were:

> "... filled with hieroglyphical characters, conveying no definite meaning. The characters on the oldest paper, apparently appear to have been traced with blood; and on each paper, a crucifix and the sun, is distinctly visible; with the figures, 6,000, 30,000, 80,000, &e.-There is likewise a piece of paper, of a late date, which, all agree, is a list of his men; if so, they were short of twenty."[19]

On June 5, 1831, Governor Floyd wrote in his diary that there was much preaching in Richmond and had been so for some time. A religious revival was in process, protected by the constitution but, without realizing the ironic meaning of his words, he noted "this fanaticism which has seized upon the minds of the people, or new zeal, or as they call it a 'revival of religion' would seek to satisfy itself by shedding the blood of their fellow citizens 'for love of the Lord they adore.'"[20]

Little did he know that 5 slaves in Southampton were at that moment planning to shed the blood of all whites in

Southampton to accomplish the command of the Holy Spirit **that the last should be first**. Nat Turner confessed:

> ... *it was intended by us to have begun the work of death on the 4th July last—Many were the plans formed and rejected by us, and it affected my mind to such a degree, that I fell sick, and the time passed without our coming to any determination how to commence.*[21]

No doubt Nat Turner realized the symbolic importance of a strike for liberty on the fifty-fifth anniversary of the nation's declaration of its freedom. There were more practical reasons, however, for the initial choice of the 4th, namely, that it was a major holiday and slaves would have more freedom of movement as whites celebrated.

The state government shut down during the holiday period. Governor Floyd left Richmond on June 29th to visit his plantation, and on the 4th still was on the road with his sick wife. He did not return to the capitol until August 1st.[22]

It is no surprise that Nat Turner became sick under the strain of formulating a plan whereby five unarmed slaves could create a slave army that would destroy slavery. But this raises a more fundamental inquiry, namely, what forces were operating in Southampton in 1831 to produce a Nat Turner, a slave audacious enough to seek the violent overthrow of slavery against overwhelming odds?

To answer this question it is useful to start in 1800, the year of Nat Turner's birth, when social-economic forces were at work that created the conditions he faced as he approached his 31st birthday. On July 4, 1831, the day Nat Turner was too weak to strike, a former President, and Governor of Virginia, James Monroe died. It's ironic that Monroe also played a major role in events in 1800 that would have a profound impact on the course of the insurrection in 1831.[23]

Chapter 2

1800 and the 30-Year Cycle of Insurrection

(A) Gabriel's Insurrection and the 30-Year Cycle of Violence

1800 was a year of political revolution in the United States, as Jefferson was running for President and subsequently would crush Federalist dominance. In Virginia's capital, however, with James Monroe as Governor, an altogether different political revolution was set to explode. Gabriel, a slave blacksmith, had planned an insurrection that had as its goal the capture of Richmond, starting with the "Capitol, the Magazine, the Penitentiary, the Governor's house and his person."[24]

Gabriel, a slave of Thomas Prosser, was born in 1776 on a plantation six miles outside Richmond. He was raised with his owner's son, also named Thomas Prosser, who was born the same year. Young Prosser became Gabriel's owner after his father died. Gabriel learned to read and write as a child and was trained as a blacksmith. In 1800, when he was 24 years old, Gabriel was married, over 6 feet tall, with a powerful chest and arms; he had short hair, a dark complexion, and a long bony face marred by the loss of two front teeth and several scars on his head. Gabriel's owner had business interests in Richmond and Gabriel spent his time between the plantation and the city where he hired himself out as a blacksmith.[25]

Gabriel was also a convicted felon. A year before, he and several others had been caught by an overseer stealing a hog and in a fight between the two Gabriel bit off part of the man's left ear, a capital offense.

Gabriel was tried for the offense in the slave court, called *oyer and terminer*, before five judges without a jury. He had a lawyer but was found guilty. He escaped the death penalty through a procedure called "benefit of clergy." If he could recite a verse from the Bible, he had the option of being branded on his left hand in open court. The brand would mark him as a person ineligible for a reprieve if he was convicted a second time. Gabriel, like many slaves, had knowledge of the Bible. Gabriel was branded and released.[26]

The next year Gabriel was plotting insurrection. The plan was to mobilize 500 to 1,000 armed slaves six miles outside Richmond, rise up and kill their masters, including his young master and the overseer he had maimed, and then proceed to Richmond. Governor James Monroe in a report to the General Assembly noted:

> "They contemplated a force of cavalry as well as infantry and had formed a plan of attack on the city which was to commence by setting fire to the lower end of the town where the houses consisted chiefly of wood, in expectation of drawing the people to that quarter, while they assailed the Penitentiary, Magazine and Capitol, intending after achieving these, and getting possession of the arms, to meet the people unarmed on their return."[27]

Gabriel planned to seize the governor, James Monroe, and to link up with simultaneous slave insurrections in Petersburg and Norfolk. Quakers, Methodists and French people were not to be harmed.

The insurrection was organized by slave artisans who had freedom of movement because of their occupations, and who attended church services, fish feasts and barbecues to recruit participants, including free blacks. Gabriel used his skill as a blacksmith to make swords for the fighters. The leaders of Gabriel's rebellion were assimilated slaves, literate, skilled, urban and knowledgeable about the political divisions among whites. They hoped to gain support from white workers. There was evidence that Gabriel had assistance from two refugees from the French Revolution.[28]

The Gabriel insurrection was to begin on August 30, 1800, a Saturday. Slaves had freedom of movement on weekends and would not alarm whites as they congregated outside the city. An unexpected storm delayed the insurrection and several slaves betrayed the plan to their masters. Immediately the roundup of conspirators began. Gabriel escaped to Norfolk with the help of a white riverboat captain, but was subsequently captured after betrayal by two black crew members. On September 28, 1800, Governor Monroe reported to the members of the Council on Gabriel's capture:

"This slave was brought to my house yesterday about four in the afternoon, and a great crowd of blacks as well as whites gathered round him. I requested Captain Giles who was present to form a guard of fifteen or twenty of the citizens he could collect on the ground and take him under its care to the Penitentiary and continue to guard him there with that number of men, in a separate cell till further orders: holding no conversation with him on any subject, or permitting any other person to do so."[29]

Governor Monroe hoped to get a confession from Gabriel but lamented on October 5th "it appeared he had promised a full confession, but on his arrival here he declined making it. From what he said to me, he seemed to have made up his mind to die, and to have resolved to say but little on the subject of the conspiracy."[30]

Sixty-seven slaves were tried between September and October 1800. Most were convicted of an offense, 27 were hanged, including Gabriel and two of his brothers, but 19 were acquitted. Gabriel's rebellion had the potential for great violence but in the end no white lives were taken.[31]

On September 15, 1800, before Gabriel was captured, Monroe wrote Jefferson, who was in the midst of a presidential campaign, to update him on the insurrection. "We have had much trouble with the negroes [sic] here. The plan of an insurrection has been clearly proved, & appears to have been of considerable extent."[32] Monroe told Jefferson that 10 were executed and 20 to 40 remained to be tried. He then expressed his misgivings about executions. The public hangings of the rebels crystallized Monroe's thoughts about capital punishment for slaves, sentiments brewing in the ruling class generally for some time. Jefferson in a 1779 draft proposal for the Virginia penal code observed "that cruel and sanguinary laws defeat their own purpose" and that execution was "the last melancholy resource."[33]

Both Jefferson and Monroe were veterans of the

American Revolution and were conscious they were living in a revolutionary age. The American Revolution had spread doctrines of political equality and human rights. The revolutionary war had resulted in the freeing of many slaves in Virginia both through the turmoil of war itself and manumissions afterward.[34]

American revolutionary ideas spread to France where they inspired the French Revolution, which abolished slavery in 1794. Events in France were closely followed in Virginia where the revolution had support among Jeffersonian Republicans. But the French revolution itself triggered a slave and free black revolution in what is now known as Haiti. Refugee planters from Haiti were arriving in Virginia with their slaves. It is estimated that 12,000 slaves from Haiti entered the United States. The port at Norfolk was a favorite entry point for the Haitian refugees. There is evidence that a refugee and a slave settled in Southampton. The events in Haiti inspired the slave rebels in Richmond.[35]

Finally, in Richmond itself, 1800 was a year of fierce political struggle between Federalists and Republicans over the year's presidential election. There were harsh threats of nullification and civil war after the passage of the Alien and Sedition Acts in 1798, which Republicans thought were designed to suppress their party. Gabriel sought to use these divisions between white elites to carry out the insurrection.[36]

Monroe interviewed Gabriel, and the other slave rebels, and understood they were revolutionaries inspired by the same ideals that had inspired his own participation in the American struggle. Monroe expressed this idea in a message to the General Assembly, seeking to explain the insurrectionary spirit among the slaves: "A variety of causes contribute to produce this effect, among which may be enumerated the contrast in the condition of the free negroes [sic] and slaves, the growing sentiment of liberty existing in the minds of the latter, and the inadequacy of the existing patrol laws."[37]

Both Monroe and Jefferson knew that executed rebels became martyrs adding fuel to the revolutionary fire. Experience had taught them, and other members of the elite, that unrestrained use of the death penalty did not deter a human being determined to gain his liberty. Only a shift to a humane policy that showed firmness but mercy could dampen the ardor for freedom. At the time of the Gabriel insurrection the Governor had no alternative punishment at his disposal, but Monroe believed the Governor should have power to grant mercy by selling a rebel out of state. In a letter to Jefferson on September 15, 1800 Monroe lamented to Jefferson:

> "When to arrest the hand of the Executioner, is a question of great importance. It is hardly to be presumed, a rebel who avows it was his intention to assassinate his master & if pardoned will ever become a useful servant. And we have no power to transport him abroad, nor is it less difficult to say whether mercy or severity is the better policy in this case, tho' when there is cause for doubt it is best to incline to the former council."[38]

The next year the ruling class reached a consensus and the legislature passed a statute that allowed transportation of slaves involved in insurrection and rebellion. There was also a strong economic motive intertwined with transportation, since the state could recoup the money it paid the owner from a sale, which it could not do if the slave was executed.[39]

Gabriel's rebellion entered into the folklore of both blacks and whites in Virginia. It was the subject of songs and lived on in the traditions of the people in the region. Both Nat Turner and John Brown were born in 1800. The former 8 days before Gabriel was hanged. Gabriel's insurrection set off a roughly 30-year cycle of major insurrections in Virginia, led by Nat Turner in 1831 and John Brown in 1859, both inheritors of Gabriel's tradition.[40]

(B) Jefferson's Election

The 1800 presidential election was won by Jefferson because of the extra electoral votes he gained from the three-fifths clause in the Constitution which allotted the South extra seats in the House of Representatives and the Electoral College based on its slave population. Jefferson got twelve to fourteen electoral votes because of the slave count, in a race in

21

which he received in total 8 more electoral votes that his opponent John Adams. This is the reason he was labeled the "Negro President."[41]

In June 1801, Governor Monroe wrote now President Jefferson informing him Virginia had passed a transportation statute and requested assistance in acquiring land for the transported slaves. Monroe noted:

> "This resolution was produced by the conspiracy of the slaves which took place in this city and neighborhood last year, and is applicable to that description of persons only. The idea of such an acquisition was suggested by motives of humanity, it being intended by means thereof to provide an alternate mode of punishment for those described by the resolution, who under the existing law might be doomed to suffer death. It was deemed more humane."[42]

Monroe had a much broader goal in mind, however, when he sought a site for the deported slaves. Monroe, like Jefferson at the time, and others of the Virginia elite, believed that slavery was at its core evil and a contradiction to the principles they had fought for in the American Revolution. Each time there was an insurrection the old revolutionaries were embarrassed by world opinion. In the same letter to Jefferson, Monroe noted: "It is impossible not revolve in it, the condition of those people, the embarrassment they have already occasioned us, and are still likely to subject us to. We perceive an existing evil which commenced under our Colonial System, with which we are not properly chargeable, or if at all not in the present degree, and we acknowledge the extreme difficulty of remedying it."[43]

In November, 1801, Jefferson replied, indicating he agreed that it was necessary to procure lands outside the U.S. "to form a receptacle for these people." Jefferson advised it was best not to have the colony on the North American continent as it was too close to the domestic slave population. The best location was in the West Indies, especially Haiti. Jefferson wrote Monroe:

> "The most promising portion is the island of St.

Domingo, where the blacks are established into a sovereignty *de facto,* & have organized themselves under regular laws & government. I should conjecture that their present ruler might be willing, on many considerations, to receive even that description which would be exiled for acts deemed criminal by us, but meritorious, perhaps, by him."[44]
The Virginia legislature did not approve Haiti as a destination because it might serve as a base for insurgents to attack the slave system in the state. Jefferson also sought a haven in Sierra Leone but the British did not want to accept insurgents and no overseas territory was acquired in Jefferson's term. The Virginia statute provided that transported felons must be sold out of the United States but the requirement was difficult to enforce.[45]

Two successes of the Jefferson administration, the purchase of Louisiana in 1803, and the closing of the international slave trade in 1808, had a profound impact on slavery in Virginia, and the rest of the nation. Both of these events were deeply influenced by the slave insurrection in Haiti, which raged from 1791 to 1806. Napoleon's decision to sell Louisiana was a direct result of the destruction of his armies in Santo Domingo. The main reason the U.S. acted so expeditiously to forbid the importation of slaves was the fear of rebellious Africans entering the South.[46]

Technological advances, especially the saw gin, coupled with the 800,000 square miles of fertile land in the Louisiana Purchase and the rising demand for cotton, led to an explosive demand for slave labor at a time when the international supply was drastically reduced. There was a massive expansion of the plantation system, with one of the largest internal migrations in U.S. history, as the slave population was redistributed from the upper South to the lower South and Southwest. In 1790 Virginia and Maryland held over 56 percent of the nation's slave population. By 1820 this proportion had declined to 35 percent and continued to drop so that on the eve of the Civil War these two states had just 15 percent of the slave population.[47]

Cotton production was the reason. Cotton was a minor

crop at the time of the American Revolution. Tobacco was king. The invention of the cotton saw gin, the most important technological innovation in the antebellum period, changed everything. At the start of the 19th century around 1 percent of all slaves lived on cotton plantations and by 1850 this rose to 64 percent.[48]

Cotton production was the most important influence on the growth of the American economy in the antebellum period. This strategic industry dominated the export trade, constituting 39 percent of the value of exports between 1816 to 1820 which increased to 63 per cent from 1836 to 1840. The wealth from cotton led to the expansion of the internal market. Income from cotton was used to pay for food production in the West and financial services in the Northeast. It provided the capital for the development and expansion of the nation's manufacturing base, particularly textiles. Before the Civil War, the manufacture of cloth was the nation's primary heavy goods industry and its textile mills and machine shops provided the tools for the industrial revolution in the U.S.[49]

Cotton also led to the relative economic decline of Virginia, even as it diversified from tobacco into production of cereal and grain. The state was not a major cotton grower. It had begun to export slaves to the newer cotton growing slave states in the 1790's and the pace of this exportation increased substantially after the ending of the African slave trade in 1808. This domestic trade reached its peak in the 1830's when over 118,000 slaves left the state. There were 469,757 slaves in Virginia in 1830, which decreased to 448,987 by 1840, despite the natural increase of the slave population. This trade, which was an important source of investment capital, had a devastating impact on the enslaved family networks, often separating spouses and teenage children from their families. The trade, along with owners migrating South with slaves, disproportionately affected young-adult slaves. Nat Turner, born in 1800, was raised in this turmoil.[50]

Chapter 3

Native Son: Nat Turner in Southampton

Nat Turner was born on October 2, 1800 in
Southampton. The baby was named Nathaniel, which meant
"the gift of God." His mother, Nancy, was an olive-skinned
African, purchased by Benjamin Turner from a slave coffle
sometime in 1799. Legend has it she was born in North Africa
near the Nile, captured while a teenager, and marched to West
Africa, sold to white traders and, after enduring the middle
passage, and the slave insurrection in Haiti, reached Norfolk in
1795.[51] At this time in Virginia history it was rare for an
African immigrant to enter the state. By the time of the
American Revolution native born slaves dominated the
Virginia slave population, when two percent were Africans. In
1800 there were only 678 Africans in the total Virginia slave
population of 346,000, less than 1 percent.[52]

Legend has it that Nancy, the name given to her by her
owner, was so distraught about bringing a child into slavery
she was tied so she would not murder him.[53] Infanticide was
not unknown in Virginia. Between 1785 and 1831 eight slave
women were either executed or transported, i.e., sold outside
the state, for this crime. Infanticide, however, was difficult to
detect or distinguish from late-term abortions or stillbirths.
Newborns were also victims of disease and accidents and to
draw the line between such a demise and an intentional killing
was difficult.[54]

The name of Nat's father is unknown. He was the son of
another slave on the Turner plantation, Old Bridget. In the
early years of his life, Nat Turner's father was present and
played a role in his early development and sense of self. Nat
was a precocious child and when he was very young had an
experience that shaped his life. He remembered:

> *Being at play with other children, when three or four*
> *years old, I was telling them something, which my*
> *mother overhearing, said it had happened before I*
> *was born—I stuck to my story, however, and related*
> *somethings which went, in her opinion, to confirm*

> *it—others being called on were greatly astonished,*
> *knowing that these things had happened, and caused*
> *them to say in my hearing, I surely would be a*
> *prophet, as the Lord had shewn [sic] me things that*
> *had happened before my birth. And my father and*
> *mother strengthened me in this my first impression,*
> *saying in my presence, I was intended for some great*
> *purpose, which they had always thought from certain*
> *marks on my head and breast.*[55]

Nat Turner's father also left another deep impression on him when he escaped slavery by running away, while Nat was still a youth.[56]

Benjamin Turner, Nat's owner, was the third generation of slave owning Turners in Southampton. Nat grew up on a plantation of several hundred acres on Rosa Swamp not far from Jerusalem. Turner owned 30 slaves by 1810 which he had acquired through inheritance, marriage, and purchase. Benjamin Turner and his wife broke with the Anglican faith of his ancestors and became Methodist after the American Revolution. He was active and did all he could do to spread the message of free will and individual salvation to residents of Southampton, including his human property. The Turners held prayer services on the plantation and took the slaves to church on Sunday.[57]

Turner raised tobacco, corn, apples and cotton. The land was so forested that only 100 acres was used to plant crops. Turner's farm was self-sufficient and had large herds of hogs and cattle. There were skilled slave artisans on the plantation who could distill brandy, preserve meat, spin, weave, and do the coopering and carpentering jobs necessary. Turner had a large store of apple brandy in the basement of his two-story house.

Benjamin Turner had three sons and two daughters, and Nat was close to the youngest, John Clark Turner, who was near his own age. Both boys received the same religious instruction. In the Sunday school a spelling book and reader were used to teach the children. Benjamin Turner's children were instructed by private tutors and teachers in small community schools. This was a break from the past as

Benjamin Turner's ancestors were not literate.[58]

In this setting, Nat Turner became literate at an early age. In his confession he said:

> *The manner in which I learned to read and write, not only had great influence on my own mind, as I acquired it with the most perfect ease, so much so, that I have no recollection whatever of learning the alphabet—but to the astonishment of the family, one day, when a book was shewn [sic] me to keep me from crying, I began spelling the names of different objects—this was a source of wonder to all in the neighborhood, particularly the blacks—and this learning was constantly improved at all opportunities.[59]*

Nat was close to his grandmother, Old Bridget, who was very religious. One can only speculate on the stories his African mother told him or the traditions she passed on to him. His grandmother must also have passed on her wisdom of survival in slavery through religious belief. Nat's master exposed him to white religious leaders who often visited. All, including his grandmother and master, observed the boy's precocity, and as Nat observed:

> *... noticing the singularity of my manners, I suppose, and my uncommon intelligence for a child, remarked I had too much sense to be raised, and if I was, I would never be of any service to any one as a slave—To a mind like mine, restless, inquisitive and observant of everything that was passing, it is easy to suppose that religion was the subject to which it would be directed, and although this subject principally occupied my thoughts—there was nothing that I saw or heard of to which my attention was not directed.[60]*

Nat grew up with a sense of his own superiority and uniqueness. He was not alone in this perception as both blacks and whites knew he was a gifted child. When Nat was around nine years old he began to experience the traumas of slavery. First, his father fled North to escape bondage, never to be seen or heard again. Then, Nat and his mother were loaned to

Samuel Turner, the eldest son of Benjamin, who had purchased 360 acres from his father, two miles south of the home plantation.

In 1810, a year later, Benjamin, in his early fifties, died after a typhoid epidemic hit Southampton. The death of a slave master was always a gut wrenching event for his human property. It opened the door to sales, breakup of families, and removal to a distant site, far from the place of birth. Nat was fortunate because Benjamin's 30 slaves were divided among his wife and five children. Nat, his mother and grandmother, were devised to Samuel Turner and remained in Southampton.[61]

Samuel Turner was in his mid-twenties when his father died. He was deeply religious like his father, and completed building a Methodist church on an acre of land donated by his father. Between ten and twelve, Nat was sent to work in the fields. His days were occupied by the farm routine often dictated by the predictable schedule of planting and harvesting the cotton, corn and other crops. Nat was a field hand and did not train as an artisan. Cotton had replaced tobacco as a major crop in Southampton after 1800 and between 1818 and 1822 there was a major depression in cotton prices which caused economic hardship to Samuel Turner and other farmers in the region. Nat Turner, while working in the fields did not focus on the economic hardship. The hard physical labor did not lessen his intellectual curiosity. Nat noted:

> When I got large enough to go to work, while employed, I was reflecting on many things that would present themselves to my imagination, and whenever an opportunity occurred of looking at a book, when the school children were getting their lessons, I would find many things that the fertility of my own imagination had depicted to me before; all my time, not devoted to my master's service, was spent either in prayer, or in making experiments in casting different things in moulds made of earth, in attempting to make paper, gun-powder, and many other experiments, that although I could not perfect, yet convinced me of its practicability if I had the

means.[62]

Despite Nat's obsession with religion, and his strict morals which forbade stealing, he was no prude. The other slaves recognized his superior ability and would take him with them *when they were going on any roguery, to plan for them.*[63]

At this time Nat Turner began to create a mystique around his person. He prayed, fasted, and lived an austere lifestyle which was noticed by both blacks and whites. Nat was aware of his uniqueness from childhood and cultivated a persona that expressed it:

> *Having soon discovered to be great, I must appear so, and therefore studiously avoided mixing in society, and wrapped myself in mystery...*[64]

This occurred during an economic depression in Southampton in the early 1820's, when the price of cotton dropped from 30 cents a pound to less than 10 cents. It was about this time that Nat Turner began to have the religious experiences that defined for him his main purpose in life. One biblical passage struck him with particular force, *"Seek ye the kingdom of Heaven and all things shall be added unto you."* The realization that, despite his gifts, he was a slave sunk into his soul. *Now finding I had arrived to man's estate, and was a slave, and these revelations being made known to me, I began to direct my attention to this great object, to fulfil [sic] the purpose for which, by this time, I felt assured I was intended.* One day while praying at his plow, the Spirit spoke to him repeating the passage above and he realized it was the same Spirit *that spoke to the prophets in former days.*[65] Nat Turner began to prepare his fellow slaves, who said his *wisdom came from God*, for his purpose *by telling them something was about to happen that would terminate in fulfilling the great promise that had been made to me.* He also married a woman on the Turner plantation named Cherry.[66]

In 1821, Samuel Turner hired a white overseer to increase production. This was unusual among the small plantations where the owner or a trusted slave usually supervised the work gangs. Apparently the overseer whipped Nat Turner who ran away for 30 days. He hid in the woods around the farm. The blacks thought he had escaped North like his father. When he returned of his own free will, the slaves on the plantation thought he was foolish for coming back since he had the intelligence to escape and not serve as a slave. But Nat Turner's return was a calculated act:

> But the reason of my return was, that the Spirit appeared to me and said I had my wishes directed to the things of this world, and not to the kingdom of Heaven, and that I should return to the service of my earthly master—"For he who knoweth his Master's will, and doeth it not, shall be beaten with many stripes, and thus have I chastened you."[67]

In 1822, Samuel Turner suddenly died, leaving a wife and children, along with 23 slaves. Nat was 22 years old and worth $450, the value of a field hand. The blacksmiths, coopers, distillers and other skilled hands were worth $600. Samuel Turner's will provided that Nat's mother and grandmother would remain with his wife. However, Nat Turner and his wife, along with 18 other slaves were sold. This was at a time when Virginia was selling slaves to the cotton fields of the deep South. Both Nat and his wife were fortunate and, even though purchased by different owners, remained in Southampton.[68]

Nat Turner was bought by Thomas Moore who had a 720 acre spread three miles from the Turner plantation. Nat's wife, Cherry, valued at only $40, was purchased by Giles Reese who had a farm in the same area. The couple did not lose contact with each other, and they remained near other family members. Cherry eventually had a daughter and one or two sons by Nat Turner. His new master was a man on the rise. Several years before he had married Sally Francis who was a member of a prominent family in Southampton and was near the same age as Nat. Sally and Nat had known each other since childhood. Nat was purchased to work the fields. Moore intended to reap the labor from his investment.[69]

Nat Turner spent hours behind a mule, plowing the fields. The mule would urinate, defecate and fart in his path. There is also evidence that Nat had an even worse experience with a mule, when one kicked him in the head and left a scar on his temple.[70] Around 1825, Nat had a powerful vision. The

Spirit appeared again:

> And I saw white spirits and black spirits engaged in
> battle, and the sun was darkened-the thunder rolled
> in the Heavens, and blood flowed in streams-and I
> heard a voice saying, "Such is your luck, such you
> are called to see, and let it come rough or smooth,
> you must surely bear it."[71]

Nat Turner was a Baptist exhorter and prophet. An
exhorter was a lay preacher who was not ordained or part of a
church. He was called by the Spirit and preached. There was a
tradition of slave lay preachers in the Baptist church and the
democratic spiritual practices of the Baptist church were
probably one of the reasons Nat Turner was attracted to it and
did not follow the Methodist faith of his prior owners. Nat,
while exhorting and singing at neighborhood meetings and in
the slave quarters, did not draw on his African mother's
tradition, even though he had gained great power over his
listeners. Nat preached with a purpose knowing he was called
to perform a great task. He did not use *conjuring and such like
tricks-for to them I always spoke of such things with
contempt.*[72]

Visions were also a part of the Baptist practice. It was
not uncommon for members to find the Lord through a
visionary experience. These visions, however, usually fit a
common pattern, involving an introspective look at the self
while the spiritual journey was made from hell to heaven with
a guide that led to an encounter with the splendors of Heaven
and God, often with an emphasis on whiteness. Nat Turner's
visions were both auditory and visual and were of a radically
different quality than the traditional ones. His visions were
violent and bloody in which white and black spirits battled on
equal terms. Moreover, his contact was with the Spirit, not
God as was common in the ordinary Baptist visions. This
separated him from other Baptist vision experiences where the
believer usually encountered Christ or God.[73]

After Nat had the vision of white and black spirits at
bloody war, he withdrew from those around him and went into
himself. He wanted to serve the Spirit more fully and entered
into communion with it. The Spirit spoke to him of the past

things it had revealed to him since childhood and it also revealed *to me the knowledge of the elements, the revolution of the planets, the operation of tides, and changes of the seasons.*[74] Nat claimed supernatural powers to cure disease and to command the weather and clouds.[75]

For three years Nat made his spiritual explorations guided by the Spirit. He fasted and prayed and continued his visionary experience with the Spirit. He gained *true knowledge of the faith* and the *Holy Ghost was with me, and said,*

> *"Behold me as I stand in the Heavens"—and I looked and saw the forms of men in different attitudes—and there were lights in the sky to which the children of darkness gave other names than what they really were—for they were the lights of the Saviour's hands, stretched forth from east to west, even as they were extended on the cross on Calvary for the redemption of sinners.*[76]

Inspired by the vision, Nat Turner continued to pray for the revelation of its meaning. Shortly afterwards, while in the fields, *I discovered drops of blood on the corn as though it was dew from heaven.* He also discovered *on the leaves in the woods hieroglyphic characters, and numbers, with the forms of men in different attitudes, portrayed in blood, and representing the figures I had seen before in the heavens.*[77]

At this point Nat Turner emerged from his isolation and began to preach to whites and blacks about what he had seen. This was a time when religious fervor of the Second Great Awakening was sweeping eastern Virginia, including Southampton. The recollections of James L. Smith, another slave exhorter in Virginia during Nat's life, suggest how he worked. Smith states that after work on a Saturday he would walk a 24 mile circuit throughout the night holding prayer meetings at packed slave cabins on the route, where singing and prayer would take place to daybreak. On Sunday he would move on to other cabins spending the day repeating the process. Then he would have to walk the long route back to his farm for Monday's labor. Smith recollected:

"The way in which we worshipped is almost

indescribable. The singing was accompanied by a certain ecstasy of motion, clapping of hands, tossing of heads, which would continue without cessation about half an hour; one would lead off in a kind of recitative style, others joining in the chorus. The old house partook of the ecstasy; it rang with their jubilant shouts, and shook in all its joints. "[78]

Nat Turner, like Smith, walked throughout Southampton spreading the news of his vision. He crisscrossed all the paths and byways of the neighborhood. The most dramatic example of his charismatic power came after a vision in which the Holy Ghost revealed itself and made plain the meaning of the bloody images Nat had witnessed; Nat realized *the great day of judgment was at hand.*[79] In 1827, he told his revelations to Etheldred T. Brantley, a respectable white overseer, who immediately ceased his sinful behavior and broke out with *a cutaneous eruption, and blood oozed from the pores of his skin.* After Nat prayed and fasted with him for nine days the pox disappeared. The Spirit again appeared to Nat Turner and told him that *as the Saviour had been baptised [sic] so should we be also.*

Nat sought to perform the baptism in one of the local white churches but was refused. Nat was undeterred and announced he would hold the dual baptism at Pearson's Mill Pond in the heart of the forest. On the day of the event a crowd of whites and slaves gathered to watch. *We went down into the water together,* Nat confessed, *in the sight of many who reviled us, and were baptised [sic] by the Spirit.* After the baptism Nat Turner rejoiced and thanked God, but Brantley became an outcast among whites and took a job in North Carolina.[80]

Baptism, the symbolic drowning and rebirth in living waters, was a central ritual in the faith among slave converts which, perhaps, had a mystic echo of the African past with its rites of passage involving water. To slaves watching Nat Turner baptize Brantley it must have reconfirmed his mystery and their belief that he was a prophet with supernatural powers. Here was a slave, a field hand no less, making concrete the fact that the least among them could lead the mighty to salvation. The whites did not view the event or Nat Turner in the same light. He was dismissed as inconsequential, an invisible man in the invisible church.[81]

It was right after the Brantley episode that Nat Turner had his most significant vision. The date was burned into his memory:

> And on the 12th of May, 1828, I heard a loud noise in the heavens, and the Spirit instantly appeared to me and said the Serpent was loosened, and Christ had laid down the yoke he had borne for the sins of men, and that I should take it on and fight against the Serpent, for the time was fast approaching when the first should be last and the last should be first. And by signs in the heavens that it would make known to me when I should commence the great work—and until the first sign appeared, I should conceal it from the knowledge of men.[82]

At last, Nat Turner saw the way. When the celestial sign appeared he *should arise and prepare myself, and slay my enemies with their own weapons.*[83] Until the sign he was not to reveal his plan to anyone. He was faithful to this stricture except that he told his owner, Thomas Moore, that slaves ought to and would be free one day. Moore whipped him for insolence.[84]

In 1828, Thomas Moore died. His wife, Sally, was named administrator of his estate. Moore left six slaves, including Nat, to his nine year old son Putnam. Under Virginia law, if Sally had received a life estate in the slaves and remarried, the slaves would belong to her new husband for the length of her life. A year later, on October 5, 1829, Sally Francis Moore married Joseph Travis, a wheelwright, who moved to her farm. He supervised Nat and the 17 other slaves, including Hark, who Nat Turner had met when both were owned by Thomas Moore.[85]

Nat Turner had managed to escape sale outside Southampton once again. Estate sales and divisions were one of the most common causes of migration of slaves outside the home county and frequently to the deep South. This was particularly true between 1815 and the 1830's, the highpoint of the domestic slave trade. Young blacks under 19 were the group most likely to leave Southampton. Nat Turner was 29 years old and this age group was much less likely to migrate. One reason was that slave owners liked to keep slave couples near each other during the peak childbearing years.[86]

Nat Turner waited for his heavenly omen while political events swirled around him. After the revelation on May 12, 1828, Nat's eyes were turned to heaven for the sign to *commence the great work.* He had to wait two years and nine months. The sign happened on February 12, 1831 when a solar eclipse darkened Southampton, along with much of the eastern seaboard. As Nat Turner entered the late summer of 1831, he and his four cohorts were still searching for the precise plan to end slavery.[87]

Insurrection Time-Line 1831[88]

13 August   <u>Saturday</u>, the Second Omen, the Sun appeared with a black spot.

21 August   <u>Sunday</u>, The seven conspirators: Nat Turner, Hark, Henry, Nelson, Sam and Jack eat the Last Supper at Cabin Pond.

22 August   <u>Monday</u>

(A) Blood Trek to Barrow Road

2:00 A.M.   Attack on Travis House and Salathial Francis

5:30 A.M.   Piety Reese

6:00 A.M.   Sunrise and attack on Elizabeth Turner & Henry Bryant

7-8:00 A.M. Whitehead House, Richard Porter, Howell Harris & T. Doyle

8:30 A.M.   Nathaniel Francis House and Peter Edwards

(B) Barrow Road to Jerusalem

9-10:00 AM	John T. Barrow, George Vaughn, Newit Harris
10:00 A.M.	Levi Waller, William Williams
11:00 A.M.	Jacob Williams, Caswell Worrell
12 Noon	Rebecca Vaughn
1:00 P.M.	Parker's Field
8-9:00 P.M.	Ridley's Quarter

23 August   Tuesday

6:00 A.M.	Sunrise Dr. Blunt's, Hark captured; flight to Newit Harris where Will killed; free blacks led by Billy Artist join rebels
8-9:00 A.M.	Curtis & Stephen captured
12 Noon	Billy Artist leads raiding party to Nathaniel Francis house
3-4:00 P.M.	Billy Artist and Thomas Hathcock return to Blunt's
Night	Nat Turner goes underground.

Chapter 4

Insurrection: *The Valley of Bones*

(A) The Last Supper

On Saturday morning, August 13, 1831 a second celestial phenomenon occurred which Nat Turner took as the Spirit's final sign. The sun on rising "seemed to have changed from the usual brilliant golden color to a pale greenish tint, which soon gave place to a cerulean blue, and this also to a silvery white. In the afternoon he [sic] appeared like an immense circular plane of polished silver, and by the naked eye a black spot could be seen. It shone with a dull, gloomy light; the atmosphere was moist and hazy."[89]

This sign erased any confusion existing in Nat Turner's mind.

> *Still forming new schemes and rejecting them, when the sign appeared again, which determined me not to wait longer.*

A week later, on August 20th, Nat Turner agreed with Henry and Hark to prepare a dinner the next day for the conspirators to decide on a final plan. They agreed to rendezvous at the Cabin Pond deep in the woods near the Travis house.

> *Hark, on the following morning, brought a pig, and Henry brandy, and being joined by Sam, Nelson, Will and Jack, they prepared in the woods a dinner, where, about three o'clock, I joined them.*[90]

Hark's stealing of the pig was symbolic of the Rubicon the conspirators were crossing. Hogs were an institution in Virginia and the law gave them special protection. Hog stealing by slaves was a perennial problem and there was a law exclusively for them that made hog stealing a capital offense on the third conviction, even though there's no evidence that any slave was ever executed for the crime. The punishment for slaves was harsher than that for whites for the same offense. But the conspirators wanted meat for the important supper and the stolen pig was small recompense for their free labor.[91]

Nat Turner, the Prophet, took his time joining the other

conspirators and, with his profound knowledge of the Bible, had probably **The Book of the Prophet Ezekiel** on his mind. The verses:

> **An end is come, the end is come: it watcheth for thee; behold it is come; And the Lord said unto him, Go through the midst of the city, through the midst of Jerusalem, and set a mark upon the foreheads of the men that sigh and that cry for all the abominations that be done in the midst thereof. Slay utterly old and young, both maids, and little children, and women...**[92]

He was aware of his aura, the mystery that surrounded him at this supreme moment. When asked why he was so backward in joining them, Nat Turner responded: *The same reason that caused me not to mix with them for years before.*[93]

Will and Jack were new recruits. The Prophet described his encounter with the core conspirators as follows:

> *I saluted them on coming up, and asked Will how came he there, he answered, his life was worth no more than others, and his liberty as dear to him. I asked him if he thought to obtain it? He said he would, or loose his life. This was enough to put him in full confidence. Jack, I knew, was only a tool in the hands of Hark.*[94]

Hark was married to Jack's sister and had brought him to the meeting. The band had still not decided on a plan. Nat Turner said it was time and took them out, one by one, and had a long conversation with each. After the talks the core conspirators met in a group with brandy when Jack, the youngest, began to protest that they were too few in number after he was told the group "intended to rise and kill all the white people." Hark told him that as they went on and killed the whites the blacks would join them. Nat Turner then improvised the insurrection on a serpentine path through the swampy countryside near Cross Keys, twenty miles from Jerusalem. The first milestone was Barrow Road, which took 6 hours and much killing to reach.[95]

> *It was quickly agreed we should commence at home (Mr. J. Travis') on that night, and until we had armed*

and equipped ourselves, and gathered sufficient force, neither age nor sex was to be spared, (which was invariably adhered to.)[96]

On the march to the Travis home, the insurgents bypassed the home of Giles Reese, who rented land in a swampy location near the Cabin Pond. Nat Turner's wife, Cherry, and his children, were Giles' property.[97]

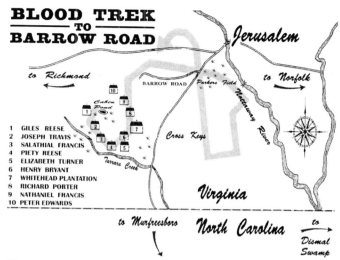

BLOOD TREK
TO
BARROW ROAD

Jerusalem

to Richmond

BARROW ROAD · *Parkers Field*

to Norfolk

Cabin Road

1 GILES REESE
2 JOSEPH TRAVIS
3 SALATHIAL FRANCIS
4 PIETY REESE
5 ELIZABETH TURNER
6 HENRY BRYANT
7 WHITEHEAD PLANTATION
8 RICHARD PORTER
9 NATHANIEL FRANCIS
10 PETER EDWARDS

Cross Keys

Nottoway River

Tamara Creek

Virginia

to Murfreesboro   *North Carolina*   *to Dismal Swamp*

This map represents the southwestern part of Southampton County.
Many of the places described in the text are represented here, as well as
the path of Nat's destructive campaign.   (shaded arrow)

Composite map.[98]

(B) Blood Trek to Barrow Road

Around 2 a.m. Monday morning, the band of seven, Nat
Turner, Henry, Hark, Sam, Nelson, Will and Jack arrived,
without firearms, at the home of Joseph Travis, his wife Sally
Francis, and three children, one of whom was Nat's legal
owner, twelve year old Putnam Moore. Putnam was Sally's
son by a previous marriage with Thomas Moore, who had died
in 1828. A year later Sally married Joseph Travis, who
established his busy wheelwright shop in her home. He
boarded a 14-year-old apprentice, Joel Westbrook, and also
took over supervision of her six slaves, until Putnam, the male
heir, reached maturity. Putnam had inherited Nat and the
others. Under Virginia law when a widow married again the
slaves she held from the estate of her deceased husband
belonged to her second husband. This result was avoided by
willing the slaves to the minor child. Joseph Travis owned
Hark, one of the original conspirators.[99]

41

Sally Francis, one of ten children, was a member of a prominent Southampton family. Her parents had a thousand-acre plantation which her brother Nathaniel had inherited, while another brother Salathial lived near by. Nat Turner, who was the same age as Sally Francis, had known her since childhood and had played with the younger Nathaniel when they were kids. Will was owned by Nathaniel Francis. The Travis family also had an infant. Travis and his family had spent the day away from the farm and did not arrive home until dark. They had attended a church service at Barnes's Church where Richard Whitehead, a young Methodist exhorter, had preached.[100]

"Two hours in the night," the group arrived at the Travis farm, where there were 17 slaves, a majority of them children. Upon arrival the seven conspirators were joined by an eighth, Austin, another slave. *They all went to cider press and drank, except myself,* confessed Nat Turner.[101] Hark approached the house with an axe to break down the front door, *as we knew we were strong enough to murder the family.* But it was unwise to alert neighbors, so it was decided to enter the house by stealth.

> *Hark got a ladder and set it against the chimney, on which I ascended, and hoisting a window, entered and came down stairs, unbarred the door, and removed the guns from their places. It was then observed that I must spill the first blood. On which, armed with a hatchet, and accompanied by Will, I entered my master's chamber, it being dark, I could not give a death blow, the hatchet glanced from his head, he sprang from the bed and called his wife, it was his last work, Will laid him dead with the blow of his axe, and Mrs. Travis shared the same fate, as she lay in bed. The murder of this family, five in number, was the work of a moment, not one of them awoke; there was a little infant sleeping in a cradle, that was forgotten, until we had left the house and gone some distance, when Henry and Will returned and killed it.*

Putnam and Joel were sleeping in an upper chamber. Witnesses to the scene indicated, "one blow seems to have

42

sufficed for two little boys, who were sleeping so close, that the same stroke nearly severed each neck." The infant was found with its cut off head in the fireplace. Legend has it that Nat said "nits make lice" when he sent Will and Henry back to kill the infant.

Broad-axes were used to commit the murders. The band now got its first firearms, *"four guns that would shoot, and several old muskets, with a pound or two of powder."* The guns were cleaned and loaded. The band also got horses that were saddled. They spent some time at the farm where Nat lined the men up and drilled them as soldiers. *"After carrying them through all the manoeuvres [sic] I was master of, marched them off to Mr. Salathul [sic] Francis', about six hundred yards distant."* The insurrectionists took Moses, a slave boy, with them to tend the horses. Moses remained with the conspirators to the end. He was the source for a newspaper article that the killings at the Travis household convinced the band that they had gone too far to recede and had to cast aside their doubts and become as "ferocious as their leader." The slave army was now armed, mounted, and blood-thirsty.[102]

The bachelor, Salathial Francis, a powerfully built man with a reputation for courage, lived with one slave, 'Red' Nelson, in a one room cabin, a crudely constructed structure, with a chimney from the fireplace for heating and cooking. It was one square room with a "jump," a neat and serviceable loft which formed a small apartment. Salathial's cabin was similar to a slave cabin and illustrated the lot of small slave-owners who existed on a subsistence level. It also explains why the other sons in the large family left the county when the older brother Nathaniel inherited the family estate after the father died, except Salathial who remained on a plot of family land nearby. Salathial had warned Sally Francis that Nat Turner was untrustworthy. His warning was ignored.[103]

The conspirators used guile to kill him. Sam and Will, trusted slaves of Nathaniel Francis, Salathial's older brother, tricked him out of his one-room cabin.

> *Sam and Will went to the door and knocked. Mr. Francis asked who was there, Sam replied it was him, and he had a letter for him, on which he got up and*

43

> *came to the door; they immediately seized him, and*
> *dragging him out a little from the door, he was*
> *dispatched by repeated blows on the head; there was*
> *no other white person in the family.*

'Red' Nelson, Salathial's loyal slave, was shot by insurgents while escaping but later helped to save the life of the wife of Nathaniel Francis.[104]

When the conspirators left some were mounted as they headed southeast a mile to Piety Reese's, arriving there around 5:30 A.M. Jack, reluctantly one of the original seven, was the slave of Piety's son William. Nat Turner noted that after Salathial's:

> *We started from there for Mrs. Reese's, maintaining*
> *the most perfect silence on our march, where finding*
> *the door unlocked, we entered, and murdered Mrs.*
> *Reese in her bed, while sleeping; her son awoke, but*
> *it was only to sleep the sleep of death, he had only*
> *time to say who is that, and he was no more.*[105]

After William's death, Jack gained courage, stole his owner's shoes and socks, and wore them until he was captured. Jack, though owned by William Reese, was working for Jordan Barnes, who had given him permission to visit his owner several days before August 22nd. When Jack returned, he told Barnes that a slave had told him of the murders at a nearby farm.

The Reese's overseer, James Barmer, tried to escape from the house but was discovered and beaten near to death by hoes and axes. He survived by playing dead and was discovered maimed several days later. He never fully recovered.[106]

The insurrectionists next marched east a mile to the home of the widow Elizabeth Turner, Nat's former mistress, which they reached at sunrise Monday. Nat Turner knew it well. He had lived at the farm from birth until he was 22 years of age when Elizabeth had sold him in 1822 to Thomas Moore for $400 after her husband Samuel Turner died. Elizabeth had also sold Nat's wife, Cherry, to Giles Reese for $40 at the same time but had kept his mother as a domestic servant. Nat had spent a decade slaving in the fields surrounding the house.

44

By 1831, Elizabeth had prospered, employed an overseer, Hartwell Peebles, and had eighteen slaves.[107]

When the conspirators arrived at the Turner farm the killing began immediately. Elizabeth Turner and her neighbor, Mrs. Sarah Newsome, were inside the house. Nat Turner confessed:

> Henry, Austin, and Sam, went to the still, where, finding Mr. Peebles, Austin shot him, and the rest of us went to the house; as we approached, the family discovered us, and shut the door. Vain hope! Will, with one stroke of his axe, opened it, and we entered and found Mrs. Turner, and Mrs. Newsome in the middle of the room, almost frightened to death. Will immediately killed Mrs. Turner, with one blow of his axe. I took Mrs. Newsome by the hand, and with the sword I had when I was apprehended, I struck her several blows over the head, but not being able to kill her, as the sword was dull. Will turning around and discovering it, despatched [sic] her also.[108]

Nat Turner noted that at each house the conspirators destroyed property while searching for money and ammunition.[109]

The band of insurrectionists grew to fifteen, nine were mounted and six were on foot. Davy, a Turner slave, was forced to join the group or face death. He joined. Another recruit went to the distillery where the dead overseer Peebles lay and dressed himself in the dead man's clothes.[110] Nat Turner split the group into two parts. The horsemen were dispatched to Cathy Whitehead's while the footmen followed a shortcut a hundred yards to Henry Bryant's. The two groups were to reunite at the Whitehead homestead.[111]

The six footmen killed Mr. Bryant, his wife Sally, their child, and Sally's mother. After plundering the house the group headed one mile east to Catherine Whitehead's homestead to join the mounted rebels. By the time they arrived the killing at the Whitehead's was over.[112]

It was early Monday morning when Nat Turner led the slave horsemen on a rapid raid to the Whitehead plantation. Catherine Whitehead, a wealthy widow, widely known throughout Eastern Virginia and North Carolina, lived with her own mother, five daughters, including two famed for their beauty (Margaret and Harriet), a grandchild, and a son Richard, a young Methodist preacher. Richard Whitehead had preached the day before at Barnes's Church, which the Travis family had attended. Local folklore states that Nat Turner preached to slaves in the courtyard of the same Church the week before the insurrection. Catherine Whitehead owned over 25 slaves.[113]

The land around the Whitehead plantation was surrounded by woods and swamps. Nat Turner knew the area well, as he had roamed it since youth. The Turner's Meeting House built by his previous owner was nearby. The insurgents were on a serpentine path to Jerusalem and the Whitehead plantation offered the prospect of additional recruits.

As the slave cavalry approached the house they saw Richard Whitehead in the cotton fields with slaves. Nat Turner noted:

> ... as we approached the house we discovered Mr. Richard Whitehead standing in the cotton patch, near the lane fence; we called him over into the lane, and Will, the executioner, was near at hand, with his fatal axe, to send him to an untimely grave.

Richard, according to folklore, did not comprehend what was happening, fell under a cedar tree, and asked why? The more he asked the more the insurgents shouted, "Kill him! Kill him"! Will cut Richard's head off with the axe. Another version had Will mince him.[114]

The horsemen continued the race to the main house. Nat Turner noted:

> As we pushed on to the house, I discovered some one run round the garden, and thinking it was some of the white family, I pursued them, but finding it was a servant girl belonging to the house, I returned to commence the work of death, but they whom I left, had not been idle; all the family were already murdered, but Mrs. Whitehead and her daughter Margaret. As I came round to the door I saw Will pulling Mrs. Whitehead out of the house, and at the

step he nearly severed her head from her body, with
his broad axe. Miss Margaret, when I discovered her,
had concealed herself in the corner, formed by the
projection of the cellar cap from the house; on my
approach she fled, but was soon overtaken, and after
repeated blows with a sword, I killed her by a blow
on the head, with a fence rail.[115]

Seven members of the Whitehead family were murdered. Two
days later, an officer from a North Carolina military unit found
Catherine Whitehead, and six others, including the grandchild,
"chopped to pieces with axes, the trees, fences and house top
covered with buzzards preying on the carcasses." Legend
states that the seven family members were buried in the
garden. As late as 1992, bloodstains were still visible on the
floor of the Whitehead house.[116]

One member of the Whitehead household escaped,
Harriet, with the help of Hubbard, a loyal family slave.
Hubbard hid his mistress between the bed and a mat when the
slave cavalry attacked. After the band departed he moved her
to another location in the swamps. But she was fearful that
Hubbard had joined the insurrectionists and moved to a new
hiding place where he could not locate her. The next day she
was discovered dirty, bitten by mosquitoes, and was taken to
Cross Keys, where she told her story. Harriet remained
unmarried for the next twenty-three years of her life and lived
at the plantation with the loyal slaves who had saved her
life.[117]

Nat Turner impressed recruits for his slave army at the
Whitehead plantation. Two Whitehead slaves, Jack and
Andrew, joined the insurgents after the slayings. In the slave
trials that began ten days later the loyal Hubbard testified the
two had fled when the insurgents arrived but returned after the
murders and, after inquiring if the conspirators had left,
mounted one horse and rode after them. There was also
evidence that the boys had ridden with a free black, Thomas
Hathcock, who was accused of participating in the
insurrection.[118]

Hubbard was also a witness against another pair of slaves
who were impressed into the slave army. Hubbard testified

that while Nat Turner was present, Joe came "one hour by sun" to the Whitehead house with Nat, not to be confused with Nat Turner. The two had come from hunting and had a raccoon. Joe said he had been hunting just after the Whitehead family was murdered. He did not ask who had committed the murders or why. Nat Turner ordered Joe to go with the insurgents; he appeared reluctant, but he went.

The killing was completed at the Whiteheads, and the footmen had returned from their murderous work at the Bryant place between 7 and 8 A.M. Monday morning. The insurgents continued to seize loot, including weapons and horses after the murders. Their number had grown and they were mounted.[119]

Nat Turner formed his men into units. He confessed:

> *We again divided, part going to Mr. Richard*
> *Porter's, and from thence to Nathaniel Francis', the*
> *others to Mr. Howell Harris', and Mr. T. Doyles. On*
> *my reaching Mr. Porter's, he had escaped with his*
> *family. I understood there, that the alarm had*
> *already spread, and I immediately returned to bring*
> *up those sent to Mr. Doyles, and Mr. Howell*
> *Harris'.*[120]

In six hours, the insurgents had destroyed 6 slave owning families, slaughtering 22 persons, mostly women and children, without warning, resistance, or any losses of their own. But now the alarm was out and Turner was aware he would have to face armed whites soon. Legend has it that slaves who had silently witnessed the Travis and Sal Francis murders had alerted the whites in other neighborhoods. The panicky whites fled to small hamlets nearby like Cross Keys and Jerusalem, while others camped in the woods. The insurrection, a letter from a Southampton judge stated, "came upon us as unexpectedly as anything possibly could and produced a pretty general panic, especially among our females."[121]

The next stop was the Richard Porter house. Porter was the owner of Henry, one of the original four conspirators to whom Nat Turner had confided his goal. Henry wanted to kill his master as the others had done. About 9 o'clock in the morning Andrew and Jack, the two Whitehead slaves, had come to the Porter house and asked if the slaves there had killed the Porter's as all the whites at their plantation were dead. Venus, a house slave, said no because the whites had fled before the insurgents arrived. They then inquired where the insurgents had gone and indicated they were going to join them. The two then left on one horse in search of the rapidly moving slave cavalry.[122]

After Nat Turner left the home of Richard Porter he retraced his steps and encountered the detachments he had sent after Doyle and Harris. Howell Harris had escaped but one detachment had killed Trajan Doyle when they encountered him with a servant on the road to the mill. The servant escaped and saved a white wife and infant, while another slave had warned Harris.[123] Nat Turner continued in search of his main mounted units. He knew that they were moving rapidly.

One detachment attacked the farm of 26-year-old Nathaniel Francis, the owner of two of the original conspirators, Sam and Will, and 13 other slaves. On Monday morning, August 22, 1831 he was there with his 19-year-old wife, Lavina, whom he had married a year before. Nathaniel's mother and two young nephews, the Browns, were also staying there, along with an overseer, Henry Doyle, who also took care of the distillery. Six free blacks also lived on his farm.

A young slave from the Travis farm ran to Nathaniel's place and said that all the whites were killed. Nathaniel rode over to his sister's to investigate. His mother, also alarmed, took a bypath to her daughter's home. By happenstance both missed the insurgents, reportedly led by Will, who rode up to the house from the opposite direction. As the slave cavalry rode up the lane to the house, the three year old nephew innocently ran to greet them and Will decapitated him with an axe. His brother screamed from a clump of woods and the slaves dealt the same fate to him. Doyle, the overseer, had run into the house yelling and when he came right back out, he was shot to death in the yard.

Lavina Francis, who was eight months pregnant, was still in the house. She was hidden in an upstairs cuddy by a loyal slave, 'Red' Nelson. Sam and Will entered the house and asked for Nathaniel and the other whites. Nelson told them that all were gone. The two made a fruitless search, found no one, and when they left spotted Mrs. Williams, a white woman, the wife of a local schoolteacher, and her child coming to visit the Francis clan. Both were killed. The slaves then went to the distillery and celebrated, recruited more slaves for the army, and left.

Inside the house Lavina had fainted while the killing was occurring outside. After the insurgents left, she regained consciousness, and left her hiding spot. She found slaves fighting over her clothes. A female slave, Charlotte, attacked Lavina with a knife but was restrained by the others. Ultimately, Nelson helped Lavina to safety and she joined her husband and mother-in-law at Cross Keys.

Nathaniel had joined the local militia to hunt the insurgents after he was informed that his family was dead. Legend has it that later Nathaniel and Lavina encountered Charlotte among a group of captive slaves, and that Nathaniel dragged her outside, strapped her to a tree, and shot her to death. Lavina went on to have nine children and lived to 1885. Nathaniel died in 1853, before Lavina reached forty.[124]

The slave detachment, after it completed *"the work of death and pillage, at Mr. Francis,"* went to the nearby plantation of Peter Edwards, one mile north of the Francis home. He owned 29 slaves and at least one indentured apprentice, Berry Newsom, who was one of the free blacks accused of insurrection. A loyal slave helped Edwards and his family escape.[125]

The detachment impressed one Edwards slave, Sam, into the slave army. His experience indicates one method the rebels used to recruit. Sam, considered a loyal slave by his owner even after the insurrection, rode with an insurgent detachment that raided plantations and murdered women and children. He rode in the rear, mounted with a gun or stick and had unsuccessfully pursued a slave at the Newit Harris plantation. After one massacre, in which he did not participate, he was seen wiping his eyes but was ordered by Nat Turner himself to get on his horse and rejoin the band as it moved on to the next killing ground. Reluctant slaves were guarded by others with orders to shoot if they tried to escape. After brandy some

50

became enthusiastic converts, while others followed in fear and would desert at the first opportunity. The slave army had a hard core of 20 led by 10 efficient killers. Henry, one of the original conspirators, was the paymaster: the recruits received $1 a day; Generals like Nat Turner, Nelson and Hark got $10, and he paid himself $5 per day from the $800 to $1,000 collected from the raids.

Sam, a reluctant follower, was apprehended the next night hiding under his mother's house in the slave quarters at the Peter Edward's farm. Loyal slaves informed a party of militia led by Nathaniel Francis of his location.[126]

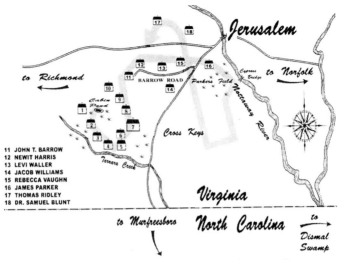

This map represents the southwestern part of Southampton County. Many of the places described in the text are represented here, as well as the path of Nat's destructive campaign.   (shaded arrow)

Composite map.[127]

(C) Barrow Road to Jerusalem

After the slave detachment left the Peter Edwards farm, it immediately reached Barrow Road, the only major thoroughfare in the area, which connected in five miles with the main road to Jerusalem. Barrow Road sanctified the name of an anti-slavery Baptist preacher, David Barrow, who fled Southampton a year before Nat Turner was born. Nat Turner must have contemplated his slave army with satisfaction as it raced to the "harlot" Jerusalem. The Spirit had allowed him to blow life into the dry bones of his followers.

> So I prophesied as he commanded me, and the breath came into them, and they lived, and stood up upon their feet, an exceeding great army.[128]

Nat Turner inspired his army by telling them "that as the black spot had passed over the sun, so would the blacks pass over the earth."[129]

The advance unit of slave cavalry raced less than a mile

to the plantation of John T. Barrow, situated at the head of Barrow Road. Barrow, a veteran of the war of 1812, and captain in the militia, was forewarned of the slave insurrection. He delayed fleeing, according to legend, while his beautiful wife, Mary Vaughn Barrow, completed her grooming. Meanwhile, the slave cavalry, led by the terrible Will, galloped down the lane to the house. A letter from Jerusalem on August 24th described the attack, after noting that Mrs. Barrow was one of the few to escape death at the hands of the slaves but:

> "...whose husband was murdered in his cotton patch, though he had received some notice in the course of the morning of the murderous deeds that were going on; but placed no confidence in the story and fell victim to his incredulity."

Other versions had him dying in the house. He fought bravely, but was killed when his throat was cut with a razor. According to folklore the insurgents saluted his bravery by saying "there were no more Tom Barrows to contend with," while in another version, the insurgents wrapped his corpse in a bed-quilt and placed it on the floor in the bedroom, with a plug of tobacco on the chest. It was also said Barrows was killed as revenge for preventing a slave marriage.

The insurgents did not take the time to hunt out the wife who escaped by hiding "between weatherboarding, and the unplastered lathing." Later she was a witness in several of the Southampton trials.

As the rebels left the Barrows they encountered George Vaughn, the brother of the wife, who was expecting to join a fox hunt at his sister's. Instead he joined the other dead left in the wake of the insurgents' race to Jerusalem.[130]

Meanwhile, Nat Turner was operating in the rear of the advance slave detachments, coordinating the movements of the rebel army, while he sought to renew contact with the forward units. The slave cavalry was moving rapidly and Nat Turner was right behind them as they moved murderously from plantation to plantation. He arrived shortly after they had left both the Peter Edwards' and John T. Barrows' homes.

I pursued on their track to Capt. Newit Harris',

> *where I found the greater part mounted, and ready to
> start; the men now amounting to about forty, shouted
> and hurraed as I rode up, some were in the yard,
> loading their guns, others drinking. They said
> Captain Harris and his family had escaped, the
> property in the house they destroyed, robbing him of
> money and other valuables. I ordered them to mount
> and march instantly, this was about nine or ten
> o'clock, Monday morning. I proceeded to Mr. Levi
> Waller's, two or three miles distant.* [131]

Nat Turner resumed his position in the rear. He had devised a
military tactic to *carry terror and devastation wherever we
went* by placing 15 or 20 of his best armed and fiercest cavalry
in front, *who generally approached the houses as fast as their
horses could run; this was for two purposes, to prevent their
escape and strike terror to the inhabitants.* [132]

The Waller plantation was three miles from the Harris
homestead on the Barrow road to Jerusalem. The home was a
community center for the local residents, with a distillery, as
well as blacksmith and wheelwright shops. There was a well-
attended boarding school nearby which Waller's children
attended. Levi Waller had 18 slaves who resided in cabins on
the place. At least 11 persons were killed at the Waller
plantation, the bloodiest family massacre of the insurrection.

Between 9 and 10 o'clock Monday morning Waller,
while at his still, was warned that the slaves had risen, were
murdering whites and were on the way to his home. He sent
his son Thomas to warn the boarding school, a quarter of a
mile away, and to bring his own children home. The
schoolmaster William Crocker returned with the Waller
children, but before they could arm themselves Crocker came
to the still and said the insurgents were on them. Waller
concealed himself in a weed-covered fence behind the garden,
opposite the house. [133]

Waller saw between 40 and 50 insurgents mounted on
horseback and armed with guns and swords, and other
weapons, ride into his yard. All his family attempted to make
their escape. Only Waller, the school master, two of his sons,
and a young girl "who had sagacity enough to creep up a

54

chimney" were successful.

Several of the insurgents went after Waller who escaped by jumping a fence and hiding in the weeds. Dred, a slave of Nathaniel Francis, was mounted with a gun or rifle when the raiding party reached the Waller house. He rode to the fence and looked for Waller. Waller knew this slave well. Dred broke off the search when the insurgents went after the blacksmith, who they thought was Waller. Levi Waller testified Dred was one of the insurgents who killed his family. Later he saw Dred drinking with the others at the still.[134]

Waller meanwhile crawled to a vantage point in a plum field where he could see what went on at the house. He saw Daniel, owned by Richard Porter, and Sam, the slave of Nathaniel Francis, along with a third insurgent, enter a log house where Waller's wife and a small girl had attempted to hide. He saw the three come from the house and Daniel had his wife's chain in his hand. The witness later entered the log house and found his wife and the small child murdered, as well as many other members of his family.[135]

An eyewitness to the scene reported that, "At Mr. Levi Waller's, his wife and ten children, were murdered and piled in one bleeding heap on his floor." Another witness said he saw, "in one room ten dead persons, women, boys, and girls, from helpless infancy to hoary age, of the family of Mr. Levi Waller, and some children who were at a schoolhouse near his dwelling."[136]

Nat Turner arrived after the murders were completed. It was now his practice to ride in the rear. He noted in his confession that:

> I never got to the houses, after leaving Mrs.
> Whitehead's, until the murders were committed,
> except in one case. I sometimes got in sight in time to
> see the work of death completed, viewed the mangled
> bodies as they lay, in silent satisfaction, and
> immediately started in quest of other victims.[137]

From his hiding place in the plum orchard, Levi Waller watched the insurgents drinking brandy at his still when Nat Turner rode in on Dr. Musgrave's horse. He also saw Hark in the yard with a gun in his hand directing a detachment of insurgents. The band addressed Hark as Captain Moore, using the last name of his original owner, the deceased Thomas Moore.

Levi Waller testified, however, that Nat Turner was clearly in charge of the 40 to 50 insurgents. He watched as Nat Turner made Sam, the slave of Peter Edwards, go with the group despite his unwillingness. Waller did not see Sam murder anyone and, in fact, "saw him at a distance wiping his eyes." Then he heard Nat Turner tell Sam to get on his horse when they were about to leave. Sam did not want to go, but did get up and go off with them. Waller did not know if Sam was forced to go or if he could have escaped.[138]

Waller also witnessed his own slave, Davy, called Brother Clements by one of the band, come to the house after the killings and survey the carnage. He then went and dressed himself clean, drank with the insurgents at the brandy still, and then rode off with them on his master's horse, in good spirits and great glee. Davy was present at the murder of several other families, got drunk, and heard Capt. Nat, as the band passed a house where some very poor white people lived, say he would not kill them because they thought "no better of themselves than they did of the negroes [sic]." While Waller was watching all this, two insurgents came after him again. He escaped to a swamp nearby.[139]

Unbeknownst to the insurgents a party of mounted white volunteers, 20 or 30 in number, led by 39-year-old William C. Parker, a young lawyer in Jerusalem, had begun to track them after they left the Newit Harris farm. Parker, a veteran of the War of 1812, had recently arrived in Southampton, owned several slaves, and was a new member of the court elite. That summer he was appointed a prosecutor in the county's Superior Court. Parker took control of the defense of Jerusalem, even though he was not a militia officer. During the Southampton insurrection trials Parker served as defense counsel, representing 14 insurgents, including Nat Turner. Col. James Trezevant, a magistrate on the court, also rode with this militia unit.

The volunteers found "the blood hardly congealed in the houses they had left." On retracing the path of the insurgents the next day, an observer described his shock at the Waller home:

> "At Levi Waller's the spectacle was truly touching; there, for the first time, I saw at one of those fated houses, a living white soul; and this consisted of a little girl about 12 years of age, looking with an agonized countenance, on a heap of dead bodies lying before her; nine of them women and children; her sister among the number. She gave me a minute account of the tragedy there acted, having witnessed it from her place of concealment."[140]

Alfred, one of Levi Waller's slaves, was apprehended on Monday by a second party of whites, who were tracking the insurgents. The two white groups pursuing the slave insurgents were unaware of each other's presence. The second group, led by A.P. Peete, a member of the oligarchy and a judge on the slave court, included Thomas R. Gray, a young lawyer who would play a prominent role in the aftermath of the insurrection, did not want its movement impeded by caring for Alfred, so they disabled him by cutting the large tendon just above the heel in each leg. Alfred, a blacksmith, around 30 years old, was left hamstrung on the road. Later a troop of the Greensville Dragoons, engaged in suppressing the insurrection, tied Alfred to a tree and shot him "as a beneficial example to the other Insurgents" who were still armed and "unsubdued" [sic].[141]

The insurgents next went to the home of William Williams, moving at a rapid pace, striking additional terror, for they never rode at less than full speed, and as their horses became tired they impressed fresh ones.[142] Williams lived three miles from Waller's shop, on the road to Jerusalem. Williams had recently married and lived in a small home near the road. The insurgent cavalry raced to him and two hired boys, Miles and Henry Johnson working in a field, and hacked the trio to death.

William Williams' wife was at home when the insurgents arrived. She ran while the rebels killed the males. Nat Turner described her fate:

> *Mrs. Williams fled and got some distance from the*

> *house, but she was pursued, overtaken, and*
> *compelled to get up behind one of the company, who*
> *brought her back, and after showing her the mangled*
> *body of her lifeless husband, she was told to get down*
> *and lay by his side, where she was shot dead.*[143]

Jacob Williams, the uncle of William Williams, and the owner of one of the original conspirators, Nelson, lived nearby. Jacob Williams had an overseer, Caswell Worrell, who supervised Nelson in the field. On the previous Thursday, Nelson, who was known as a conjurer, told Worrell that "they might look out and take care of themselves—that something would happened before long—that anybody of his practice could tell these things."

In the early morning on Monday, August 22nd, Worrell arrived at the main house on the Jacob Williams plantation to take the slaves to work new ground. Nelson was not at the house when he arrived. Nelson, arriving after Worrell had taken the work crew to the fields, seemed very sick, went to his house and changed into his best clothes. About an hour later, Nelson went to the new ground where the other slaves were working and said he was too sick to work. Nelson had his work clothes with him and put them on and said he wanted to go to the house, which he did, returning to the field just before the insurgents arrived. Worrell believed that Nelson wanted to trap and kill him.

Jacob Williams had left the plantation early on the 22nd on business. He returned around 11 A.M. and saw Nelson dressed in his best clothes, and from Nelson's manner the Master, even though he had not heard about the insurrection, felt the slave had the intention to attack him. Jacob Williams did not confront Nelson but instead went to the woods to measure timber, not returning until the evening when he found his family murdered.

Around 11 A.M. the main party of the insurgents arrived. As they rode to the house they encountered Edwin Drewry, an overseer from the nearby James Bell plantation, who had come to load corn. As he saw the mounted slaves rapidly approaching he said to Stephen, a slave accompanying him, "Lord, who is that coming" and immediately the insurgents rode up and shot him to death. He was also disemboweled.

The insurgents rode on to the house and killed the master's wife and three children. Nelson changed back to his dress clothes. While the insurgents were in the yard, Nelson came into the kitchen and asked for some meat. He took meat meant for Mrs. Williams out of the pot and cut a piece off. He told Cynthia, who worked in the kitchen, "You do not know me. I do not know when you will see me again." Nelson left the kitchen, stepping over the dead bodies of the wife and children, without any manifestation of grief.

The insurgents then rapidly rode to the nearby home of the overseer, Caswell Worrell and killed his wife and child. Worrell escaped. Nelson then reluctantly left with the insurgents for the plantation of Rebecca Vaughan. The evidence indicated he did not participate in the murders there, but did drink with the insurgents and had "his tickler filled by his own request."

The probable reason Nelson was reluctant to leave his master's is surmised from the fact that, while Jacob Williams was at the house later the evening of the 22nd, grieving over his dead family, he saw the insurgents again approaching and distinctly saw Nelson riding in the front of the detachment. Jacob Williams escaped.[144]

There was a newspaper report four days later that volunteers from Norfolk and Portsmouth had killed Nelson, who the insurgents called Gen. Nelson, cut off his head and were taking the skull to Norfolk. The report was false as Nelson was captured alive, tried on September 3, 1831, convicted and hung.[145]

The insurgents' next target, the home of the widow Rebecca Vaughan, was a quarter of a mile away. She lived there with her two sons George and Arthur. Earlier George Vaughan, expecting a fox hunt at the Barrows, where his sister was the mistress, was killed by the insurgents. His mother was unaware of his death or the insurrection.

Around noon Mrs. Vaughan was preparing dinner on the porch when she saw a cloud of dust from mounted horsemen and wondered what it could mean. In a second the insurgents mounted and armed came into view, spewing curses as they rode into the yard. Mrs. Vaughan, white as a sheet, screamed and ran into the house. The conspirators dismounted and surrounded the house, pointing their guns at the doors and windows. Mrs. Vaughan appeared at a window and begged for her life, inviting the band to take all she had. The insurgents answered the prayer by shooting her to death through the window.

Upstairs was her 18-year-old niece, Ann Elizabeth, one of the beauties of Southampton, who rushed downstairs begging for her life. She was shot to death, a few steps from the door, by a 21-year-old insurgent, Marmaduke, who was later severely wounded himself. One observer noted that Marmaduke, while in custody, "bore his suffering with magnanimity as though he was a hero."

Vaughan's 15-year-old son, Arthur, was at the still when he heard the shots. He thought it was his brother returning from the fox hunt and ran to the house where the insurgents shot him to death. He was the last white to die in the insurrection. After the killing was done, the insurgents made an old slave woman, who had witnessed the murders, provide them food and drink. She said the band now became nice and damned the brandy as vile stuff.[146]

By this time, noon on Monday, August 22nd, the alarm on the insurrection was widespread. White families, particularly the women and children had fled to populated centers like Jerusalem and Cross Keys. The countryside was deserted of whites who had left their plantations and homes unbarred and in charge of loyal slaves. The insurgents had wreaked havoc on a 20 mile trek across Southampton, leaving over 50 dead, most hacked to death with axes. Nat Turner was aware that time was short. *I determined on starting for Jerusalem,* he confessed. *Our number amounted now to fifty or sixty, all mounted and armed with guns, axes, swords and clubs.*[147]

(D) Battle at Parker's Field

It was early afternoon, twelve hours after the first killings at the Travis place, and the insurgents were now 3 or 4 miles from Jerusalem, the county seat, and site of the courthouse. Jerusalem was a sanctuary for 400 women and children, guarded by a few men, while the others were out hunting the insurgents. It was the prime objective of the insurrection. Nat Turner knew his forces were poorly armed and were using clubs and axes to do most of the killing. Jerusalem had arms, ammunition, and other staples, including food, a successful army needed. It also had hostages. One observer, who later questioned "Capt. Nat" said: "His object was freedom and indiscriminate carnage his watchward [sic]. The seizure of Jerusalem and the massacre of its inhabitants, was with him, a chief purpose."[148]

The verses of **Ezekiel 16:20 and 40** must have rung in Nat Turner's mind as he rode to Jerusalem:

> **Moreover thou hast taken thy sons and thy daughters, whom thou hast borne unto me, and these hast thou sacrificed unto them to be devoured. *Is this* of thy whoredom a small matter.**

and

> **They shall also bring up a company against thee, and they shall stone thee with stones, and thrust thee through with their swords.**

Three quarters of a mile from the Vaughan homestead was the lane gate that led to the home of James W. Parker, 31 years old, a prosperous slave owner, and a judge on the Southampton slave court. Parker, and his family, had fled the plantation when word of the insurrection reached them.

When the rebels reached the gate Nat Turner did not want to stop. However, several insurgents had relatives who were Parker's slaves and wanted to recruit them. *I objected, as I knew he was gone to Jerusalem, and my object was to reach there as soon as possible.* Nat was overruled and remained at Parker's gate with 7 or 8, while over 40 insurgents rode the half mile to the house.

When the band did not return promptly Nat Turner said: *I became impatient, and started to the house for them, and on our return we were met by a party of white men, who had pursued our blood-stained track, and who had fired on those at the gate, and dispersed them, which I knew nothing of, not having been at the time rejoined by any of them.*

The whites were the company of 18 volunteers, including Thomas R. Gray, led by Captain A.P. Peete. The company had routed the insurgents at the gate and were marching on the house. Peete had ordered his men to hold fire until they were within 30 paces of the insurgents. Nat Turner described what happened next:

> *Immediately on discovering the whites, I ordered my men to halt and form, as they appeared to be alarmed—The white men, eighteen in number, approached us in about one hundred yards, when one of them fired. And I discovered about half of them retreating, I then ordered my men to fire and rush on them; the few remaining stood their ground until we approached within fifty yards, when they fired and retreated. We pursued and overtook some of them who we thought we left dead; after pursuing them about two hundred yards, and rising a little hill, I discovered they were met by another party, and had halted and were re-loading their guns.*

Unknown both to the insurgents and the column of volunteers, the other group of whites led by William C. Parker and Col. James Trezevant, had set an ambush on the road, knowing that the insurgents were nearby, and were waiting their return to the road. This second group was not aware of the presence of the column led by Captain Peete. When they heard the shots they rushed to the scene and arrived just in time to save Peete's column. Five or six of Nat's bravest men were wounded, while *the others became panick struck and squandered over the field.* Hark had his horse shot from under him but Nat Turner caught another for him. Outgunned he retreated carrying his wounded with him; none were left on the field. A witness saw Daniel, an insurgent, riding Dr. Musgrave's horse. He shot at Daniel who escaped.[149]

Nat Turner was still intent on laying siege to Jerusalem after the defeat at Parker's Field. He realized that the whites thought he would try to enter Jerusalem by the main bridge over the Nottoway River. So he decided to cross at the Cypress Bridge, but ran into complications described in his confession:

> *Finding myself defeated here I instantly determined
> to go through a private way, and cross the Nottoway
> river at the Cypress Bridge, three miles below
> Jerusalem, and attack that place in the rear, as I
> expected they would look for me on the other road,
> and I had a great desire to get there to procure arms
> and ammunition. After going a short distance in this
> private way, accompanied by about twenty men, I
> overtook two or three who told me the others were
> dispersed in every direction. After trying in vain to
> collect a sufficient force to proceed to Jerusalem, I
> determined to return, as I was sure they would make
> back to their old neighborhood, where they would
> rejoin me, make new recruits and come down
> again.*[150]

Nat Turner took his hard-core army of twenty south and
then made a looping maneuver, which retraced their original
path, and took the band north to the Belfield Road and the
plantation of Thomas Ridley. The looping maneuver confused
and threw the militia units off the track. A member of one of
the search parties, probably Thomas R. Gray, wrote about the
chase: "And though pursued the whole night, fortune seemed
to sport with us, by bringing us nearer together, and yet,
making us pursue separate routes." Ridley's quarter was
located four miles from Jerusalem. Nat Turner described his
tactic as follows:

> *On my way back, I called at Mrs. Thomas's,*[151] *Mrs.
> Spencer's, and several other places, the white
> families having fled, we found no more victims to
> gratify our thirst for blood, we stopped at Majr.
> Ridley's quarter for the night, and being joined by
> four of his men, with the recruits made since my
> defeat, we mustered now about forty strong.*[152]

Thomas Ridley's plantation was one of the two largest in
Southampton, with 145 slaves. The slave army set up a camp
for the night and posted pickets. Nat Turner wanted to sleep.
In the *Confessions* he explains what happened next:

> *After placing our sentinels, I laid down to sleep, but*

> *was quickly roused by a great racket; starting up, I*
> *found some mounted, and others in great confusion;*
> *one of the sentinels having given the alarm that we*
> *were about to be attacked, I ordered some to ride*
> *round and reconnoitre [sic], and on their return the*
> *others being more alarmed, not knowing who they*
> *were, fled in different ways, so that I was reduced to*
> *about twenty again.*[153]

The slave sentries panicked for no reason. Even though the militia leaders in Jerusalem had intelligence Monday night that the slave army was bivouacked at Ridley's quarter, they incorrectly thought it was 200 strong and if they came after it with the 60 men guarding the county seat, the slave army might outflank them and enter the town. So they stayed put.[154]

(E) Free Blacks Join the Insurrection

At daybreak on Tuesday, August 23rd, Nat Turner was determined to rebuild his army. The nearest plantation belonged to Dr. Samuel Blunt, who owned over 60 slaves, and was aware he was a target. Crippled by gout, he decided to stay and fight. Blunt, his 15-year-old son, Simon, the overseer, and three white neighbors fortified the house and, along with armed loyal slaves, waited in ambush for the slave army. Nat Turner described what happened:

> *Dr. Blunt's was the nearest house, which we reached*
> *just before day; on riding up the yard, Hark fired a*
> *gun. We expected Dr. Blunt and his family were at*
> *Maj. Ridley's, as I knew there was a company of*
> *men there; the gun was fired to ascertain if any of the*
> *family were at home; we were immediately fired upon*
> *and retreated, leaving several of my men. I do not*
> *know what became of them, as I never saw them*
> *afterwards.*[155]

Dr. Blunt's racially mixed force acquitted itself well. Simon, his 15-year-old son, distinguished himself through his bravery and came to the attention of President Andrew Jackson. Jackson rewarded him with an appointment to the Naval Academy, which embarked Simon on a military career.[156]

At least one of the slave rebels was killed at Blunt's, while several were captured including the wounded Hark, one of the original conspirators. Hark was armed, called Captain Moore, and when arrested at Dr. Blunt's admitted his involvement. He had a pocketbook that belonged to the murdered Trajan Doyle, as well as powder, shot, and some silver in his pocket.[157]

Free blacks joined the insurrection on Tuesday, the second day. Five were prosecuted in subsequent trials. The acknowledged leader of the free blacks was William "Billy" Artist, who lived on a swampy 14-acre farm near Nat Turner's birthplace. The tall, light-skinned rebel had a slave wife and six children. Early reports had him riding with Nat Turner as a co-leader. Early Tuesday morning Billy Artist and his wife came by the Blunt plantation. Artist asked two slaves to go with him, one of whom was named Ben. Ben had foreknowledge of the insurrection and had warned a fellow slave the day before. Ben led them to Peter Edward's where his brother, Nathan, lived. Nathan joined the other three and around 12 noon they went to the Nathaniel Francis homestead, where they entered and took out three bundles of clothes. Ben helped carry the goods.[158]

After the ambush at the Blunt homestead, Nat Turner fled with the insurgents along a path to the farm of Captain Harris which they had visited the day before. There was a party of white men at the house and all of Turner's men deserted except two, Jacob and Nat. Legend has it that Will, the executioner, was shot to death during a skirmish there.[159]

Sometime that morning, Nat Turner dispatched two of Ridley's slaves, Curtis and Stephen to recruit fighters at the Newsom and Allen quarters. At about 8 or 9 o'clock Tuesday morning, August 23, 1831, the two riding mules were intercepted by a mounted and well-armed party of whites. Both admitted that they spent Monday night with the insurgents, and had joined the party that raided Capt. Harris' the second time, but both claimed they were on the way home, even though they were moving in an opposite direction from the Ridley plantation.

They were taken to Cross Keys, questioned further, and confessed that Nat Turner had told them to go to the Newsom and Allen quarters to get other Negroes to join them and that they were on the way for that purpose. The trial court found the confessions voluntarily made, with no threats or promises. According to folklore, however, the two were interrogated by a brutal militia company at Cross Keys. There were reports that suspected insurgents were tortured with a red-hot iron to induce confessions.

When captured both were under the influence of alcohol and said the insurgents had given them brandy. When asked how they expected to get through all the armed whites in the area, they said Nat Turner had told them the white people were too much alarmed to interrupt them. Scipio, another Ridley slave, testified that both Curtis and Stephen were forced to join the insurgents and were surrounded so they could not escape.[160]

The final act in the insurrection occurred when Billy Artist, his wife, and Ben returned to the Blunt place around 3 or 4 o'clock in the evening with another free black, Thomas Hathcock, who had three slave boys with him. Billy Artist waved his hat and loudly said he would "cut his way, he would kill and cripple as he went." Billy Artist was creating his own free black/slave detachments to carry on the insurrection.[161]

Nat Turner escaped and went into hiding. He was a fugitive for months. The other leader, William "Billy" Artist was not as fortunate. He was wounded but escaped into the forest. On September 2nd he was found allegedly shot by his own hand, with his pistol lying by his side, and his hat on a stake nearby. Some doubted he committed suicide. Legend has it that when the slave army impressed Billy Artist into service he wept like a child. But once he had tasted blood he was like "a wolf let into the fold."[162]

One can only speculate what direction the insurrection would have taken if chance had not intervened at Parker's Field and instead the slave army had overcome Peete's unit. This would have opened the door to Jerusalem, which was nearby. An observer noted: "Every house, room and corner in this place is full of women and children, driven from home, who had to take the woods [sic], until they could get to this place."[163] It was barely defended as most of the militia units were in the field searching for the insurgents. Nat Turner's army would have ridden into Jerusalem intoxicated by its defeat of the white militia, and under the homicidal influence of the potent apple brandy. It would have captured the hundreds of women and children concentrated there, and would have held them hostage or worse. Instead of the 55 to 60 whites killed in the insurrection, the number could have reached the hundreds.

There is no evidence that at any time the insurgents raped white women or burned homesteads and farms. This differentiated the Southampton insurrection from the first slave uprising in Haiti where widespread rape and burning occurred.[164] But the captives in Jerusalem would have rightly trembled with fear since the verses of **Ezekiel 9:6, 7** would have rung in Nat Turner's mind:

> **Slay utterly old and young, both maids, and little children, and women: but come not near any man upon whom is the mark; and begin at my sanctuary.**
>
> **And he said unto them, Defile the house, and fill the courts with the slain: go ye forth. And they went forth and slew in the city.**

The chance convergence of the two militia companies at Parker's field broke the insurrection and prevented the capture of Jerusalem. Nat Turner escaped and literally went underground. His broken army collapsed into two and three men units, some returning to their home plantations, while others hid in the swamps from white patrols.[165]

Chapter 5

Slave Trials

(A) The Fog of War

News at the time of the insurrection was spread by written messages carried on horseback. The first report of the Southampton affair did not reach Richmond, seventy miles away, until early Tuesday morning, August 23, 1831. John Floyd, the first person elected Governor from western Virginia and of partial Indian ancestry, received the eyewitness notice from James Trezevant, who was later to serve as a judge in the slave trials. Trezevant's report indicated that there was an insurrection of slaves, several families were massacred, and it would take considerable force to put down the insurrection. Governor Floyd wrote in his diary: "This will be a very noted day in Virginia."[166]

Rumors began to spread as soon as the news became known. One newspaper noted: "The intelligence has burst very unexpectedly upon us. No one has had the slightest intimation or dream of such movement."[167] Several newspapers reported the rumor that 150 or 200 runaway slaves from the Dismal Swamp were responsible for the insurrection. Another newspaper reported that, "The rumors have been so numerous and contradictory that we are unable to state to our readers, at present, the precise state of affairs in that county."[168]

There were also rumors that the British were in Southampton leading the insurrection. A white woman, Nancy Parson, was on her way to her sister's house on Monday when she saw several blacks standing by the Charlton plantation near the upper end of the county. She had heard of a disturbance but did not know of what character and was told the British were in the county. When she asked Issac, one of the slaves standing nearby, if he was afraid, the slave said no, and that if they came he would join them and assist in killing all the white people, that if he succeeded he would have as much money as his master. Issac was convicted of conspiracy to rebel, and, though valued at $300 by the court, was sold out of state for $400.[169]

There was also an early newspaper report that whites were leading the insurrection. During the trials Henry, a slave, testified that he had also heard Monday that the "British were in the County killing the white people."[170] These false rumors were a historical echo of the raids by British cavalry during the Revolutionary War and the brutal Chesapeake depredations by the British in 1813, when 600 runaway slaves received sanctuary. In one version whites were leading a slave army.[171]

The rumors were "numerous and contradictory." There were reports that the slave army was on its way to Belfield in Greensville, an adjacent county, near the North Carolina Border. Another rumor had it that 80 to a 100 whites were dead, "their heads severed from their bodies."[172]

By Wednesday, August 24th, the details of the actual plot emerged. A dispatch from Jerusalem published in a Richmond newspaper reported that, "A fanatic preacher by the name of Nat Turner (Gen. Nat Turner) who had been taught to read and write, and permitted to go about preaching in the country, was at the bottom of this infernal brigandage."[173] As the reality sunk in that local slaves and free blacks had created the insurrection, the whites reacted with a terrible vengeance.

(B) Vigilante Response and the Restoration of Order

The last slave killing had occurred Monday noon and by Tuesday enraged citizens and militia units were scouring the countryside to kill or capture insurgents, who had either returned home or broken down into small bands of three or four and were "dodging about in the swamps." The whites were animated with a spirit of "vindictive ferocity," reported John Hampden Pleasants, a journalist who was a member of the Richmond Troop, noting that "summary justice in the form of decapitation has been executed on one or more prisoners." The insurgents were shown no quarter. Another report noted "the slaughter of many blacks, without trial, and under circumstances of great barbarity. How many have thus been put into death (generally by decapitation or shooting) reports vary."[174]

Southampton had its own militia units that engaged the black rebels at Parker's field and pursued them afterward. But as word of the insurrection spread to Richmond, the Governor John Floyd took control. He was worried that the insurrection was not localized to Southampton.

On Tuesday, August 23rd, Governor Floyd placed Brigadier-General Richard Eppes in charge of the militia sent to Southampton and also gave him command of all forces converging on the area. A troop each of cavalry and light artillery, as well as two companies of infantry—along with 1000 stand of arms—were sent to Southampton. They joined the numerous militia units and armed whites pouring into the county from across the state.

Floyd placed Brigadier-General William H. Broadnax in charge of the troops and arms sent to counties adjacent to Southampton because of the fear of widespread insurrection. There was a popular rumor the slaves had planned an insurrection across several counties and that those in Southampton had risen prematurely. One report from Richmond noted:

> "We understand that the confessions of all the prisoners go to show that the insurrection broke out too soon, as it is supposed, in consequence of the last day of July being a Sunday, and not, as the negroes [sic] in Southampton believed, the Saturday before. The report is that the rising was fixed for the fourth Sunday in August, and that they supposing Sunday, the 31st of July to be the first Sunday in August, they were betrayed into considering the 3d Sunday as the 4th. This is the popular impression founded upon confessions, upon the indications of an intention of the negroes [sic] in Nansemond and other places to unite, and upon the allegation that Gen. Nat extended his preaching excursions to Petersburg and this city."

The Richmond Troop arrived in Jerusalem on Thursday morning, August 25th "after a rapid, hot and most fatiguing march from Richmond." Jerusalem was packed with militia units, 300 to 400 frightened women, and three artillery companies of U.S. troops and a detachment of sailors and marines, around 100 men, under a field officer, from Fortress Monroe near Norfolk. The Federal forces had entered unbeknownst to the Governor at the request of officials from Norfolk. The Governor, a states rights advocate and fierce opponent of the Federal government, was not happy to learn of the Federal troop deployment.[175]

The insurrection was crushed by the time the Richmond Troop arrived. The first order of business was to stop the widespread killing of valuable slave-property in the countryside. General Eppes issued a stern order to halt the bloody depredations. On Sunday, August 28, 1831, from his headquarters in Jerusalem, General Eppes felt:

> "... himself bound to declare and hereby announces, to the troops and the citizens, that no excuse will be allowed to any other acts of violence after the promulgation of this order, and further to declare in the most explicit terms that any who may attempt the resumption of such acts shall be punished, if necessary by the rigors of the articles of war."

In his Order Eppes noted that "acts of cruelty and barbarity" had occurred and that the blacks had "felt the fury of outraged humanity." "Ample sacrifice" had been made and most of the participants were shot or in custody. It was time to let the judicial process run its course.[176]

The Federal troops on the scene never entered the fray. Governor Floyd thought it was a mistake for them to have come to Southampton in the first place. In 1831, Virginia had a militia force of 101,488 men including cavalry and artillery units. Floyd felt Virginia could defend itself without Federal help and the movement of Federal troops to Southampton might give the insurgents the wrong idea. He wrote:

> "I felt reluctant to ask of the United States that which we could so easily do ourselves, because if the negroes [sic] believed we were under the necessity of obtaining aid from that quarter, on this occasion, it is not difficult to perceive the train of thought which would be indulged, should the United States at any future day have use for their forces in the prosecution

of a foreign war."

Floyd also felt the Federal forces were needed to protect the rear areas in case the insurrection was widespread.[177]

At Fort Monroe, Norfolk, a recently arrived, newly wed Lieutenant, Robert E. Lee, observed the insurrection even though he did not join the Federal troops dispatched to Southampton. In a letter to his wife's parents he decried the vigilante excesses and general white panic, but repeated the rumor that the scope of the insurrection reached beyond Southampton.[178]

President Jackson was personally briefed on the events in Southampton on September 8th. Jackson was so moved by the courage of Dr. Blunt's 15-year-old son that he commissioned him a midshipman. Jackson was deeply interested in the insurrection both as the owner of around 150 slaves, and as a military man. The record is silent on what role, if any, he had in the deployment of Federal troops but there is no doubt that Floyd disdained the Federal intrusion. On August 27th the commander of the Federal troops, who had placed a small guard at the jail in Jerusalem, notified General Eppes that he was withdrawing because his troops were not needed, but would return to his base by a different route through an adjacent county, so his show of force could "operate a moral influence" on "the misguided wretches who have been the cause of so much atrocity and ingratitude."[179]

The Governor was joined in his disapproval of Federal troops by a Richmond newspaper which on September 3, 1831 noted it was "sorry to learn that a paper signed by a few names in Southampton, should have been addressed to the President of the United States requesting the continuance of some of the U.S. troops in that quarter."[180] Virginia, it maintained, had no need for them. National politics had momentarily intruded into the Southampton affair with the arrival of Federal forces but swiftly went away with their prompt withdrawal.

By Thursday, August 25th, thousands were hunting the rebels. General Eppes reported to Governor Floyd on the 25th that he had enough force to quell the rebellion.[181] On Sunday, the 28th, Eppes informed the Governor that the insurrection was crushed and there was no danger any longer in

Southampton. He had captured over 50 suspects who would stand trial. The estimates range as to how many blacks died in the bloody aftermath but modern estimates agree over 100, with many of them innocent of any participation in the insurrection. Eppes in his dispatch on the 28th also confirmed some bad news: the ringleader, Nat Turner, "a Baptist Preacher," "a great enthusiast—declares to his comrades, that he is commissioned by Jesus Christ, and proceeds under his inspired directions—that the late singular appearance of the sun was the sign for him," had escaped.[182]

One memento of the bloody reprisals remains to this day. Since the insurrection, the crossroads of the Barrow Road and the Jerusalem-Cross Keys Highway has been known as Black Head Signpost. A grimaced head of an insurgent, many claimed it was Nat Turner's, was impaled on a post there as a reminder to blacks of the cost of rebellion. Parker's cornfield was 500 yards away. The message was plain "that another insurrection will be followed by putting the whole race to the sword."[183]

(C) The Southampton Trials

Governor Floyd was aware from the beginning that the insurrection was a major historical event. His intense interest in the judicial process was a response to two realities. First, there was great concern on his part and others that the insurrection was much wider than Southampton county. Second, he was aware that the private property of the elite was threatened by the summary justice of outraged citizens and the courts had to exert control over the dispensation of justice. The reputation of Virginia as a civilized polity was also at stake. Floyd was equally concerned about his own political future as the crisis was a test of his leadership.[184]

Virginia authorities, including Floyd, relied on the courts to determine the facts of the insurrection, particularly its scope. He wanted the investigation to determine if it was true that the Southampton slaves, part of a larger conspiracy, had risen prematurely on the third Sunday of August, rather than the fourth. He sent a message to county courts in five counties, including Southampton, to send him certified transcripts of the evidence of all insurrection trials resulting in the death penalty. The trial evidence from confessions and eyewitnesses was the practical way to determine what happened. Speedy trials were also the way to assert the rule of law and rapidly punish the guilty.[185]

The Southampton trials began on Wednesday, August 31, 1831, nine days after the first killing, and were completed by November 21, 1831. There were 44 trials with 50 defendants; several of the trials had either two or three defendants. Approximately 22 magistrates heard the 44 Southampton trials, usually sitting in five man panels; slaves had no right to a jury trial. The judges were members of the county's slave-owning elite, and were bound together by ideological, familial, religious, political, social, and recreational ties. They shared a common outlook, even though the class had its liberal and conservative wings. The judges were serious in fact finding and demonstrated mercy in punishment. The criminal law provided that the burden of proof was satisfied by a slave's confession, the testimony of one white witness, or the testimony of people of color, bond or free, sustained by pregnant circumstances.[186]

The magistrates, most of them not lawyers, were members of the planter hierarchy, and welcomed the state militia's efforts to restore order. Slaves were valuable property and summary executions resulted in financial loss to the owners, unlike the compensation they would receive if the slave was executed by the state or sold out of state. There was a core of seven judges who heard the most cases: James Trezevant (31), Carr Bowers, (26), Ores Browne (26), James W. Parker (21), Jeremiah Cobb (21), Alexander Peete (19) and William Goodwyn (19). These seven were representative of the class.

Goodwyn, a doctor and owner of 64 slaves, was a member of a family that owned the county's largest plantations. C. Bowers was a prominent doctor, served in the legislature, was widely read, with the best library in the county. While he owned slaves and supported slavery he was from the liberal wing of the elite. He sheltered hunted free

74

blacks in his home right after the insurrection and his last political act before death was to vote against Virginia's secession from the Union. J. Cobb had 32 slaves and was a longtime member of the court. He was elected to office and was a leading breeder of racehorses. Of the remaining judges, three—A. Peete, J. Trezevant and J.W. Parker—were slave owners and from prominent families. Peete was active in the Jerusalem Jockey Club that brought so many members of the elite together, as well as the militia. He led the unit that encountered the insurgents at Judge Parker's cornfield.[187]

There were 45 slave defendants and 5 free blacks. Of the 45 slaves tried, 15 were acquitted and 30 were convicted. Of the 30 convicted, 18 were hung, while 12 received mercy and were sold out of state.[188] The trials took place in a highly inflamed political climate. Usually court day was a festive occasion, generating a large turnout of the population to socialize, buy and sell goods, to drink and observe.[189] But this was not an ordinary time. Nat Turner was a fugitive, the only person in the leadership to escape. Twin emotions of fear and revenge surged in the populace. There were threats that the mob would provide vigilante justice if any of the suspects were acquitted.[190] On September 6th, the court asked General Eppes to leave a guard of 50 men because "a strong guard is necessary to the safe keeping of the prisoners now in jail until such as are condemned may be executed."[191] In his August 28th order, General Eppes told Southampton residents that, "A sufficient force is now assembled for the security of the prisoners, and to sustain and enforce the sentence of the Courts, as well as to cause to be respected its judgments of dismissal."[192]

The court heard four cases its first day, August 31st. Its decisions that day showed a pattern that continued throughout the trials. One slave was acquitted, three were convicted, but only two were hung, while one had his sentence commuted and was sold out of state.[193]

The one acquittal on the first day, a 25% acquittal rate, was actually lower than the actual rate throughout the Southampton trials. Fifteen of the 45 slave defendants tried were discharged or acquitted, roughly 33%. The court records are silent on the evidence in acquittals, since testimony was summarized only in trials where death or transportation was at issue. A contemporary newspaper account indicated that several of the acquittals occurred because the only witness was a female slave and "under our act of Assembly, the testimony of a slave or free negro [sic], unless supported by pregnant circumstances, is insufficient to convict in any case."[194]

The transcript of only one case provided the reason for acquittal. On October 17th Jack and Shadrach were jointly "charged with treason against the Commonwealth." The court, composed of the usual five members, discharged both defendants on the ground that "a slave cannot be tried in this Court for Treason." This was one of the few cases where no defense lawyer was appointed.[195]

An 1803 statute stated that the law against high treason did not apply to slaves. In 1819, legislation was passed which prohibited the prosecution of slaves for treason in *oyer and terminer* courts. The law was premised on the principle that persons of color, free or slave, were not citizens or members of the body politic. In an 1824 case, *Aldrige v. Commonwealth* 2 Va. Ca. 447, the court held that the Bill of Rights did not extend to persons of color, since they were denied the privileges of citizenship like voting, they were not covered by the protections of either the Federal or state constitutions. Treason is a crime that only a citizen can commit since it involves breach of an allegiance to the state. The court determined that a slave could revolt against constituted authority, i.e. participate in an insurrection, but owed no allegiance to the state.

The same insight that the slave owed no allegiance to the polity was reflected in the famous 1830 case, *State v. Mann*, from neighboring North Carolina, which held that a master's power over his slave was absolute since this was the only way to control a piece of property that had no duty of obedience or loyalty. The master-slave relationship was ultimately grounded on force and nothing else. Jack and Shadrach were the only defendants charged with treason, the others faced charges of insurrection.[196]

The existence of a one third acquittal rate was a

reflection of the independence and power of the magistrates of the *oyer and terminer* court. The slave owning elite could disregard the passions of the white masses to pursue its own interests in both fact finding and deterrence.

The 30% acquittal rate in the Southampton trials also suggests that slave defendants received a finer quality of justice from the county's elite judges than they would have received if juries had heard the cases. Between 1786 and 1865 in Southampton there was an acquittal rate in excess of 30 percent for insurrection, so the results in the 1831 insurrection trials only served to confirm this pattern. These results indicated a degree of judicial integrity in the fact finding process and justified the confidence that the lawyer-correspondent John Pleasants expressed in a dispatch from Jerusalem on September 3rd: "We trust and believe that the intelligent magistracy of the county, will have the firmness to oppose the popular passions, should it be disposed to involve the innocent with the guilty, and to take suspicion for proof."[197]

(D) The Guilty: Death or Transportation

Of the 30 convicted slaves, 18 were executed and 12 had their sentences commuted. The slave courts were designed to speedily determine guilt and to punish. A speedy execution for the most culpable had the greatest deterrent effect. General Eppes told the vengeful populace to safeguard suspected rebels, because "if preserved and delivered to the civil authority, a public execution in the presence of thousands will demonstrate the power of the law, and preserve the right of property."[198]

On Saturday, September 3rd, Jerusalem postmaster, Theodore Trezevant, the 41-year-old younger brother of magistrate James Trezevant, sent a dispatch to the editors of the Constitutional Whig in Richmond to update them on the trial proceedings. Noting that families were returning home, but the trials were progressing slowly because of the numerous witnesses traveling from different parts of the county, he indicated the testimony was, "strong and conclusive as respects conspirators," showing that the insurrection was local. He indicated the pace of trials was accelerating, and the court had condemned 14 out of 15. In an addendum added Sunday night he noted: *"We commence hanging tomorrow."*[199]

The trial transcripts indicate that between August 31 and September 6, twenty slaves and one free black were tried. Nineteen of the slaves were convicted. Two, Daniel and Moses were hung at 12 noon Monday, September 5th. These public executions in the presence of large crowds demonstrated the power of the authorities since there was usually a 30-day wait between conviction and execution. Insurrection was an exception to this rule and the hangings usually occurred within days of conviction. Six more slaves were executed on Friday, the 9th, and two more on Monday, September 12th. The court recessed for a week on September 12th, having completed trials of 29 of the "principal offenders." The hard-core offenders, including the surviving original conspirators, were tried early on and executed.[200]

(1) Lawyers & The Cabin Pond Conspirators

Nearly all the prosecuted slaves were provided with counsel. James L. French, a 24-year-old Jerusalem attorney handled more insurrection cases, 21, than any of the four other lawyers who participated in the trials. William C. Parker, with 14, and Thomas R. Gray, with 5, handled the bulk of the other trials. The newcomer, Parker, who owned several slaves, had led one of the militia units that defeated the rebels. The downward mobile 31-year-old Gray, the son of a prominent planter, had become a lawyer within the last year, resigned his seat on the county court, and began to practice law. The lawyers were paid $10 per case by the court. The trials of the core conspirators illustrated that lawyerly skills had influence on the trial process.

Of the six co-conspirators at Cabin Pond with Nat Turner two, Will and Henry, were killed during the insurrection. Will was killed in the final skirmish near the Newit Harris home, while Henry, the paymaster of the slave army, was decapitated in the bloody aftermath and one newspaper reported his "skull is in the possession of one of the surgeons of the detachments who visited Jerusalem." Another version had angry citizens cut off his head and carry it around the county.[201]

On September 3rd, while Nat Turner was still a fugitive, the four surviving Cabin Pond conspirators, Sam, Hark, Nelson, and Jack were tried. The first tried, Sam, was owned by Nathaniel Francis and represented by Thomas R. Gray. When interrogated Sam "denied that there had been anything like a general concert among the slaves. It was confined to the immediate neighborhood of the scene." Sam was convicted of insurrection and murder on the testimony of one white witness, Levi Waller. Waller testified that he had known Sam for several years and saw him "go with others" into the house where his family was murdered on Monday, August 22nd.[202]

Hark, owned by the Estate of Joseph Travis, came second, charged with insurrection, represented by William C. Parker, and was convicted on his own confession and the testimony of two white witnesses. Levi Waller testified he saw Hark in the yard at his home with the other insurgents, a gun in his hand, the other insurgents called him Captain Moore. Thomas Ridley testified Hark confessed he was with the insurgents who went to Dr. Blunts. When the prisoner was searched he had property from the murdered Trajan Doyle.[203]

Nelson, owned by Jacob Williams, represented by James L. French, was convicted on the testimony of two whites and two slaves. His owner, whose small farm was 4 miles from Jerusalem, testified he saw Nelson on Monday, August 22nd, about 11 A.M. dressed in his best. Even though the master had not heard about the insurrection he became fearful of Nelson's demeanor and fled. He returned later in the day and found his wife and 3 children murdered. Nelson also tried to trick Worrell, the overseer, to come to the main house so the insurgents could kill him. Several slaves also implicated Nelson in the insurrection, one noting that after he ate his dead mistress' meat he stepped over the dead bodies of Mrs. Williams and the children "without any manifestation of grief." On September 9th Nelson, Sam and Hark were publicly hung.[204]

(2) Reasons for Transportation

Jack's case, the fourth of the Cabin Pond conspirators to face trial, took a different turn than the others. Jack, a 20-year-old slave owned by the deceased William Reese, a victim of the insurrection, was represented by Thomas R. Gray. Gray's legal skills came into play in the case. The most common reasons to commute a slave death sentence were either the age of the insurgent, and/or whether or not he was forced to join the band, and whether he cooperated in the investigation. Gray raised all these defenses in Jack's case. In an anonymous letter to a Richmond newspaper Gray outlined the defense, stating the slave army had a hard core of ten, and:

> "... they did not make one dozen efficient recruits, along their whole route of slaughter-they certainly made many more, but instead of being of any service, most them had to be guarded, by some two or three of the principals, furnished with guns; with orders to shoot the first man, who endeavoured [sic] to escape. Many persons have expressed their surprise, how so few could guard so many. To me it appears, that the orders to shoot down whoever attempted to escape, explains the riddle."[205]

The trial began on September 3rd when Moses, a slave, testified that Jack came to the home of his master, Joseph Travis, on the Sunday night before the murders. He complained of being sick and wanted to go home but Hark would not let him go. Hark had Jack's sister for a wife. Jack sat with his head between his hands resting on his knees. Moses testified that the insurgents made Jack go with them after the Travis family was murdered.

Thomas C. Jones testified that Jack had confessed that he had been taken by Hark on the Sunday before the outbreak to a dinner where the plot was explained to him. Jack protested that they were too few but was countered by Hark who said the blacks would join them.

This testimony supported the defense that Hark dominated the younger Jack and forced him to go with the insurgents. The next witness, Sampson C. Reese, devastated the defense case, testifying that when Jack was arrested he was wearing the shoes and socks of William Reese, his murdered owner. Even though owned by William Reese, he was hired out to Jordan Barnes, who testified Jack knew of the Whitehead murders when he returned to the home on the morning of August 22nd. The court found Jack guilty and ordered him hung, fixing his value at $350. However, by a majority of one it recommended that the Governor commute the punishment to transportation.[206]

On its face, the recommendation for transportation appears bizarre, even from a divided court, which included the four most versed of the magistrates, J. Cobb, C. Bowers, J. Trezevant, and O. Browne. Jack was at the crucial meeting when the insurrection was launched, wore the stolen shoes and socks of his murdered owner, and fled the scene of the crime.

Transportation itself was a severe punishment since an insurgent would never see his family again, next to death the slave's most profound fear. Also effective representation had an impact on the punishment. Thomas R. Gray did successfully get the court by a majority of one to recommend it. It was probably Hark's control, Jack's youth, as well as his first full account of the meeting at Cabin Pond that moved the majority of the court to recommend mercy.

The final decision on the transportation was left to the Governor and Council. Governor John Floyd had ordered all the court records on the trials of those sentenced to death sent to him. On September 3rd he received the records from the trials on August 31 through September 1st, in which two slaves were condemned to death and two were recommended for transportation. He agreed with the recommendations, including the two transportations, noting in his diary that day:

> "Through out this affair the most appalling accounts have been given of the conduct of the negroes [sic], the most inhuman butcheries the mind can conceive of, men, women, and infants, their heads chopped off, their bowels ripped out, ears, noses, hands, and legs cut off, no instance of mercy shown."

The Governor, like General Eppes, was ill during the insurrection and its aftermath. On September 10th, after commuting the sentence of five insurgents by transportation, Floyd noted in his diary: "I am so unwell this afternoon that I have to go to bed."[207]

In the Southampton trials Governor John Floyd needed the advice of the Council before making the decision on transportation. This was a state constitutional requirement that the Governor intensely disliked. However, both the Council and the Governor agreed that Jack should not receive clemency. In a September 10, 1831 letter to Brig. General Eppes, the Governor noted with respect to the case:

> "It is advised that the Judgements [sic] and recommendations of the Court be adhered to-which I am inclined to pursue, except as to Jack-who is recommended to be reprieved for transportation by a Majority [sic] of one. Two Magistrates not on the bench protest against the reprieve and the Council advise against the recommendation of the Court-I will therefore not interfere."

Jack was hung.[208]

In cases with facts less egregious than Jack's, the court and the Governor were inclined to grant mercy when the most common mitigating factors were the youth of the offenders coupled with evidence they were impressed into the slave army. The newspapers reported that three transported slaves—Nathan, Tom and Davy, owned by Nathaniel Francis—were "boys of 14 or 15 years of age and all of them being forced to join the band of murderers."[209] The evidence at their joint trial indicated that after the raid on the Francis home, the three were taken and placed one behind each of the company, and forced to ride with the insurgents the whole of Monday. They went unwillingly, witnessed many of the murders, but were constantly guarded by armed insurgents who were ordered to shoot them if they attempted to escape.[210]

There were occasions when the Governor needed to act quickly and no councilors were in Richmond. On August 23rd, when he first learned of the insurrection, he could not dispatch militia units until a councilor appeared; there were none in Richmond at the time. He noted in his diary that the requirement of advice of counsel was a "vain and foolish ceremony" and that once he had met he could do as he pleased. However, the absence of a councilor had a devastating impact on the life of one insurgent in the Southampton cases. On September 27th, Floyd lamented in his diary:

> "I have received a record of the trial of three slaves, for treason [sic] in Southampton. Am recommended to mercy, which I would grant but the forms of our infamous Constitution makes it necessary before the Governor does any act involving discretionary power, first to require advice of Council, and in this case I cannot do so, because there is not one member of the Council of State in Richmond, wherefore the poor wretch must lose his life by their absence from their official duty."[211]

There was one insurgent who rode with the slave army from the beginning who survived. His case illustrates again the impact adequate defense counsel could have on a case. Moses, a slave boy owned by the Joseph Travis estate, and represented by Thomas R. Gray, had joined the conspirators at the Travis house and rode with the insurgents throughout the massacre. Moses was arraigned as a boy slave. A white testified that Moses had cooperated freely and voluntarily during the trials, sometimes for the prosecution and sometimes for the defense.

Moses also had confessed, after he was advised he was not compelled to testify and that he would get no benefit from the confession. He said he was compelled to go with the insurgents and remained with them until they were repulsed at Parker's field. The court convicted Moses of conspiring to rebel and make insurrection. However, it unanimously recommended that the Governor transport Moses. And he did so.[212]

The court records and sale prices of the slaves in the Southampton insurrection indicate most insurgents were male field hands. Lucy, age 20, was the only slave woman charged in the Southampton insurrection trials. She was the property of the deceased John T. Barrow. Mrs. Barrow testified that Lucy had seized and held her about one minute when she tried to escape after the insurgents had entered her yard. Another slave intervened and took Lucy away. Mrs. Barrow, while not certain, thought Lucy tried to detain her so the insurgents could kill her.

Other testimony placed Lucy with the insurgents at the door to the house after Mr. Barrow was executed. Robert T. Musgrave testified that Lucy had told him the lie that she had fled through the kitchen and concealed herself in the cornfield when the insurgents arrived. Finally, Bird, another Barrow slave, testified that several weeks after the murder she found four pieces of money in a bag of feathers and covered with a handkerchief in a room occupied by Lucy and Moses, another Barrow's slave, who was executed for his role in the insurrection. Lucy was convicted and hung. She was valued at $375.[213]

The slave army was primarily composed of male field hands. However, there was one artisan, Frank, owned by Solomon Parker, a blacksmith valued at $600, who was convicted of insurrection. Frank was defended by James L. French, and only one witness, Becky or Beck, a 16- or 17-year-old house servant owned by Solomon Parker, testified against him.

Becky swore that she was "seldom in the outhouses," but the day the insurrection began she heard black persons in the slave quarters at Solomon D. Parker's, including Frank, say that if the insurgents came that way they would join and help them kill the white people. There were several slaves present and Frank said that "his master had cropped him and he would be cropped before the end of the year." The slaves told Becky the conversation was a secret and if she told the white people they would shoot her.

Becky's mistress, Parker's wife, fled to the adjacent county of Sussex during the insurrection and when her mistress wondered if her slaves were concerned Becky told her about the conversation. Becky said she did not tell before because she did not understand its importance. Apparently Frank testified in his own behalf, but the court convicted him even though there was no evidence to corroborate the testimony of a single slave, except the pregnant circumstance that he was owned by Solomon Parker and present at the plantation when Becky said the conversations occurred.

On the same day Becky also testified against two field hands, Jim valued at $300 and Issac at $400. Jim and Issac were the property of Samuel Champion and lived a mile from the Solomon Parker plantation, in the adjacent Sussex county. Becky testified the same as she did in Frank's trial. The prosecution called Bob, a slave, who testified that both defendants told him they were at Solomon Parker's before and after the insurrection. The court convicted both defendants.

When it came to sentence, the court treated the valuable blacksmith and the field hands differently. It recommended Frank receive mercy through transportation while the two field hands were condemned to death. An economic motive, an intra-ethnic class bias, must explain the distinction. The evidence in the two cases was virtually the same, except for the lack of corroboration in Frank's case. Moreover, Frank was the most threatening and aggressive of the three, with his threat to cut off his owner's ears. The Governor exercised his discretion and transported all three of the felons. The three cases also demonstrate how the authorities punished harshly mere "insurrectionary statements," without any acts in furtherance, so as to maintain their own authority and control.[214]

(E) Slaughter of the Innocents

There were approximately 80 trials attributed to the Turner insurrection, 50 of which occurred in Southampton. Thirty trials occurred in adjacent counties. These slaves were charged with participation in the Southampton insurrection and were hung or transported. The same Becky, the slave of Solomon Parker, also testified in trials in Sussex county, repeating a version of her Southampton testimony about overhearing talk of a plot, and at least seven slaves in Sussex were convicted and some hanged.[215]

Becky's testimony was the only evidence of a long planned and widespread slave plot across several counties.

Becky swore she had heard the insurgency discussed 18 months before the outbreak, and had seen slaves in Sussex and Southampton join. Newspaper reports began to raise questions regarding her credibility. In February 1835 her perjured testimony was repudiated when James L. French, representing a slave in Sussex county convicted on Becky's testimony, had his sentence commuted to transportation.[216]

Sussex county was not alone in trying slaves for the Southampton insurrection. Trials also occurred in Nansemond, Prince George, Spottsylvania and Greensville counties.[217] Since the trials in Southampton revealed that the insurrection was local, the slaves convicted and punished outside the county were innocent victims of the panic and hysteria of the times. On September 17th, a writer of a letter from Jerusalem lamented: "Those who have been condemned to death and those actually shot, exceed the number attributed to the insurgents. It follows then, as a necessary consequence, that several innocent persons must have suffered." He noted that "superstitious remarks" made by slaves on the singular appearance of the sun, or a statement by a slave of what he would do if Nat came his way, even after the insurrection was suppressed, could result in conviction and death.[218]

The slave trials established several facts. First, the insurrection was confined to Southampton county, led by the fugitive Nat Turner. Second, the slave army was composed primarily of male field hands, with some members, often the youth, impressed against their will. Third, the magistrates' actions in the Southampton trials illustrated the lesson the elite had learned that justice measured with mercy was the surest deterrent of future slave violence. One member of the elite expressed it this way: "I am of the opinion that security is to be found only in the rigid enforcement of the laws, regulating this class of our population, united with humane and just treatment in their owners." Neither Southampton, nor Virginia as a whole, experienced significant slave insurrections after the suppression of the Nat Turner rebellion.[219]

There was also evidence that free blacks joined the insurrection on Tuesday, the second day. Five free blacks had their initial hearings in the slave court and four were bound over to the Superior Court for trial. An examination of their hearings sheds additional light on the African-American rebellion in Southampton.

Chapter 6

Free Black Prosecutions

(A) Southampton Free Blacks

In 1830 there were 1,745 Southampton free blacks, in excess of 10% of the county's total population, and one of the highest concentrations of free blacks in the state. Southampton county had a tradition of manumission that was a result of anti-slavery agitation by Southampton's Quakers and Baptists. The American Revolution furthered the process and led to an increase of the free black population both in Southampton and the rest of the state. In 1800 there were 829 free blacks in Southampton, which increased to 1,745 by the time of the Nat Turner insurrection.[220]

Only a small number of Southampton's free blacks owned property. Most worked as farm laborers, while a few were artisans. Nearly half of the free black families were headed by women and many free blacks were married to slaves.[221] Free blacks were not citizens of Virginia and could not vote but had some legal rights, the most important of which was the right to own property.

The hybrid status of free blacks, neither slave nor citizen, and the kinship ties between free blacks and slaves, led whites to view them with suspicion. Free blacks had a central role in the Haitian revolution and there was fear the same might occur in Virginia. These fears were heightened in 1830 when 30 copies of free black David Walker's <u>An Appeal to the Colored Citizens of the World</u>, which told slaves that God "will give you a Hannibal" and "God will indeed, deliver you through him from your deplorable and wretched condition under the Christians of America," were intercepted on their way to a free black in Richmond. In April 1831, reacting to the pamphlet, Virginia passed a statute that barred all free blacks from getting together for educational purposes and also outlawed whites from teaching slaves to read or write. Fear of a joint free black-slave insurrection was palpable.[222]

In 1831, however, free blacks retained legal rights to habeas corpus and a jury trial. The slave courts, formally known as *oyer and terminer,* had no jurisdiction to hear free black cases. Instead, the magistrates reconstituted themselves as a regular county court to examine the free black cases. Five free blacks were examined during the Southampton insurrection trials. One was discharged, while four were bound over for jury trial in the Superior Court.[223]

(B) The Free Black Examinations

On September 5, 1831 the county court's five magistrates, including Jeremiah Cobb, James Trezevant and James W. Parker, heard the first free black case. The accused was Arnold Artes, arraigned as a "free man of color charged with counseling, advising and conspiring to rebel." Artes was in custody and represented by counsel at the time of the proceeding. The court heard sundry witnesses and discharged Artes from custody. As with the acquittals in the slave trials, the record is silent on the testimony of the witnesses. Testimony was not reported in the free black cases because it was only a probable cause hearing and the defendants would have a jury trial in the Superior Court where both white and black defendants were tried.[224]

On September 12th, the court heard the case of Thomas Hathcock, aka Thomas Haithcock, a 39-year-old, free man of color, with a wife and stepdaughter. He was 5ft. 6 inches tall with "scars near the corner of his left eye and left side of his forehead." He was charged with "conspiracy to rebel and make insurrection." Hathcock was remanded to custody for trial in the Superior Court because the magistrates after "hearing the testimony and from all the circumstances of the case are of the opinion that the prisoner ought to be tried for the said offense at the next Current Superior Court."[225]

Hathcock's trial record, like the others, is silent on the evidence that supported the court's ruling but a clue is provided by testimony from the slave cases. In a slave trial there was testimony that on Tuesday, the second day of the insurrection, Hathcock and four boys came to the home of Benjamin Edwards and said that "Genl. Nat would be there Wednesday or Thursday and Mr. Edwards had 4 likely boys that he would take with them as prisoners and two others said they would join." Hark, one of the core conspirators, testified in the same case that Hathcock and four boys came to the Edwards place and "said they had separated from Nat and they were going to join them again."[226]

In a companion case a slave witness testified that on Tuesday morning Hathcock and four boys came to the Benjamin Edwards place and told him and others that "Capt. Nat and company had a fight with the white people at Parkers field-that Capt. Nat was then making towards Belfield and would return and be at Mr. Edwards on Wednesday or Thursday and that Mr. Edwards had four likely men who should join them."[227]

In another case, a slave witness testified that on Tuesday at about 3 or 4 o'clock in the evening Thomas Hathcock and 3 boys came to his place along with another free black, Billy Artist, a leader of the insurgents who was later killed. Artist waved his hat or brandished his hatchet, as the group rode off, saying in a loud voice "he would cut his way, he would kill and cripple as he went."[228]

Hathcock, himself, had testified as a defense witness in one of the early slave cases, indicating that two slaves, "the prisoner and Andrew came to his house, asked what they should do, much grieved-and went with him to several houses."[229] It is probable the slave testimony was repeated in the examination and was found sufficient to send Hathcock to trial.

Two other free men of color charged with conspiring to rebel and make insurrection, Exum Artist and Isham Turner, were also sent to trial in the Superior Court. The record is silent on the reasons, but does indicate two slaves, Burwell and Ben, owned by William Dick, were the key witnesses against Exum Artist. Dick had to post a $300 bond to ensure their appearance at the Superior Court trial. Isham Turner was represented at his hearing by James L. French.[230] Like all free blacks bound over for trial the two were jailed without bail.

The final defendant, Berry Newsom, "an indentured apprentice to Peter Edwards," was the most intriguing of the lot. His trial record was the only one silent on ethnic background, in which no charge was stated, no defense counsel appointed, and no plea was entered. His hearing, like that of the other free blacks, does not record the testimony but simply held him to answer in the Superior Court. The record indicated that two slaves, Harry and Henry, were the witnesses against him.[231 232]

While most historians agree Newsom was African-American, at least one has speculated that he was white because it was doubtful that there was an indenture system for blacks in Virginia in 1831. However, the evidence is to the contrary. The 1830 census indicated that most of the 1,745 free blacks in Southampton lived on farms with white families as either servants or farm hands. Moreover, contracts for apprenticeship were widely used by free blacks so Newsom's contract with Peter Edwards was not uncommon. The contract was advantageous to Newsom because he might learn a trade, earn money, and receive food and board. Virginia had a very harsh law that required all freed slaves to leave the state one year after emancipation or face public sale. Even though this law was not enforced vigorously, indenture to a powerful planter like Peter Edwards provided Newsom a measure of protection.[233]

Despite the silence of his trial record, testimony from the slave trials indicated his participation in the insurrection. Henry testified in the trial of Hardy, a slave owned by Benjamin Edwards, that on Monday he went to the fields and Berry Newsom in the company of Hardy, "stated that the damned Rascal, meaning the witness' master, had been there, that they would get him before night." Henry testified that he went to a neighbor's farm and heard "that the English were in the County killing white people," that he told Hardy and Berry Newsom and that Hardy "made light of it and said it was nothing and ought to have been done long ago-that the negroes [sic] had been punished long enough."

Harry, a slave witness against Berry Newsom, testified Henry had said in front of Hardy and Newsom that "Genl. Nat had sent them word that he would be at their home on Wednesday or Thursday next for them to join him" and all agreed. Newsom was jailed on this evidence and sent to trial in the Superior Court.[234]

The Superior Court trials began in the Spring of 1832. Berry Newsom was the only free man of color convicted and hung. His crime partner, the slave Hardy, was convicted but sold out of state. The two convictions and harsh punishments were another example of the severe consequences resulting from insurrectionary thoughts or words, even without an overt act to further them. The other free blacks, Hathcock, Artist, and Turner, were acquitted in the Superior Court, probably because of the rule of evidence that required pregnant circumstances to corroborate the testimony of slaves and other persons of color. The trial records were destroyed during the Civil War.[235]

The free black examinations demonstrated free blacks participated in the insurrection to some degree, especially on the second day. Billy Artist was the main free black insurgent but the evidence supports the assumption that there was wider free black participation. It is ironic that the racist dualism regarding the worth of white and black testimony, might have freed free blacks where there was no evidence to corroborate slave testimony. The role of free blacks in the insurrection was secondary, however, since it was the field slaves who were the hard-core fighters in the insurgent army.

Chapter 7

Capture and Trial of Nat Turner

(A) Flight and Capture

Nat Turner was the only hard-core insurrectionist to escape. On Tuesday night, after he sent his last two men to contact Henry, Sam, Nelson and Hark, Nat Turner was alone. He spent that night and the next day near the Cabin Pond where the group had met the Sunday before, waiting for the others. When he saw white patrols in the area he concluded he was betrayed.

> *On this I gave up all hope for the present; and on Thursday night after having supplied myself with provisions from Mr. Travis's, I scratched a hole under a pile of fence rails in a field, where I concealed myself for six weeks, never leaving my hiding place but for a few minutes in the dead of night to get water which was very near.*[236]

It was first reported that Nat turner was killed trying to cross the bridge to Jerusalem after the skirmish at Parker's field. By Sunday night August 28, General Eppes reported to Governor Floyd that the reports Nat Turner was killed near the Jerusalem bridge were unfounded and, "The insurgents all taken or killed, except Mr. Turner the leader, after whom there is a pursuit." Eppes noted: "… it is believed he cannot escape."[237]

The insurrection trials began the next Wednesday on August 31 and the first hangings occurred the following Monday, on September 5th. On September 7th a report from Jerusalem confirmed the two executions on Monday and reported that several others would hang on Friday. It noted: "The only one going at large is the ring leader, *Nat*. All are at a loss to know where he has dropped to."[238]

On September 10th there was a false report that the "famous gen. [sic] Nat, of the Southampton negroes [sic]" was captured in Baltimore and turned over to Virginia. In fact, Governor Floyd had given up hope that his troops would capture Nat Turner and on September 13, 1831, he informed

General Eppes that he would offer a reward for the capture of the rebel leader but "I must now request you to furnish me with a full description of his person, as throughout this whole affair I have not seen any description of him."[239]

William C. Parker, at a time when photographs did not exist, sent the Governor a description of "Nat the Contriver and leader of the late insurrection in this county," which the Governor included in a Proclamation for a reward of $500, which he issued on September 17th. On the reverse side of the Proclamation was the description:

> "Nat is between 30 & 35 years old, 5 feet 6 or 8 inches high, weighs between 150 and 160 lbs, rather bright complexion, but not a mulatto—broad shouldered—large flat nose-large eyes—broad flat feet-rather knock-kneed-walks brisk and active—hair on the top of the head very thin—no beard except on the upper lip, and the tip of the chin—a scar on one of his temples—also one on the back of his neck-a large knob on one of the bones of his right arm near the wrist produced by a blow."

The Proclamation left out the details provided by Parker that the scar on the temple was caused by the kick of a mule and the scar on the neck by a bite.[240]

Intensive efforts were made to apprehend the rebel leader. A September 17th report from Jerusalem indicated that his wife, Cherry, who resided near his hideout on the Travis property, was whipped until she turned over papers "filled with hieroglyphical characters, conveying no definite meaning. The characters on the oldest paper, apparently appear to have been traced with blood; and on each paper, a crucifix and the sun, is distinctly visible."[241] If she knew, she did not disclose his whereabouts.

In early October, six weeks after going into hiding, Nat Turner noticed that the patrols had diminished and he began to reconnoiter the countryside.

> *Thinking by this time I could venture out, I began to go about in the night and eaves drop the houses in the neighborhood; pursuing this course for about a fortnight and gathering little or no intelligence,*

afraid of speaking to any human being, and returning
every morning to my cave before the dawn of day.[242]

He kept a stick on which he notched the days spent in hiding. He made several attempts to leave the area but could not travel by day and the patrols prevented flight at night. He also considered surrender and once walked within two miles of Jerusalem before he changed his mind. During this period false reports were frequently made in the press of his death, capture, or sighting from Southampton to Botetourt County 180 miles away, to Baltimore.[243]

In mid-October Nat Turner's luck ran out. While out one night a dog, smelling meat in his hole, discovered his hiding place.

A few nights after, two negroes having started to go
hunting with the same dog, and passed that way, the
dog came again to the place, and having just gone
out to walk about, discovered me and barked, on
which thinking myself discovered, I spoke to them to
beg concealment. On making myself know they fled
from me. Knowing then they would betray me, I
immediately left my hiding place.[244]

The hue and cry increased to a roar as the search for the rebel leader intensified. Nat Turner, even though seen several times by blacks, managed to evade capture for another two weeks. *During the time I was pursued, I had many hair breadth escapes.* After he left the Travis place, Turner hid in haystacks on the farm of Nathaniel Francis, until Francis discovered him on October 28th, and narrowly missed wounding him when his pistol-shot went through Turner's hat. Immediately a party of 50 men turned out to hunt for Turner in the woods and swamps around the Francis place. They searched for two or three days without success.[245]

Despite the sighting in Southampton, reports of his presence in other parts of the state continued to come to the Governor. On October 26, Governor Floyd wrote in his diary the he had "received news of the supposed appearance of Nat, the Southampton leader of insurrection, being in Greenbrier, Not true." On October 30th, the Governor noted: "Received news that the dead body of the negro [sic] which was supposed to be Nat had been taken up and examined by General Smith of Kanawha and found not to answer the description."[246]

On Sunday, October 30th, around 12 noon, Nat Turner was captured. Benjamin Phipps, a poor white, who for the first time hunted Turner, had taken his shotgun that morning and alone retraced the steps of the 50 man tracking party. A mile and half from the Travis house, on the plantation of Nathaniel Francis, he came to a place where a number of pines were cut down. He saw movement among the pines, approached cautiously, and saw a head protruding from a:

> ... little hole I had dug out with my sword, for the
> purpose of concealment, under the top of a fallen
> tree. On Mr. Phipps' discovering the place of my
> concealment, he cocked his gun and aimed at me. I
> requested him not to shoot and I would give up, upon
> which he demanded my sword. I delivered it to him,
> and he brought me to prison.

Phipps had Nat Turner lay on the ground as he securely tied his hands. Turner, who was emaciated and ragged, wore the hat with the pistol-shot holes left by Nathaniel Francis. Phipps walked him a mile alone to the Peter Edwards estate where in less than an hour over 100 persons gathered. At the Peter Edwards farm the mother of a slave rebel "ran out and struck Nat in the mouth, knocking the blood out and asked him, 'Why did you take my son away?' In reply Nat said, 'Your son was as willing to go as I was.'" After spending the night Phipps marched Turner on Monday, followed by a large crowd, to the jail in Jerusalem. Phipps received several rewards which totaled $1,100.[247]

(B) The Passion of Nat Turner

Nat Turner arrived well guarded and in chains in Jerusalem at a quarter after one o'clock. He was delivered to two magistrates of the court, James W. Parker and James Trezevant, who interrogated him for nearly two hours. Both had sat through numerous insurrection trials and had insight into the uprising. Other knowledgeable investigators participated, including William C. Parker, who would represent Nat Turner at the trial set for November 5th.

During the interrogation Nat Turner "evinced great intelligence and much shrewdness of intellect." He freely confessed he was a Prophet, and had revelations that led him to believe he could conquer Southampton as the whites did in the revolution. The dark appearance of the sun was the signal to begin.

For William Parker this was the first time he had seen his client. He noted:

> "He answers exactly the description annexed to the Governor's Proclamation, except that he is of a darker hue, and his eyes, though large, are not prominent—they are very long, deeply seated in his head, and have rather a sinister expression. A more gloomy fanatic you have never heard of."[248]

The interrogators were interested in the operation of his mind. William Parker asked questions himself on this subject. He wanted to know how his "idea of emancipating the blacks" was connected to the signs he saw, his conversation with the spirits, and his supernatural powers to heal disease and to control the weather. "I examined him closely upon this point, he alway [sic] seemed to mystify." However Nat Turner did not "conceal that he was the author of the design, and that he imparted it to five or six others." After the interrogation, Turner, in chains, was jailed with the four free black prisoners who were awaiting trial.[249]

Nat Turner was to spend the last 11 days of his life in the Southampton jail. During the first three days of his incarceration he was interviewed by Thomas R. Gray, the young, downward mobile, defense lawyer, which resulted in a seminal document in American history, which revealed for the first and only time the inner working of the mind of a slave rebel leader. The young Gray was a member of a prominent Southampton family, and as recently as 1829 had owned 21 slaves and 800 acres of farmland. By 1831, however, young Gray had lost all this, except for one slave and 300 acres. He was motivated by economic interest to publish *The Confessions of Nat Turner* so he could remedy his economic situation. Gray painted a vivid portrait of the jailed slave leader:

> "The calm, deliberate composure with which he spoke of his late deeds and intentions, the expression of his fiend-like face when excited by enthusiasm, still bearing the stains of the blood of helpless innocence about him; clothed with rags and covered with chains; yet daring to raise his manacled hands to heaven, with a spirit soaring above the attributes of man; I looked on him and my blood curdled in my veins."[250]

In a period when most white males were barely literate, and there was near total illiteracy among slaves and women, Turner's superior intelligence, literacy, and knowledge of the scriptures negated the intellectual distance between him and Gray, a member of the elite. Gray's respect for Turner was further reinforced by the slave leader's sobriety. Gray noted: "It is notorious, that he was never know to have a dollar in his life; to swear an oath, or drink a drop of spirits." Gray also realized that while Turner had no formal education, he could read and write "and for natural intelligence and quickness of apprehension, is surpassed by few men I have ever seen."[251]

From the *Confessions* it is clear that Nat Turner saw himself as a Prophet and the second coming of Christ. *And on the 12th of May, 1828, I heard a loud noise in the heavens, and the Spirit instantly appeared to me and said the Serpent was loosened, and Christ had laid down the yoke he had borne for the sins of men, and that I should take it on and fight against the Serpent, for the time was fast approaching when the first should be last and last should be first.* When Gray asked Nat Turner if he was mistaken in his action, the slave rebel replied: *Was not Christ crucified.*[252]

In the *Confessions* Turner makes several references to the Bible, all of them to the New Testament, with Luke 12 the most frequently cited passage. Nat Turner was an expert on the Bible and must have known that Jesus did not leave a first person account of his passion and no one was present who left an eyewitness account. With Thomas R. Gray recording his state of mind and witnessing his passion, Nat Turner remedied the lack of firsthand accounts left by the first Jesus.[253]

Nat Turner noted that it was the passage from Luke 12:31 **Seek ye the Kingdom of Heaven and all things shall be added unto you** that inspired him to begin his revolutionary quest. The Jesus of Luke 12 is not the passive turn the other cheek Jesus found elsewhere in Luke and the other Gospels. The Jesus of Luke 12 says: **I am come to send fire on the earth; Suppose ye that I am come to give peace on earth. I tell you, Nay; but rather division: For from henceforth there shall be five in one house divided, three against two and two against three. The father shall be divided against the son, and the son against the father; the mother against the daughter, and the daughter against the mother; the mother-in-law against her daughter-in-law, and the daughter-in-law against her mother-in-law.** And Luke also taught Nat Turner that he, like Jesus, would meet his death in Jerusalem.[254]

(C) The Trial of Nat Turner

On November 5, 1831 Nat Turner was tried. He was arraigned as "Nat, alias Nat Turner, a Negro man slave," the only Southampton slave defendant accorded a last name. Only free persons received a last name. All the slave defendants had only a first name in the record. Free black defendants had a first and last name, like whites. The granting of Nat the last name Turner reflected his stature in the eyes of the elite.

An additional reflection of his stature was the fact that ten of the most experienced magistrates heard his case, unlike the other slave trials in which 5 presided, and an extra guard was provided. Turner was charged with conspiring to rebel and make insurrection. He pled not guilty, saying to his counsel William C. Parker, "that he did not feel so."[255]

The evidence against Turner consisted of his confession to magistrates James W. Parker, who also served as one of the trial judges, and Samuel Trezevant in which he admitted killing Margaret Whitehead and striking the first blow against the Travis' before they were killed. He also admitted participating in the insurrection from beginning to end. Levi

Waller testified that he witnessed the murders at his home and saw Nat Turner, whom he knew well, ride up and assume command of the insurgents. Nat Turner presented no defense and was convicted by a unanimous panel and sentenced to hang on November 11, 1831. The court placed his value at $375 and allowed Parker $10 for the defense.[256]

During the trial Trezevant recounted the interrogation in which Nat Turner stated he had "signed omens from God" that he should undertake the insurrection and he "could by the imposition of his hands cure disease" and "that he went on to detail a medley of incoherent and confused opinions about his communication with God" and "his command over the clouds." A newspaper article on November 4th had noted: "His profanity in comparing his pretended prophecies with passages in the Holy Scripture should not be mentioned, if it did not afford proof of his insanity."[257]

The insanity defense was first used in a Virginia criminal case in 1661 and underwent a rapid evolution in English and American law at the time of the American Revolution, when slaves received benefit of the defense. In part this evolution was a product of the mental illness of King George III as well as an assassination attempt against him in 1800 by James Hadfield. The test used to declare Hadfield insane was not the absence of an ability to think and know the difference from right and wrong, but rather whether or not the defendant was operating under a delusion.[258]

It is clear from the evidence, including the statements of Nat Turner himself, that he had a mental illness by modern standards. He had both visual and auditory hallucinations. On more than one occasion the Spirit spoke to him. He saw visions in the sky on several occasions culminating *on the 12th of May, 1828, I heard a loud noise in the heavens, and the Spirit instantly appeared to me and said the Serpent was loosened, and Christ had laid down the yoke he had borne for the sins of men, and that I should take it on and fight against the Serpent.*

In addition to the hallucinations, there is also evidence that Nat Turner had suffered a serious head injury. He had a scar on his temple allegedly caused by a kick of a mule. It is well established that a serious head injury, especially if it compromises the frontal lobes, and is combined with significant physical and psychic abuse, can produce a serial killer. Nat Turner was whipped and had scars on the back of his neck and on his right arm near the wrist produced by a blow. With his symptoms Nat Turner today would receive a diagnosis of psychotic schizophrenia.[259]

While it is useful to consider the theoretical applicability of the insanity defense to the Nat Turner case, the defense attorney did not present it for good reasons. William Parker was present at the interrogation of Turner by the magistrates and asked questions himself which probed the rebel's mental state. By 1831, the law of insanity held that mental illness was not enough to excuse criminal culpability so long as the perpetrator maintained his cognitive abilities intact and could distinguish between right and wrong. It is clear from his confession that Nat Turner was well aware of what he was doing once the killing began and his detailed recitation of the facts of the insurrection demonstrated his precise knowledge. Parker's decision not to raise the issue of insanity was grounded in the reality that it was futile in light of what Turner had done. He must die both as payback for his acts and to deter. In addition, he was not legally insane under existent law.[260]

(D) Execution

There was no right of appeal from the slave court and, of course, clemency by the Governor was out of the question. On November 11, 1831 Nat Turner was executed. The hangman was Edward Butts a deputy sheriff who certified the execution of the sentence, indicating that he had "executed the within slave named Nat according to the sentence of the court." The execution occurred precisely at noon before a small crowd. A witness noted, "He betrayed no emotion, but appeared to be utterly reckless in the awful fate that awaited him and even hurried his executor in the performance of his duty."[261]

Meanwhile, Thomas R. Gray was aggressively pursuing the publication of the *Confessions*. On November 10th he copyrighted the pamphlet in Washington D.C. and by November 20th had 50,000 copies printed in Baltimore. Two days later they were on sale for 25 cents a copy. A second edition was printed in 1832 but the proceeds did not alleviate Gray's economic woes. He moved to Portsmouth in 1839 and died impoverished there in 1845.[262]

Immediately after Nat Turner's death rumors began about the disposal of his remains. One stated he "sold his body for dissection, and spent the money for ginger cakes." Another indicated his corpse was skinned, grease was made of his flesh, and a money purse of his skin. Legend has it that Turner's head, which resembled that of a sheep, was separated from his body and for a time ended up in a college in Wooster, Ohio. It was reported that his headless skeleton was misplaced around 1900. The dissection of Turner's body reflected an attempt by the state to control his memory and spirit after death. It denied him a Christian burial, deprived his family and friends of final rites, and sought to diminish his status as a martyr.[263] Even though the whereabouts of his remains are uncertain, there is no doubt that his spirit, reflected in his words, actions, and foresight to record his state of mind, still resonates in the collective consciousness of the nation.

Chapter 8

Aftereffects

(A) The Short-term

President Andrew Jackson in his Third Annual Message in December 1831 did not mention the events in Southampton or touch at all on the subject of slavery. This stance reflected the policy of ignoring slavery in the legislative forum. However, he adopted the exactly opposite position on the question of Native Americans. In the message he explicitly referred to his policy of Indian removal, noting:

> "The internal peace and security of our confederated States is the next principal object of the General Government. Time and experience have proved that the abode of the native Indian within their limits is dangerous to their peace and injurious to himself."

He indicated it was his intention to remove major tribes in the Southeast from the United States by persuasion if possible, but by other means if necessary. The goal was to extinguish Indian title to all the land in the cotton growing South, as well as other regions.[264]

Virginia's Governor John Floyd delivered his end of the year message on December 6, 1831. While preparing the message, he had written the Governor of South Carolina, James Hamilton, and indicated he would propose a plan of gradual slave emancipation by requiring slaves to "work for a time on the Rail Roads" earning enough to pay their transportation out of the country.[265] On November 21st he confided in his diary, "Before I leave this Government, I will have contrived to have a law passed gradually abolishing slavery in this State, or at all events to begin the work by prohibiting slavery on the West side of the Blue Ridge Mountains."[266]

In his lengthy address to the House of Delegates on December 6th, however, he dropped the gradual emancipation plan, focusing instead on the insurrection, internal improvements and Federal relations. He reported that the insurrection was "new, unexpected and heretofore unknown to the State," that sixty-one whites, mostly women and children, were killed by "a banditti of slaves," numbering up to 70. He noted the insurrection was quickly suppressed by the morning of the second day, and the military force, including Federal troops, was overwhelming. The most profound cost of the insurrection, he stated, was the loss of security, noting that, "All communities are liable to suffer from the dagger of the murderer and midnight assassin, and it behoves them to guard against them."[267]

Governor Floyd blamed "negro [sic] preachers" for the insurrection, noting that the "spirit of insurrection" was widespread as the prosecutions in other counties proved. The black preachers, under the influence of northern elements that preached equality and abolition, used mass religious services to spread their seditious ideas. "The public good requires the negro [sic] preachers to be silenced."[268]

Floyd ignored the evidence of free black participation in the insurrection, instead saying "some proof is also furnished that for the class of free people of color, they have opened more enlarged views, and urge the achievement of a higher destiny, by means for the present less violent, but not differing in the end from those presented to the slaves." Floyd argued that the free blacks should leave the state, proposing that the state appropriate money to assist in their removal. He also proposed reform of the state militia into an effective military force to maintain the "due subordination" of the blacks.[269]

The bulk of the Governor's address was devoted to two subjects: internal improvements and Federal relations. The two subjects were deeply linked since both involved fractures that would most clearly manifest themselves thirty years later in the Civil War. Floyd was the first westerner elected Governor of Virginia and wanted to construct internal improvements, either a canal or railroad, linking the west with the rest of the state. The west was relatively slave free when compared with the eastern part of the state. Anti-slavery sentiment was more widespread there than elsewhere in Virginia. This part of Virginia would side with the Union and become the state of West Virginia in the coming war.

Floyd was an advocate of states rights, viewing the

Federal government as an "Agent of the State," only authorized to handle foreign affairs. The Federal government had usurped powers and had engaged in policies like the tariff that redistributed wealth from the producing states in the South to non-producing states elsewhere. Floyd confided in his diary on December 6th:

> "My message was well received, though many think it a bold state paper. It may be their attachment to Jackson has blunted their patriotism. I think so. But it is the true doctrine of the Federal Constitution and States Rights. I will maintain it as long as I am Governor even to the utmost hazard."[270]

The Legislature accepted the reasoning of the Governor regarding the insurrection and passed a statute that prohibited any slave or free black from preaching, day or night, or attending any nighttime religious services, even if the preacher was white. These statutes were enforced by whipping for a first offense, and enslavement and sale out of the country on a second. Draconian restrictions were placed on free blacks with respect to movement and entry into the state, as well as prohibitions against the purchase of real property and/or slaves other than family members, possession of firearms, and commerce, including the training of other blacks in skilled trades, except barbering. The most drastic change was in the legal status of free blacks, who, except for homicide or where the punishment was death, were stripped of the right to jury trial and other due process protections, and were relegated to the slave courts for trial before magistrates, where there was no right to have an indictment or information filed, or any right to appeal.[271]

The harsh measures initially induced panic among Southampton's free blacks. A sixth of the most skilled left in December 1831 for Liberia on a voyage sponsored by the American Colonization Society. More followed in 1832. Others fled north, especially to Boston, Chicago, Cincinnati and Canada. The panic, however, subsided and the county's free black population actually increased for the rest of the decade.[272]

Southampton lost population between 1830 and 1840.

The census data indicates that the county's population declined to 14,427 by 1840. While the free black population increased to 1,801, both the number of whites (6,143) and slaves (6,483) declined. In 1840 nearly 65% of the lower county's population was black, compared to a little over 49% in the upper.[273] The decline in the white and slave population was a reflection of the redistribution of the southern population in the 1830's, through migration and slave sales. The Southampton economy was marginal for many and the best source for cash was the sale of a slave.[274]

The most dramatic short-term effect of the insurrection was the first and only open debate on the abolition of slavery in the South in the antebellum period. In the same legislative session discussed above, a measure to gradually abolish slavery was introduced and voted upon. In his diary on the 26th of December 1831, Governor Floyd noted that even though legislative members from the slave owning East opposed it, the subject of gradual abolition of slavery was beginning to be discussed and it "must come if I can influence my friends in the Assembly to bring it on. I will not rest until slavery is abolished in Virginia."[275]

In January the Governor's allies from the Trans-Allegheny region of the state, the future West Virginia, outmaneuvered the slave interests and turned a vote to shut off debate on abolition into a victory that opened the debate on that subject. The grandson of Thomas Jefferson, a slaveholder himself, introduced a bill to submit to voters legislation that would gradually abolish slavery, a modification of a plan originally proposed by his grandfather. Randolph, partially motivated by his wife's terror after the Southampton massacre, proposed that all slaves born after July 4, 1840 become state property, males at 21 and females at 18, and be transported outside the United States. The hired labor of the slaves would help defray the cost of the deportation. Emancipation and colonization went together in this *post-nati* emancipation plan because, like his grandfather, and most whites North and South, he did not believe that it was possible to incorporate persons of African descent into the body politic. In the *Notes on the State of Virginia* Thomas Jefferson made the classic

106

statement of this point of view:

> "It will probably be asked, Why not retain and incorporate the blacks into the state, and thus save the expense of supplying, by importation of white settlers, the vacancies they will leave? Deep rooted prejudices entertained by the whites; ten thousand recollections, by the blacks of injuries they have sustained; new provocations; the real distinctions which nature has made; and many other circumstances, will divide us into parties, and produce convulsions which will probably never end but in the extermination of the one or the other race."

Jefferson then went on to detail his racist beliefs about the "real distinctions which nature has made."[276]

The Virginia House divided into three groupings on the issue, which had a regional-racial dimension. The conservative slaveholding eastern interests, with heavy free black and slave populations, wanted silence and no action at all. The moderates, from the central regions of the state, with moderate free black and slave populations, proposed colonization of free blacks as a first step to emancipation, while the Trans-Allegheny with few free blacks and slaves, supported gradual abolition and colonization. In the end, gradual abolition was defeated, state funded colonization of free blacks and manumitted slaves passed the House, but was killed by the Senate, and the harsh black codes discussed previously were the only successful legislative outcome of the session. Governor Floyd noted in his diary that the debate ended with threats by delegates from the slave owning areas "to divide the State by the Blue Ridge Mountains sooner than part with their negroes [sic], which is the property of that part of the State."[277]

(B) The Long-term

(1) Thomas R. Dew

Nat Turner, like the Jesus of Luke 12, came to divide and to sow disharmony and ultimately bloodshed and did so. The insurrection was a precipitating factor in the sectional division

107

that led to the Civil War and provoked a radical shift in the ideological justification for slavery in the antebellum period.

One of the significant long-term effects of the open debate on slavery in the Virginia legislature was Thomas R. Dew's <u>Review of the Debate in the Virginia Legislature of 1831 and 1832</u>. Governor Floyd appointed the 29-year-old conservative, who was the foremost intellectual in the state, to conduct the study. Dew, the son of a Tidewater planter, highly educated in the best schools, a European traveler, a professor of political law at his alma mater, William and Mary, was a disciple of Adam Smith and an advocate of free trade. In the fall of 1831 he was a delegate to the Free Trade Convention that met in Philadelphia.

His pamphlet, which he initially published anonymously, is often cited as the seminal document in the shift from the Revolutionary generation's view that slavery was an evil system to an outlook that argued it was a positive good. Dew's purpose was to "demonstrate upon every ground the complete justification of the whole southern country in a further continuance of the system of slavery which has been originated by no fault of theirs, and continued and increased contrary to their most earnest desires and petitions."[278]

Dew's main goal was to demolish the argument that it was possible to emancipate and deport the state's slave and free black populations or any portion thereof. He was a student of Malthus and argued that the state could not economically deport either free blacks or slaves fast enough to offset the natural increase in the black population. When it came to tampering with the "elastic and powerful spring of population…"

> "The energies of government are for the most part feeble or impotent when arrayed against its action. It is this procreative power of the human species, either exerted or dormant, which so frequently brushes away *in reality* the visionary fabrics of the philanthropists, and mars the cherished plots and schemes of statesmen."[279]

Dew argued that both the expense and the consequences would defeat any effort to deport the state's black population.

Dew stressed that slaves constituted one third of the wealth of the state and to divest itself of this wealth, particularly slave labor, would bankrupt the state. "It is in truth the slave labour in Virginia which gives value to her soil and habitations-take away this and you pull down the atlas that upholds the whole system." If the slave population were to be removed from the state, Virginia would become a "waste howling wilderness... the grass shall be seen growing in the streets, and the foxes peeping from their holes."[280]

Moreover, there was no satisfactory place to deport Virginia's blacks. The existing colony in Liberia could not absorb large numbers and the immigrants would ultimately have to wage wars to take the space needed. Dew argued that the real choice was between slavery or emancipation with permission to remain. The latter course would not work because free blacks, "the *drones* and *pests* of society" had demonstrated that they would not work. Experience showed that slave labor was vastly more efficient and productive than free black labor. Moreover, blacks and whites could never be equal and eventually blacks would drag whites down to their own level.[281]

In the long run, Dew argued, the only way Virginia could rid itself of slavery was to industrialize the economy and shift away from the agricultural production of staples. It could then sell its slaves to the staple producing South and attract a free white population to work its factories. Dew's views were grounded in studies he conducted on the cost of slave versus free labor at the J.R. Anderson and Tredegar Iron Works in Richmond.[282]

(2) John Brown

The Nat Turner insurrection destroyed the feeling of security and confidence of slave owners throughout the South. Through the 1840's and 1850's the South used its control of the political process to eradicate all barriers to the nationalization of slavery. The culmination of the process was the *Dred Scott* decision by the Supreme Court in 1857. Dred Scott, born in the early 1800's, was raised in Southampton, seven or eight miles from Nat Turner, until he began the odyssey that led him to Missouri, where in 1846 he sued for his freedom. The case wound its way to the U.S. Supreme Court and the South gained its most significant triumph when the justices held that the Constitution protected the owners' property rights in their slaves and there was no legal restriction to their taking this species of property anywhere in the nation. In addition, blacks, free or slave, were not citizens and had no rights worth respecting. Slavery was made a national institution reversing a policy that had restricted it regionally since the Revolution.[283]

Slave insurrections precipitously declined after the suppression of the Turner insurrection. There were only 12 Virginia slave convictions for insurrection after 1831, nearly all for speech or plans. It was at this point that a white man, John Brown, born the same year as Nat Turner, a religious mystic, and inspired by the Southampton insurrection, continued the roughly 30-year cycle of insurrection in Virginia, and precipitated the final series of events leading to civil war. As Frederick Douglass so eloquently noted on slavery:

> "When the explosive force of this controversy had already weakened the bolts of the American Union; when the agitation of the public mind was at its topmost height; when the two sections were at their extreme points of difference; when, comprehending the perilous situation, such statesmen of the North as William H. Seward sought to allay the rising storm by soft, persuasive speech, and when all hope of compromise had nearly vanished, as if to banish even the last glimmer of hope for peace between the sections, John Brown came upon the scene."[284]

On October 16, 1859 John Brown's interracial band of 18 captured the Federal arsenal at Harper's Ferry, Virginia, took hostages, including a slave owning relative of George Washington, freed a few slaves, and held out for 36 hours until Federal marines led by Col. Robert E. Lee and Lt. J.E.B. Stuart broke into the small engine house where he had retreated, and subdued Brown, who had two sons killed during the insurrection.[285]

Brown and five of the other survivors were tried a week later. While Brown was tried for insurrection, he denied this was his objective, and instead claimed he only planned to take the arms seized from the armory to the nearby mountains and establish a liberated zone where fugitive slaves could seek refuge. He had written a Constitution for his mountain republic in which blacks, slave or free, were equal citizens.

The evidence at Brown's trial, as well as his statements afterward, revealed similarities between him and Nat Turner. Both were religious mystics who believed their violent acts were God inspired, both believed their martyrdom would hasten the end of slavery, and both were accused of acting on insane religious delusions. Finally, both believed that in the end only violence would end slavery. Brown's last words, written on the day of his execution were: "I John Brown am now quite *certain* that the crimes of this *guilty, land: will* never be purged *away*; but with Blood. I had *as I now think: vainly* flattered myself that without *verry [sic]* much bloodshed; it might be done."[286]

(3) The Civil War

In 1861, nearly 30 years after Nat Turner's insurrection, the Civil War began, fulfilling his prophecy of a violent end to slavery, with division among kin. The people of Southampton, both white and black, had an impact on the outcome. For most of the War, Southampton was a backwater in southeastern Virginia, often part of a no-man's land between the two armies, supplying men and supplies to both sides. Many whites, as well as some blacks, fought on the Confederate side, while Southampton slaves were impressed to work on fortifications and perform other tasks for the men in gray. In 1862, Union forces took Suffolk, the key town in the region, which became a magnet for escaped slaves. Slaves helped the Union forces as spies or workers. Eventually significant numbers joined the Union army when Lincoln finally opened its ranks to black soldiers.[287]

1863 was a disastrous year militarily for the South, with

defeats at Gettysburg and Vicksburg. The only bright spot was a September victory at Chickamauga, Georgia. A total rout and destruction of the Union army in the West was prevented by Union Maj. General George H. Thomas, who rallied his forces to hold a critical point while the rest of the Union army withdrew to Chattanooga. For his heroics, Thomas earned the sobriquet "The Rock of Chickamauga."

General Thomas was born into a slave owning family in Southampton in 1816, and was 15 during the Nat Turner insurrection. The insurgents raided his farm and impressed several of the Thomas slaves into the insurgent army. The Thomas family fled to Jerusalem just ahead of the rebels. Years later Thomas, even though a slave owner, stayed loyal to the Union and became a leading General in the blue, and commanded African-American troops. Lincoln thought that Thomas was the perfect General to organize black soldiers. After Chickamauga, he became Sherman's second-in-command on the march to Atlanta. He was disowned by his family and friends as a traitor. In the words of Luke 12, **Suppose ye that I am come to give peace on earth. I tell you, Nay; but rather division: For from henceforth there shall be five in one house divided, three against two and two against three.**[288]

In late 1863 and early 1864, Lincoln directed General Ben J. Butler, commander of the Army of the James, which included Virginia and North Carolina, with its headquarters at Fort Monroe, to recruit black troops, both slave and free. Lincoln saw this as a war measure that would insure Union victory. Butler, the first Union general to arm blacks, while he was in command of New Orleans in 1862, was a strong advocate of the use of African-American soldiers. One of the units Butler formed at Ft. Monroe was the 2nd U.S. Colored Cavalry, which included recruits from Southampton. This unit was based at Suffolk in March 1864, and in a sense, were ghosts of Nat Turner's slave army. A major reason the 2nd Colored Calvary was sent to Suffolk was their familiarity with the area's waterways, swamps and complicated road system.

Southeastern Virginia was not a major theater in the war. Control over the area was generally in Union hands but the population was hostile, especially when black troops were garrisoned there.

In March 1864 elements of James Longstreet's army were operating in North Carolina under General George E. Pickett of Gettysburg fame. The Union's black units were also operating in the area and battled Pickett's forces. One of Pickett's divisions, led by General Matthew Ransom, was known to show no quarter to black troops.

Pickett sent Ransom to Suffolk to destroy the black units based there. On March 9th Ransom's forces, consisting mainly of infantry and artillery, crossed from North Carolina on a rapid march and entered the Suffolk area without the Union force's knowledge. A 2nd Colored Calvary unit on reconnaissance outside the town was surprised by Ransom's troops around noon as the troops were preparing to eat. The black soldiers mounted rapidly and fiercely fought their way out of an encirclement. The fight occurred under a "black flag," without quarter. Neither side took prisoners. An army report noted: "Almost entirely surrounded by ten times their number, they fought their way out, losing no prisoners or horses except those that were killed."[289] Some had to take to the swamps to escape, often after they were wounded or had their horses shot from under them. Their superior knowledge of the roads and swamps helped them survive.

Eight were trapped in a house in Suffolk, which was burned to the ground with the black soldiers fighting to the last man. The Confederate troops, desperate for food and clothing, looted the 2nd Cavalry base camp, after they had driven the Union forces out of Suffolk. The Union General Benjamin Butler noted the black troops "behaved with utmost courage, coolness, and daring." Shortly thereafter Union troops again took control of the area.[290]

1865, the last year of the war, was a time so desperate for the Confederates that General Robert E. Lee, with the approval of Jefferson Davis, was urgently requesting that the army recruit slave soldiers. Lee, who had witnessed the Nat Turner insurrection from Fort Monroe in 1831, and commanded the Federal troops who captured John Brown in 1859, wrote Jefferson Davis on March 10, 1865: "I do not know whether the law authorizing the use of negro [sic] troops has received your sanction, but if it has, I respectfully recommend that measures be taken to carry it into effect as soon as practicable."[291] But it was too late. On April 2nd and 3rd 1865, Union troops broke through Richmond's defenses and black Union troops were in the vanguard that entered the conquered Confederate capital. The war was over. On April 10, 1865 Lee issued his final order informing his troops of the defeat and surrender of his army.[292] Thirty-four years after the execution of Turner his prophecy was fulfilled when slavery died a violent death.

Chapter 9

Lessons of the Insurrection

(A) Vengeance

Today a debate rages in the United States about how to react to the 9/11 terrorist attacks. At the heart of the controversy is whether the rule of law and due process, including the traditional right of habeas corpus, should extend to suspected terrorists, including American citizens. Embedded in the debate is also the issue of whether the government should have the right to torture suspects to gain intelligence.

After September 11, 2001, the U.S. government initiated a no quarter war on global terrorism, which set aside traditional American values of due process and the rule of law. The President, using the authority of a Congressional resolution and his claimed inherent war powers, created off shore prisons in which persons he defined as "unlawful combatants" were held incognito, without charges, without access to an attorney, for an indefinite duration, without access to any judicial body, including U.S. Federal courts. On November 13, 2001, President Bush signed the Military Order that established this gulag. The Order had a broad definition of persons subject to its provisions. In addition to members of al-Qaeda, or persons who harbored them, it also included persons who harbored or "aided or abetted, or conspired to commit, acts of international terrorism, or acts in preparation therefore, that have caused, threaten to cause, or have as their aim to cause, injury to or adverse effects on the United States, its citizens, national security, foreign policy, or economy." The President or his designate decides who has violated the Order.[293]

While the order stated it did not apply to American citizens, in practice the U.S. government used its provisions to detain U.S. citizens incognito without any constitutional rights.[294]

On February 7, 2002 President Bush signed a second document, ironically entitled the "Humane Treatment of al-

Qaeda and Taliban Detainees," which stripped all detainees, except those captured in Iraq, of prisoner of war status and Geneva protections. The President found that the anti torture provisions of the Geneva Conventions did not apply to such detainees. Bush designated these detainees "unlawful combatants" and stripping them of prisoner of war status opened the door to their torture.[295]

The cornerstones of the American gulag are military prisons in Guantanamo Bay, Cuba, Afghanistan, and Iraq. These were supplemented by a series of secret prisons for high value terrorist suspects run by the CIA in Jordan, Pakistan and other undisclosed locations. Eleven senior al-Qaeda members, including Khalid Sheikh Mohammed, Abu Zubaydah, and Riduan Isamuddin were held at secret prisons. The CIA used coercive interrogation methods at these secret prisons that the U.S. government does not define as torture, even though most of the world disagrees.[296] Deaths in U.S. custody were not uncommon. The U.S. also used the process of "rendition," sending detainees to other nations for interrogation and torture.[297]

The use of torture, what the U.S. government calls "counter-resistance techniques," grew out of a real need to gain intelligence from savvy unlawful combatants. On October 25, 2002, James T. Hill, Commander, U.S. Southern Command sent a memorandum to the Joint Chiefs of Staff in which he noted, "However, despite our best efforts, some detainees have tenaciously resisted our current interrogation methods." General Hill and the Defense Department wanted to identify more coercive interrogation techniques "we can lawfully employ."[298]

After internal discussions the government approved a set of "counter-resistance techniques" which included water boarding, the practice of strapping a person down and pouring water over the cloth-wrapped face to induce fear of drowning; hooding; sleep deprivation; starving; stress positions; loud noises; sexual humiliation; assaults; nudity in cells; exposure to intense heat and cold; use of dogs; use of medical personnel to assist interrogators, among others. The same interrogation techniques migrated from Guantanamo and Afghanistan to

Iraq as the photographs from Abu Ghraib demonstrate so clearly.

The initial reaction in the war on terror, like the initial reaction to the Nat Turner insurrection, was a brutal no quarter response, in which American traditions of due process of law were banished and captives were detained and interrogated in violation of international standards governing war.[299]

(B) Dualism and Hierarchy

Throughout its history the United States has practiced a dualism in its treatment of whites and people of color. This ethnic dualism persists in the U.S. today. One only has to examine census statistics to see it reflected in data from infant mortality to life expectancy, employment, income, incarceration rates, and so on for each measure of social well being or economic status. This dualism also remains in the criminal system, notably in sentencing.[300]

Now this dualism has taken on an international character in the war on terror, manifesting itself in the treatment of Muslims, most of whom are people of color. The U.S. executive has created a parallel system of courts, called military commissions, to try terror suspects. Ironically, the military courts are similar to the Virginia slave courts of *oyer and terminer*. There are no juries but instead panels of three to seven military officers who will hear the cases, with a two-thirds majority required for conviction. Hearsay evidence is admissible. There is no right to appeal or right of habeas corpus. The President has the final say on any conviction or sentence.[301]

The Turner insurrection revealed the existence of a hierarchy that actually ruled behind a democratic façade. This is still the reality today in the United States as wealth and political power are concentrated in the hands of the richest one percent of the population. Wealth is as concentrated today in the United States as it was in 1831, or any other time, and the rate of concentration is increasing. Today the top 1 percent of the U.S. population, those with more than 5.9 million in net worth, control over 40% of the nation's wealth and each year the concentration is increasing. The wealth even within the top 1 percent is concentrated, with the top 0.5% of the upper class controlling over a quarter of the nation's wealth.[302]

The elite maintains control through the use of its wealth and the manipulation of ethnic dualism. Economic power correlates with political power, as the elite, both as individuals and through its corporate instruments, spends enormous sums to gain political influence and access. Political divisions, however, remain among the elite. The 2004 Presidential election is an apt metaphor for the point. Both George Bush and John Kerry were wealthy scions of upper class families, educated in elite schools, members of the same fraternity, Skulls and Bones, and 9th cousins twice removed. The intense political fight between the two relatives illustrates that there are deep political divisions within the upper class.[303]

The challenge for the mass of the United States population is to unite and to utilize the great wealth of the nation for all, instead of the present system wherein the interests of the richest one percent dominate.

(C) The Rule of Law

In the summer of 2004, the Supreme Court took initial steps to assert the rule of law by granting limited due process rights to terror suspects. On June 28, 2004, the U.S. Supreme Court decided three cases, *Rumsfeld v. Padilla, Rasul v. Bush, and Hamdi v. Rumsfeld*, that collectively held that detainees in the war on terror are entitled to bring petitions for habeas corpus in federal court, rejecting in the process the government's argument that off shore prisons were not subject to federal jurisdiction. The court held that as long as the custodian of the gulag, i.e., Rumsfeld, the Secretary of Defense, was available for process inside the U.S., the Federal courts had jurisdiction over the detainees.[304]

Even though the Military Order signed by Bush on November 13, 2001 indicated that it only applied to international terrorists or their associates who were non-citizens, the administration also detained American citizens under its provisions, claiming that it had the authority to indefinitely detain, without charges, or a right to an attorney, U.S. citizens it designated "unlawful combatants" and the federal court could not intervene. Jose Padilla was an American citizen seized by the government on American soil who the Bush administration claimed plotted with al-Qaeda. Bush designated Padilla an unlawful combatant in June 2002, claiming that Padilla was a soldier for al-Qaeda and planned to explode a radioactive bomb on U.S. soil. In *Padilla* the Supreme Court ducked the key issue and decided the case on a procedural point that Padilla filed his petition for habeas corpus in the wrong district. In a dissent, Justice Stevens, joined by three other justices, wrote:

> "At stake in this case is nothing less than the essence of a free society. Even more important than the method of selecting the people's rulers and their successors is the character of the constraints imposed on the Executive by the rule of law. Unconstrained Executive detention for the purpose of investigating and preventing subversive activity is the hallmark of the Star Chamber. Access to counsel for the purpose protecting the citizen from official mistakes and mistreatment is the hallmark of due process."[305]

In November 2005, the government, in order to avoid a Supreme Court review of its authority to hold Padilla as an unlawful combatant, filed three counts of conspiracy to aid terrorists and to murder US nationals overseas against him in federal court, transferred him from military custody, and rendered moot the constitutional issue raised by his case. Padilla was convicted on all the charges and sentenced in 2008 to 17 years, 4 months in prison.[306]

In *Hamdi v. Rumsfeld*, the Supreme Court also dealt with the government's contention that it could hold an American citizen as an "enemy combatant…indefinitely—without formal charges or proceedings—unless and until it makes the determination that access to counsel or further process is warranted." Hamdi was born in the United States in 1980 and raised in Saudi Arabia. In 2001 he resided in Afghanistan when he was seized by the Northern Alliance and turned over to the U.S. military. The government presented hearsay evidence that Hamdi was a trained member of a Taliban military unit who, when defeated in battle against the Northern Alliance, was armed when he surrendered. Hamdi denied the allegation. The court rejected the Bush administration's position and held that a citizen detainee had a right to counsel, and a "meaningful opportunity to contest the factual basis for that detention before a neutral decision maker."

The *Hamdi* decision, however, left the contours of the due process afforded to "enemy or unlawful combatants" unclear. In the plurality opinion, in which four judges joined, it was held that the President—pursuant to an Authorization for Use of Military Force passed by Congress in the wake of 9/11—could declare an American citizen an enemy combatant and detain him for the duration of the war on terror, without charges so long as the detainee had a chance to contest the charges, with counsel, before a neutral decision maker. For the plurality, however, the due process requirement—after balancing the interests of the citizen against the state, due to the exigencies of the war on terror—only required that detainees appear before neutral judges in military commissions in which there was a presumption in favor of the government's evidence and the burden was on the detainee to rebut it. The government could use hearsay evidence. After the ruling, Hamdi was allowed to return to Saudi Arabia when he renounced his American citizenship.[307]

The executive branch, and its allies in Congress, resisted these tentative steps toward due process, asserting the President has independent authority under his war powers to detain terror suspects, including American citizens, and to deny them due process, habeas corpus, and access to lawyers and the courts. It also asserted it had the authority to use coercive interrogation techniques, a euphemism for torture, to gain actionable intelligence. In December 2005 President Bush signed a law that barred federal courts from hearing habeas corpus petitions by Guantanamo detainees attacking their detention. Immediately afterward the Army issued new regulations that permitted executions at the Cuban base, with no federal court review.[308]

In June 2006, The Supreme Court revisited the issue of

the trial of detainees before Presidential military commissions in *Hamdan v. Rumsfeld*. The *Hamdan* decision held that the President did not have authority to establish such commissions absent congressional authorization. The primary flaw with the commissions established by Bush was they authorized convictions based on evidence the accused would never see or hear. In addition the court held that Congress had not stripped it of jurisdiction to adjudicate detainee cases and, most importantly, detainees were protected by Article 3 of the Third Geneva Convention, which provided that detainee cases should be heard by regular military courts established by Congress. These military courts provided basic due process protections including the right to personal presence to hear and confront evidence. The Supreme Court in *Hamdan,* in effect, reasserted the traditional doctrine of separation of powers by indicating it was Congress, not the President, which had the authority to establish the trial procedures for detainees in the war on terror.[309]

What the ruling means for the future is uncertain and probably depends, in part, on the outcome of the ideological struggle to control the Supreme Court. On June 12, 2008 the Supreme Court by a 5 to 4 decision decided *Boumediene v. Bush*, which grants detainees a federal constitutional right to habeas corpus. It will take time to understand the full impact of this decision. The outcome of the struggle is uncertain. It is still possible the advocates of unlimited Presidential authority will prevail and set the nation on an uncharted course of despotism with respect to terror suspects.[310]

The rulers in the United States should draw on the wisdom of its past experience with terrorism and heed the lessons of the Nat Turner insurrection, particularly the insight that justice tempered with mercy is an antidote to terrorist violence. Today the United States is at a crossroads and the Nat Turner insurrection in many ways is a microcosm for exploring reactions to terrorism that speak to us today. The Turner insurrection was inspired by intense religious beliefs that motivated followers to acts of great courage and self sacrifice, as well as deeds of chilling brutality and carnage.

The aftermath of the Turner insurrection unfolded in a

strikingly similar manner to the reaction to 9/11. Initially the reaction was vengeance, torture and indiscriminate slaughter in an atmosphere of hate and fear. Then the courts stepped in and asserted the rule of law. Impartial tribunals were used to determine the facts and to mete out justice. Vengeance was replaced with due process and mercy. This reaction was a conscious response and geared to avoid the creation of martyrs and to dissipate the hatred and desire for revenge inspired by governmental brutality.

In Virginia the response worked to deter future insurrections. The Nat Turner uprising was the culmination of an upsurge in insurrectionary violence between 1800 and 1831. After the Turner trials there were no more slave insurrections in Virginia until an outsider, John Brown, sought unsuccessfully to provoke one nearly 30 years later. He failed to garner any significant slave support. This experience teaches that the way to deter future terrorist violence is to combine due process of law with mercy, while resisting the temptation to resort to primitive instincts of an eye for an eye and a tooth for a tooth.

Appendix 1: The Legal Concept People of Color

In 1820, Chief Justice Marshall, sitting as a circuit judge, decided *The Brig Wilson v. The United States* which provided a judicial gloss on the concept "people of color." The Brig Wilson was a privateer commissioned by the government of Buenos Aires with a crew of 80 or 90, primarily free people of color, which had also received a commission from Venezuela. Privateers were privately owned ships authorized by governments to commit acts of piracy on its enemies. The Brig Wilson, before it entered the port at Norfolk, had raided several Spanish ships and an English vessel carrying Spanish cargo. Several members of the crew, persons of color, left the ship in Norfolk. Virginia authorities seized the ship and cargo for violation of a federal statute, enforcing a Virginia law forbidding the importation of persons of color.[311]

Marshall had to determine the intent of the statute, as well as the meaning of the concept people of color. In his decision he held that the statute was intended to prohibit the importation of blacks and mulattoes and other persons of color, free or slave, who were cargo or not members of the crew, and did not apply to the crews themselves. In the opinion Marshall wrote:

> "We had, at that time, a treaty with the Emperor of Morocco, and with several other Barbary powers. Their subjects are all people of colour. It is true, they are not so engaged in commerce, as to send ships abroad. But the arrival of a Moorish vessel in our ports, is not an impossibility, and can it be believed, that this law was intended to refuse an entry to such a vessel?"[312]

Marshall was prescient to include Moslems as people of color. In post 9/11 America the dualism noted in the creation of the slave courts in Virginia is today embodied in the military commissions established by the President to prosecute persons of color held as terror suspects. These military commissions follow procedures that closely parallel those of the slave courts, including no jury trials.

Appendix II: Note On African-Virginian Crime

The first Africans imported into Virginia in the early 17th century came from the Caribbean and were acculturated into western ways, including language and religion. This changed in the late 17th and early 18th centuries when there was large importation of slaves directly from Africa who did not speak English and were not Christians, nor acculturated. The Africans brought customs and traditions that were reflected in their criminal behavior.

The Africans imported into Virginia came primarily from three ethnic groups, the Ibo from Nigeria, the Akan from Ghana, and Senegambians from the region around present day Senegal.[313] Each of these ethnic groups had its own peculiar characteristics or reputation. The Ibos, the most numerous of the imports into Virginia, were not favored in slave societies in South Carolina and Jamaica because of their reputation for suicide. The Akan, also called Coromantee, were favored for their physical strength and capacity to work. The Senegambians were prized for their agricultural experience.[314]

The large-scale importation of Africans into Virginia fundamentally changed slavery in the state, leading to the creation of a slave based society, centered on plantations cultivating tobacco. The family system among slaves initially broke down as there was a disproportion of males in the immigrants and death rates rose.[315] The Virginia slave population by 1720, however, reached an equilibrium by which it was able to reproduce itself by an excess of births over deaths, the first New World slave population to do so. This was a profound event since it meant that material conditions were such that the African Diaspora in Virginia could survive without immigration from Africa or elsewhere. By the end of the 18th century the black population was increasing without imports at an annual rate of 2 percent.[316]

Poisoning was the major method of killing whites in the early period. Between 1720 and 1770 African imports into Virginia were at their peak and many of the new Africans went to the Piedmont areas, which was a key site for poison prosecutions. A significant number of the new Africans were Akans or Coromantee from Ghana who were famous for their obeahmen, who practiced a "science" brought from West Africa, which often utilized roots and herbs. Obeahmen were mysterious figures, respected and revered by slaves, who consulted them for all types of problems and for their conjuring powers. The obeahmen and women were also doctors who could cure or kill using roots and herbs. Obeahs were known for their ability to make poisons. In 1778 a Virginian slave named Obee was prosecuted for poisoning a white. Probably he was an obeahman.[317]

Before the American Revolution slave violence against whites was infrequent and most crimes against whites were committed individually not collectively. Between 1740 and 1784 poisoning and illegal administration of medicine by slaves were prosecuted more often than any other offense except burglary. The use of poison by slaves was a reflection of the domination of Africans in the slave population who utilized a West African tool to resist slave owners and other slaves.[318] Poisoning was difficult to detect and the fatal doses were often dispensed as medicine by slave doctors. In 1745, Eve was the first Virginia slave executed for murdering her owner after placing a poisonous substance in his milk. Eve received a form of execution usually reserved for traitors or witches; she was carried to the execution site on a sledge and burnt at the stake.[319]

In 1748, Virginia passed a law that sought to stop poisoning, which read:

> Whereas many negroes, under pretence of practising physic, have prepared and exhibited poisonous medicines, by which many persons have been murdered, and others have languished under long and tedious indispositions, and it will be difficult to detect such pernicious and dangerous practices, if they should be permitted to exhibit any sort of medicine, *Be it therefore enacted, by the authority aforesaid,* That if any negroe, or other slave, shall prepare, exhibit, or administer any medicine whatsoever, he, or she so offending, shall be adjudged guilty of

felony, and shall suffer death without benefit of
clergy.[320]

Between 1706 and 1784, 179 Virginia slaves were tried
for poisoning offenses, with 35 sentenced to hang, most for
killing a white victim. Poisoning was a technique the African
immigrants used to combat their enemies, and as the African
proportion of the Virginia slave population declined, it was
only 2 percent by 1790, the native born, so called Creoles,
turned to murder and insurrection to show their rejection of
slavery.[321]

This reality is reflected in the crime figures for the two
periods. Despite the fear reflected in the passage of slave
codes and the conviction of 25 of the 28 persons prosecuted
for insurrection or conspiracy from 1706 to 1785 no whites
were ever harmed, much less killed, in the insurrections. This
changed in the period from 1785 to 1831 when 236 persons
were tried for conspiracy and insurrection, and 123 of these
were hanged or transported.[322] This reality is also reflected in
the data on poisoning which from 1785 to 1865 comprised less
than 13 percent of the prosecutions for murder, attempted
murder and insurrection. The native born African-Americans,
without direct knowledge of West African poisoning and
conjuring practices, used violence differently than their
African ancestors.[323]

Appendix III: The Echo of Nat Turner in Post 9/11 America

An examination of the Southampton insurrection reveals processes still at work in American life, including ethnic dualism in the criminal law, domination of political life by an economic oligarchy, and a court system that seeks to restrain executive power through the rule of law. An understanding of the historical evolution of these processes is relevant today as the nation responds to the war on terror in the wake of the attacks on 9/11.

(A) Dualism

The concept and practice of a parallel system of courts, without constitutional protections for non-citizens, especially the ethnic other, manifested in the military commissions established by President Bush after 9/11, traces its roots in American jurisprudence to colonial Virginia. In 1692 the state created slave courts of *oyer and terminer* to hear capital slave offenses. Before 1692 slaves were tried in the same courts as other defendants. Virginia introduced this dualism into its legal system in an effort to control the rapidly increasing African population, which grew from 300 in 1650 to 120,156 by 1756.[324]

Before the rapid increase in the African population the social boundary between slave and servant was fluid. There was mixture and interplay between black slave and white servant. In the late 17th century Virginia was still a society with slaves and not a slave society. This changed in 1676 when Bacon's rebellion occurred, the first insurrection against colonial authority on American soil. The twenty-nine year old Nathaniel Bacon was a planter member of the ruling elite who led a motley army, which included as its most loyal core an alliance of slaves and white servants. What started out as a war against Indians for land, ended as an insurrection that burned Jamestown to the ground and overthrew the colonial government in Virginia. Bacon died shortly after the triumph and the rebellion was quickly suppressed, although the last

127

holdouts were a company of eighty slaves and twenty white servants.[325]

The oligarchy learned a fundamental lesson from Bacon's rebellion. At any cost it must prevent an alliance between blacks and working-class whites, and the method to do so was to ensure poor white disdain for people of color was more powerful than the antipathy toward the ruling class. Even though the legal distinction between black and white began to evolve before the Bacon rebellion, it accelerated in its aftermath. The centerpiece of the legal separation was the creation in 1692 of slave courts, called *oyer and terminer*, for the speedy prosecution of slaves for capital crimes.[326]

The 1692 statute noted in its archaic language the speedy prosecution of slaves was absolutely necessary, "that others being detered [sic] by the condign punishment inflicted on such offenders, may vigorously proceed in their labours [sic] and be affrighted to commit the like crimes and offences."[327]

The racial dualism of the slave courts was reflected in special procedures. Slaves were denied trial by jury, instead the cases were heard by justices of the peace, usually five in number, all of whom had to agree on a verdict. There was no indictment or information. Slaves were provided appointed counsel at the owner's expense, but otherwise did not receive the constitutional protections granted free men. The central process was to speedily jail, try, and punish the slave, in an effort to deter others.

Slave sentences, another reflection of the dualism, were harsher than those of whites for the same offense. There were 71 offenses for which death was the penalty for slave offenders, whereas whites received only a prison term. The judges made a conscious policy to draw a distinction between free and slave, reserving the harshest punishments for slaves even when the offenses were the same. The dualism was designed to preserve the slave system by protecting persons and property, as well as by domination of the black population. Speed was the essence of the slave judicial process. It was important, since the courts were instruments of social control, to impress upon the slave population the consequences of criminal behavior.[328]

Sentences were final since there was no right to appeal but the Governor was given statutory authority in 1801 to commute a death sentence by transportation, i.e., the selling of a slave out of state. When a slave was executed his owner was compensated for his value from tax funds. When a slave was transported, he was sold to the highest bidder, and the state had an opportunity to recoup all or part of its value. In the 1800's transportation became a common alternative to execution. Between 1785 and 1865, 635 Virginia slaves were hung, while 974 were spared the gallows through transportation. The law required that the transported slave be sold outside the United States, but subterfuges were employed to reintroduce them into the domestic slave trade.[329]

Another great dualism in Virginia's criminal law was the admissibility of the testimony of persons of color. Before 1732, slaves, except to confess, could not testify in court. The underlying rationale was that Africans were not Christians, did not believe the Old and New Testament were God's word, and therefore could not take an oath. Slave owners soon realized that it was often impossible to prove offenses against blacks without the testimony of other blacks, so in 1732, the law was changed to allow slave and free blacks, as well as Indians, to testify in slave courts only against other persons of color. This rule became one of the iron laws of criminal jurisprudence in Virginia and was grounded in the belief that persons of color were "such base and corrupt natures" that their testimony was unreliable.

The dual treatment of white and black testimony was reinforced by the standard of proof in slave courts. It was sufficient to convict a slave on his own confession alone, or the testimony of one white person. For the testimony of a person of color, to convict another black it required corroboration by so-called "pregnant circumstances," i.e., circumstantial evidence.[330]

The parallel court system for slaves was the central institution in Virginia's slave system. The dualism it reflected between the treatment of people of color and whites, of all class strata, was the technique that the ruling elite used to gain the allegiance of other white males. Racial hatred was generated as social cement between whites, with the dualism providing material benefits to white males socially and economically.[331]

(B) Oligarchy

The 1831 Southampton insurrection occurred early in the Jacksonian era. Despite an expansion of the vote among white males, North and South, as property holding requirements were relaxed, America remained a society ruled by economic elites. There was a concentration of wealth in the propertied class who dominated the economic and political system, not unlike the present day in which one percent of the U.S. population controls 40 percent of the nation's wealth.[332] During the Jacksonian era, the elites realized that they could maintain dominance despite the expansion of the vote to property-less white males. America, in short, remained a hierarchical society dominated by a propertied elite with a democratic façade.[333]

Southampton's economic, social and political life was dominated by an oligarchy, composed of elite property owners. Slaves and land were the two main forms of property in Southampton. Wealth was concentrated in the 13 percent of the slave owning population who held 20 or more slaves. Within the elite there was further concentration of wealth, as little more than 2% owned 50 or more slaves. Three men, the crème of the elite, owned over 145 slaves. One of them, Thomas Ridley, owned the plantation where the slave army spent the night during the Nat Turner insurrection.[334]

The county court in Southampton, as elsewhere in Virginia, was dominated by members of the oligarchy. In Southampton county all magistrates on the court owned slaves: 81 percent of its members owned 10 or more, and 20 percent owned 20 or more. For the county as a whole, nearly 50% of the population owned no slaves, while another 30% owned less than 10.[335] By statute the Governor appointed the magistrates but in practice the county courts were "self-perpetuating bodies" because the current members nominated their successors.[336]

The county court in Southampton, as in the rest of Virginia, was the dominant local institution, with legal, legislative and executive functions. Magistrates, often called justices of the peace, sat on the court. The court appointed all local officials, including the influential county clerk. It also had a decisive say in the selection of the Sheriff, the other powerful local office. The county court supervised elections, certified lawyers, controlled the militia, regulated inns, repaired the roads, appointed the slave patrols, recorded the deeds. It also selected from its own membership the persons to sit on the slave courts of *oyer and terminer*.[337]

The social backgrounds of the most active magistrates during the 50 Southampton insurrection adjudications provide insight into the oligarchy. The court's Chairman, Jeremiah Cobb, a long time member of the court and its only lawyer, was a central figure in the local oligarchy, residing with his family in an impressive home in the lower part of the county, seven miles northwest of the courthouse in Jerusalem. He owned 32 slaves. In August 1831 he was elected to the House of Delegates.[338]

Dr. Carr Bowers, another senior member of the court, also had one of the highest participation rates during the trials. Dr. Bowers, from an upper county family, with liberal sympathies, had ties and influence in the lower part of the county through his membership in the Black Creek Baptist Church, which was located northeast of Jerusalem. Dr. Bowers, the most powerful Baptist layman in the county, was a worldly man who was known for his extensive library, which contained classics of English literature, including Shakespeare. During the 1820's he had helped remove a minister from the church because of the minister's anti-slavery views. Bowers was known for his philanthropy and intellectual curiosity. He also served several terms in the state legislature. In the weeks after the insurrection he was one of few whites willing to harbor terrified free blacks in his home. He was a long time member of the court and one of its progressive members; he and Jeremiah Cobb had ties that went back to 1818 when they served together on the county's first Board of School Commissioners.[339]

There were extensive social connections between the men that sat on the court. The most concrete form of contact was the several pairs of family members who heard cases. Two members of the Goodwyn family, William and Robert, heard over 20 cases between them, at times sitting together on a five-man panel. William was a doctor, who like others had used his medical practice to build personal contacts to enter politics. He owned 64 slaves and had served on the Board of School Commissioners with Cobb and Bowers. The Goodwyn family, one of the most influential families in lower Southampton, was Methodist.[340]

Family members Alexander and Meriwether Peete also sat on the insurrection trials, with Alexander hearing a large number of the cases. Alexander Peete was a horse breeder and secretary of the Jerusalem Jockey Club, which was formed in 1830 and sponsored horse races. William B. Goodwyn was the president. Jeremiah Cobb, another member, was also a prominent breeder with three pedigreed studs. Alexander Peete led one of the militia units that pursued the insurgents during the insurrection. It was at Parker's cornfield, owned by James W. Parker, another magistrate on the court, that the insurgents encountered the first armed resistance.[341]

James Trezevant, a member of a prominent Southampton family, congressman, and a colonel in the militia, sat on more cases than any other magistrate during the insurrection trials. Trezevant, whose family was one of five Huguenot families in Southampton, where most whites had English ancestors, was intimately involved with the entire affair from beginning to end. It was his nearly illegible handwritten note on August 21, 1831 that told officials in Richmond the insurrection was occurring in Southampton and that a considerable military force was necessary to suppress it.[342]

Trezevant was active in Democratic politics before he left Southampton following the insurrection and relocated to Tennessee in 1831. He represented Southampton in Congress and was one of three delegates to the constitutional convention that met in Richmond from October 1829 to January 1830 to extend the vote to property-less white males.[343]

(C) The Courts: Due Process and Mercy

Another way the Nat Turner insurrection resonates today is the similarity in response by courts, both then and now, to a war, without quarter or due process, against suspected terrorists. After 9/11 the Bush Administration unleashed a war on Islamic terrorists without quarter, encompassing torture and death in secret prisons. The government contended its detainees had no legal rights under either American or international law. In 2004 the U.S. Supreme Court decided cases that began to assert the rule of law and grant due process to terrorist detainees.

A similar judicial intervention occurred after the Nat Turner insurrection, when the courts intervened and fairly treated detainees. In Southampton County, 45 slaves were tried for crimes arising from the insurrection. Of these, 15 or over 30% were acquitted, while 30 were convicted, of whom 18 were hung, and 12 were granted mercy and sold out of state. The Southampton court went so far as to recommend mercy for one of the original conspirators, who, the evidence showed, had participated in the killing of his master, and was apprehended wearing his dead owner's shoes and socks. This show of mercy by the oligarchy was not happenstance, but was the evolutionary product of long experience with slave violence and insurrection.[344]

To understand the evolution of the use of mercy by the elite, it is necessary to understand the evolution of slave violence in Virginia, since the two are intertwined. It is useful to divide this evolution into two periods, the first from 1706 to 1785 and the second from 1785 to 1831. These dates correspond roughly to the pre-revolution colonial and the antebellum American Republic periods respectively.

The early period was characterized by the rapid growth of the African population, and the use of death penalty for control of slave behavior especially for theft offenses. Between 1706 and 1784, 56.5% of the slaves condemned to death were for crimes against property, while only 24.7% were for crimes against persons. Less than 4% of the death sentences were for insurrection or other crimes against the system, with only 25 slaves convicted for insurrection in the early period. Between 1706 and 1785 prosecutions in the slave courts for poisoning and administering illegal medication, an African cultural artifact, outnumbered the combined totals for murder, attempted murder, and insurrection/conspiracy.[345]

As the Africans were assimilated into the native born Virginia slave population the pattern of criminal violence changed. After the American Revolution and until the Nat Turner insurrection in 1831 there was a rising crescendo both of individual slave violence against whites and insurrection. Convictions for murder and insurrection soared, while those for poison offenses dropped. Between 1785 and 1834, 142 slaves were convicted for insurrection or conspiracy.[346]

The court's imposition of the death penalty in the antebellum period reflected the change in slave criminal violence. It's imposition for property crimes dropped, while it increased for crimes against person and conspiracy, as the oligarchy sought to stem the rise in violence.

In 1801, in the wake of the Gabriel insurrection, the legislature granted the Governor power to transport an insurgent, that is, commute a death sentence and sell the slave out of state. Between 1801 and 1831, transportation was increasingly used even though the level of slave violence, including insurrection, increased.

The extensive use of transportation in the antebellum period was a product of more than a century of experience by slave owners with the execution of slaves in the colonial period. Slave owners learned, as slavery evolved, that the important thing was to maintain the dualism between sentences for slave and free, which increasingly meant between black and white, so that if the harshest punishments were reserved for people of color, it was not necessary to execute all slaves convicted of capital offenses. The oligarchy, many of them former revolutionaries themselves, did not wish to needlessly create martyrs. Of course, there was also an economic motive since the value of an executed slave was paid from the public treasury, while a transported slave was sold and reimbursed the state for the payment to the owner. But the main motivation was that mercy, along with swift

134

executions for the most culpable, deterred better than mass executions. In Virginia, in the antebellum period "more than twice as many slaves were transported as were hanged for capital crimes."[347]

The court showed mercy during the Southampton insurrection when almost half of the convicted insurgents were transported. The policy of mercy, rather than vengeance, was a factor, among others, including firm police measures that deterred insurrections in Virginia after 1831. The rising crescendo of insurrection between the Revolution and 1831 climaxed with Nat Turner and afterwards African-Americans turned from insurrection to arson to resist slavery. This reality is reflected in the statistics. From 1785 to 1834, 142 Virginia slaves were convicted of insurrection and 76 were hung. After 1834 only 12 were convicted of insurrection, of whom 2 were hung, while, for arson, 11 were executed and 97 transported.[348]

Post 9/11 America should turn to its own rich past to draw lessons for today. The Nat Turner insurrection is a particularly rich historical resource from which to gain insight into techniques to deter terrorism.

Notes

1   *The Atlantic*, December 2006 at 78.

2   Charles Francis Adams, Editor, *Memoirs of John Quincy Adams* (J.P. Lippincott & Co., 1876) Vol. VIII, at 313-314; Louis P. Masur, *1831* (Hill and Wang, 2001) at 2, 32, 64.

3   Charles H. Ambler, *The Life and Diary of John Floyd* (Richmond Press, Inc., 1918) at 31-38, 78-79, 94-102, 205. Alison Goodyear Freehling, *Drift Toward Dissolution* (Louisiana State University Press, 1982) at 84-85.

4   Henry Irving Tragle, *The Southampton Slave Revolt of 1831*, (The University of Masssachusetts Press, 1971) at 249-250; Freehling, *Drift Toward Dissolution* at 84.

5   Daniel W. Crofts, *Old Southampton* (University Press of Virginia, 1992) at 107; Freehling, *Drift Toward Dissolution* at 48.

6   Eva Sheppard Wolf, *Race and Liberty In The New Nation* (Louisiana State University Press, 2006) at 185-195; Freehling, *Drift Toward Dissolution* at 76-81.

7   James Hugo Johnston, *Race Relations in Virginia & Miscegenation in the South, 1776-1860* (University of Massachusetts Press, 1970) at 127-135; William W. Freehling, *The Road to Disunion. Vol.1, Secessionists at Bay 1776-1854* (Oxford University Press, 1990) at 174-177.

8   William Sidney Drewry, *The Southampton Insurrection* (Johnson Publishing Co., 1968) at 20; Tragle, at 13-14, 328-329; Oates, at 1-2.

9   Tragle at 15; Stephen B. Oates, *The Fires of Jubilee* (Harper Perennial, 1975) at 1.

10 Crofts at xii; Oates at 2.

11 Crofts at 18; Oates at 2.

12 Crofts at 18; Oates at 2-3. Robert William Fogel, *Without Consent or Contract* (W.W. Norton & Company, 1989) at 74-75.

13 Crofts, at 3-5; 8.

14 Tragle at 310.

15 Drewry at 35, 71; Oates at 52-53; Tragle at 231, 244.

[16] Oates at 53; Tragle at 193, 231; David F. Allmendinger, Jr., "The Construction of *The Confessions of Nat Turner*" in Kenneth S. Greenberg, Editor, *Nat Turner* (Oxford University Press, 2003) at 28.

[17] Philip J. Schwarz, *Twice Condemned* (Louisiana State University Press, 1988) Table 25 at 235.

[18] Id., at 234, 262.

[19] Tragle at 92.

[20] Ambler, *The Life and Diary of John Floyd* at 145-146.

[21] Tragle at 310.

[22] Ambler, *The Life and Diary of John Floyd* at 147-152; Masur at 160.

[23] Masur at 105.

[24] H.W. Flournoy, *Calendar of Virginia State Papers and Other Manuscripts From January 1, 1799 to December 31, 1807* (Richmond, 1890) Vol. IX at 147. (Confession of Solomon)

[25] Herbert Aptheker, *American Negro Slave Revolts* (Sixth Ed., International Publishers, 1993) at 219-226; Douglas R. Egerton, *Gabriel's Rebellion* (The University of North Carolina Press, 1993) at 18-25.

[26] Egerton, at 32-33, 179-181.

[27] Stanislaus Murray Hamilton, *The Writings of James Monroe* (G.P. Putnam's Sons, 1900) Vol. III, at 239.

[28] Egerton at 50-64, 182-185; Gerald W. Mullin, *Flight and Rebellion* (Oxford University Press, 1972) at 140-163.

[29] *The Writings of James Monroe* at 211-212.

[30] Id., at 213.

[31] Egerton, at 69-115, 186-188; Schwarz, *Twice Condemned*, 324-327.

[32] *The Writings of James Monroe* at 208.

[33] Thomas Jefferson, *Writings* (The Library of America, 1984) at 349.

[34] Ira Berlin, *Slaves Without Masters* (The New Press, 1974) Table 2 and Table 4 at 46-47.

[35] Egerton at 45-49; James Sidbury, *Ploughshares into Swords* (Cambridge Univrsity Press, 1997) at 32-49; Tommy L. Bogger,

Free Blacks in Norfolk, Virginia 1790-1860 (University Press of Virginia, 1997) at 23-24; Drewry at 122.

36   Egerton at 34-41.

37   The Writings of James Monroe at 329.

38   The Writings of James Monroe at 209.

39   John Chester Miller, The Wolf By The Ears (The University Press of Virginia, 1991) at 126-128; Schwarz, Slave Laws in Virginia (The University of Georgia Press, 1996) at 103-106.

40   Sidbury at 256-264; many historians contend that Gabriel was executed on October 7, 1800. See, for example Drewry at 26; however, Egerton documents that Gabriel had his execution delayed to the 10th of October and thus Nat was born 8, not 5, days before Gabriel's death. Egerton at 109-111, 219.

41   Garry Wills, "Negro President" (Houghton Mifflin Company, 2003) at 2-5, 49.

42   The Writings of James Monroe at 292.

43   The Writings of James Monroe at 294.

44   Jefferson, Writings at 1097-1098.

45   Miller at 128-129; Schwarz, Slaves Laws in Virginia at 106-108.

46   Wills, "Negro President" at 114-115; W.E.B. Du Bois, "The Suppression of the African Slave-Trade," in Writings (The Library of America, 1986) at 97; James Sidbury, "Thomas Jefferson in Gabriel's Virginia" in James Horn, Jan Ellen Lewis & Peter S. Onuf, The Revolution of 1800 (University of Virginia Press, 2002) at 207-210.

47   Robert W. Fogel and Stanley L. Engerman, Time on the Cross, (W.W. Norton & Co. Inc, 1989) at 44; Angela Lakwete, Inventing the Cotton Gin (The John Hopkins, University Press 2003) at 47-96; Roger G. Kennedy, Mr. Jefferson's Lost Cause (Oxford University Press, 2003) at 78-82.

48   Fogal and Engerman at 43; Douglas C. North, The Economic Growth of the United States 1790-1860 (W.W. Norton & Co., Inc., 1966) at 52; Fogel, Without Consent or Contract, at 30.

49   North at 68, 75, 162, 167, 189.

50   Michael Tadman, Speculators and Slaves (The University of Wisconsin Press, 1989, 1996) Table 2.1 at 12 and 169; James C. Ballagh, History of Slavery in Virginia (Johnson Reprints, 1968) at 25.

138

51 Oates at 10-11.

52 Phillipp D. Morgan, *Slave Counterpoint* (The University of
    North Carolina Press, 1998) Table 10 at 61.

53 Drewry at 27.

54 Schwarz, *Twice Condemned*, at 252-254.

55 Tragle at 306.

56 Oates at 13.

57 F. Roy Johnson, *The Nat Turner Slave Insurrection* (Johnson
    Publishing Co., 1966) at 14 and 27; Oates at 8-10.

58 Johnson, *The Nat Turner Slave Insurrection*, at 16-20; Oates at
    8.

59 Tragle at 307.

60 Id., at 307; For the Baptist religious context in Southampton see:
    Randolph Ferguson Scully, *Religion and the Making of Nat
    Turner's Virginia* (University of Virginia Press, 2008).

61 Johnson, *The Nat Turner Slave Insurrection*, at 27, Oates at 13,
    and Thomas C. Parramore, *Southampton County, Virginia*
    (University Press of Virginia, 1978) at 77. Several historians
    contend that Samuel Turner was the brother of Benjamin Turner.
    Drewry at 26, Kenneth S. Greenberg, "Name, Face, Body," in
    Kenneth S. Greenberg, Editor, *Nat Turner* (Oxford University
    Press, 2003) at 6.

62 Tragle at 307; Johnson, *The Nat Turner Slave Insurrection*, at
    32; Oates at 13-14, 20-22.

63 Tragle at 307.

64 Id., at 307.

65 Id., at 307-308; Oates at 27-28.

66 Tragle at 308.

67 Oates at 27-28; Tragle at xv, 308; for a provocative analysis of
    Nat Turner and the slave community before the rebellion see:
    Patrick H. Breen, "A Prophet in His Own Land," in Kenneth S.
    Greenberg, Editor, *Nat Turner* (Oxford University Press, 2003)
    at 103.

68 Johnson, *The Nat Turner Slave Insurrection*, at 28, 32-33; Oates
    at 29.

69 Johnson, *The Nat Turner Slave Insurrection*, at 51-52; Tragle at
    327; Oates at 29-32.

70   Tragle at 420-421; B.B. King and David Ritz, *Blues All Around Me* (Avon Books, 1996) at 60.

71   Tragle at 308-309.

72   Id., at 308; Tragle at 93.

73   Mechal Sobel, *Trabelin' On* (Greenwood Press, Inc., 1979) at 109-117, 159-168.

74   Tragle at 309.

75   Tragle at 137, 222.

76   Tragle at 309.

77   Id., at 309.

78   "Recollections of James L. Smith," in Eric Foner, Editor, *Nat Turner* (Prentice-Hall, Inc., 1971) at 73-74; see also: Peter P. Hinks, *To Awaken My Afflicted Brethren* (The Pennsylvania State University Press, 1997) at 161.

79   Tragle at 309; Oates at 36-39.

80   The three quotations come from Tragle at 309-310; see also Oates at 39-40, Drewry at 33, Johnson, *The Nat Turner Slave Insurrection*, at 58-59.

81   Sobel at 90, 130-131, 139-140; E. Franklin Frazier, *The Negro Church in America* (Schocken Book, Inc., 1974) at 23-25; for a different take on the baptism see Breen at 111-113. He argues it showed Nat Turner as an "outcast," "failed prophet," "a man 'reviled' by both blacks and whites alike."

82   Tragle at 310.

83   Id., at 310.

84   Oates at 41-42.

85   McCargo v. Callicott, 2 Munford 501, February 1812 cited in Helen Tunnicliff Catteral, *Judicial Cases Concerning American Slavery and the Negro* (Negro University Press, 1968) Vol. 1, at 122; Johnson, *The Nat Turner Slave Insurrection*, at 63; Oates at 51-53; Tragle at 231.

86   John Thomas Schlotterbeck, *Plantation and Farm: Social and Economic Change in Orange and Greene Counties, Virginia 1716 to 1860* (University Microfilms, 1980) at 138-146; Ulrich Bonnel Phillips, Edited by Eugene D. Genovese, *The Slave Economy of the Old South* (Louisiana State University Press, 1968) at 44-45.

[87]   Tragle at 310.

[88]   Tragle at xiii, xv-xvii.

[89]   Tragle at 361-362. See pp. 36-37 for a time-line of the insurrection.

[90]   Tragle at 310.

[91]   June P. Guild, *Black Laws of Virginia* (Negro Universities Press, 1969) at 159; Schwarz, *Twice Condemned* at 21; Table 13 at 127; Maurice Duke, Editor, *Don't Carry Me Back!* (The Dietz Press, 1995) at 93, 132 on slaves' attitudes toward stealing from the master.

[92]   Ezekiel, Chapter 7, verse 6; and Chapter 9, verses 4, 6; Oates at 69.

[93]   Tragle at 310.

[94]   Tragle at 310.

[95]   Tragle at 93, 196.

[96]   Tragle at 310-311.

[97]   Oates at 30, 69; For details on the issue of the wife see: Mary Kemp Davis, "What Happened in This Place?" in Kenneth S. Greenberg, Ed., *Nat Turner* (Oxford University Press, 2003) at 174-175.

[98]   The two maps in this chapter are composites with additions of maps found in Oates at 73 and Martin S. Goldman, *Nat Turner & the Southampton Revolt of 1831* (Franklin Watts, 1992) at 74-75.

[99]   Oates at 30, 51, 66; Tragle at 78, 231, 244; Johnson, *The Nat Turner Slave Insurrection* at 63; Catteral, Vol. 1 at 122.

[100] Oates at 30-31, 74; Drewry at 35-37.

[101] Thomas C. Parramore, "Covenant in Jerusalem," in Kenneth S. Greenberg, *Nat Turner* (Oxford University Press, 2003) at 58; Oates at 52-53, 69; Tragle at 222, 311.

[102] Tragle at 67, 95-96, 311; Drewry at 36; Johnson, *The Nat Turner Slave Insurrection*, at 80-81; Parramore, "Covenant in Jerusalem" at 59.

[103] Johnson, *The Nat Turner Slave Insurrection*, at 58; F. Roy Johnson, *The Nat Turner Story* (Johnson Publishing Co., 1970) at 95; Drewry at 28, 38; Oates at 31; Morgan, *Slave Counterpoint*, at 109, 124.

104 Tragle at 311; Parramore, "Covenant in Jerusalem" at 59; Drewry at 38.

105 Tragle at 195, 311; Parramore, "Covenant in Jeruslaem" at 59, Oates at 67-68, 71; Johnson, *The Nat Turner Story*, at 86.

106 Tragle at 197; Drewry at 40.

107 Oates at 29-30, 71.

108 Tragle at 311-312; Oates at 74.

109 Tragle at 312; Parramore, "Covenant in Jerusalem" at 65.

110 Oates at 74; Tragle at 185.

111 Parramore, "Covenant in Jerusalem" at 60, Tragle at 312; Johnson, *The Nat Turner Story*, at 98.

112 Drewry at 42-43; Parramore, "Covenant in Jerusalem" at 60.

113 Tragle at xvi, Drewry at 42, Oates at 74-75; Crofts at 8. The estimates on the number of Whitehead slaves range from 27 to 40. Mary Kemp Davis, "What Happened in This Place?" at 168.

114 Tragle at 312, Drewry at 42-43, Oates at 74, Parramore, "Covenant in Jerusalem" at 60.

115 Tragle at 312.

116 Johnson, *The Nat Turner Story* at 100; Tragle at 161; Crofts at 8.

117 Johnson, *The Nat Turner Story* at 100, 196; Drewry at 43-44; Oates at 76; Parramore, "Covenant in Jerusalem" at 60.

118 Tragle at 180-182, 229-230; Oates at 76; Parramore, "Covenant in Jerusalem" at 60. Hathcock is also spelled Haithcock. Hathcock is used in the court transcripts. Tragle at 237-238.

119 Tragle at 207.

120 Tragle at 312.

121 Tragle at 44, 80; Oates at 77-78; Parramore, "Covenant in Jerusalem" at 65.

122 Tragle at 181.

123 Tragle at 312; Drewry at 44-45, Parramore, "Covenant in Jerusalem" at 61, Parramore, *Southampton County* indicates the correct spelling is Doyel. See fn. 21 at 246.

124 Crofts at 15-16; Oates at 53, 77-79, 96; Drewry 45-48; Tragle at 410-412.

125 Tragle at 312; Oates at 79-80, 82; Drewry at 49;

126 Tragle at 44, 50, 69, 92, 94, 217-219, 222, 242; Parramore, "Covenant in Jerusalem" at 65.

127 The two maps in this chapter are composites with additions of maps found in Oates at 73 and Martin S. Goldman, *Nat Turner & the Southampton Revolt of 1831* (Franklin Watts, 1992) at 74-75.

128 Ezekiel 37:10, 16:35; Oates 80; On David Barrow see: Scully, *Religion and the Making of Nat Turner's Virginia*, at 122-123.

129 Tragle at 93.

130 Drewry at 50-52; Parramore, "Covenant in Jerusalem" at 63; Oates at 80; Tragle at 44-45, 96.

131 Tragle at 313.

132 Tragle at 313.

133 Oates at 83-84; Drewry at 55-58, Tragle at 221.

134 Tragle at 44, 198-199, 233.

135 Tragle at 177-179, 191, 222.

136 Tragle at xvi, 51, 60, 178, 222.

137 Tragle at 313.

138 Tragle at 218, 222.

139 Tragle at 194-195.

140 Tragle at 96-97; David F. Allmendinger, Jr., "The Construction of the *Confessions of Nat Turner*" at 26, 29-30, 32.

141 Tragle at 462-464; David F. Allmendinger, Jr., "The Construction of *The Confessions of Nat Turner*" at 32.

142 Tragle at 97.

143 Tragle at xvi, 313; Oates at 87; Drewry at 59; Parramore, "Covenant in Jerusalem" at 64.

144 Tragle at xvi-xvii, 193-194, 313; Oates at 85-86; Parramore, "Covenant in Jerusalem" at 64; Drewry at 59-61.

145 Tragle at 50, 193-194, 232.

146 Tragle at 52, 68-69; Drewry at 61-62; Oates at 86-87; Parramore, "Covenant in Jerusalem" at 64.

147 Tragle 50, 67, 313; Drewry at 62; Parramore, "Covenant in Jerusalem" at 64-65.

148 Tragle at 44, 67, 95; Parramore, *Southampton County* at 89.

[149] Oates at 88-89; Drewry at 62-66; Parramore, "Covenant in Jerusalem" at 65-66; Tragle at 60, 67, 96, 178, 313-314; David F. Allmendinger, Jr., "The Construction of *The Confessions of Nat Turner*" at 29-30, 32.

[150] Tragle at 39, 314.

[151] George H. Thomas, the future Union General, 15 years old at the time, escaped the slave army with his family. Oates at 90.

[152] Parramore, "Covenant in Jerusalem" at 67; Tragle at 60, 96, 314-315; Oates at 90; David F. Allmendinger, Jr., "The Construction of *The Confessions of Nat Turner*" at 32.

[153] Tragle at 315; Oates 90-91, 94.

[154] Tragle at 61.

[155] Tragle at 45, 67-68, 315; Oates at 94-95.

[156] Tragle at 67, 77-78, 96; Parramore, *Southampton County* at 119.

[157] Tragle at xvii and 192, 231-232.

[158] Oates at 88; Parramore, *Southampton County* at 95-96; Tragle at 48, 227; Parramore, "Covenant in Jerusalem" at 68.

[159] Oates at 95; Tragle at xvii, 315.

[160] Tragle at 186-188, 230-231; Drewry at 71-72.; Parramore, *Southampton County* at 99; Parramore, "Covenant in Jerusalem" at 67-68. On the law of slave confessions in general see: Mark Tushnet, *The American Law of Slavery 1810-1860* (Princeton University Press, 1981) 127-139.

[161] Tragle at 227.

[162] Tragle at 45, 48, 61, 72-73, 75, 80, 97; Oates 98-99.

[163] Tragle at 44.

[164] C.L.R. James, *The Black Jacobins* (Vintage Books, 1989). "They knew that as long as these plantations stood their lot would be to labour on them until they dropped. The only thing was to destroy them. From their masters they had known rape, torture, degradation, and, at the slightest provocation, death. They returned in kind." at 88.

[165] Tragle at 49-50, 52-53, 70.

[166] Tragle at 31, 35-36, 251-252; Charles H. Ambler, *The Life and Diary of John Floyd* (Richmond Press, Inc., 1918) at 11-12, 31-33.

[167] Tragle at 37.

[168] Tragle at 36, 38, 46-47.

[169] Tragle at 189-190, 231, 452.

[170] Tragle at 46, 202, 204.

[171] Parramore, *Southampton County*, at 36-46; Thomas C. Parramore, *Norfolk* (University Press of Virginia, 1994) at 143-146; Donald R. Hickey, *The War of 1812* (University of Illinois Press, 1990), at 154; Tragle at 46.

[172] Tragle at 38-39.

[173] Tragle at 44.

[174] Tragle at 42, 52, 69.

[175] Tragle at 16-19, 37, 39, 50-51, 65,70-71, 249, 251-252, 264-268, 270-272; Oates at 61-65.

[176] Tragle at 16-20, 73-76, 251-253.

[177] Tragle at 17, 65-66, 270-272.

[178] Emory M. Thomas, *Robert E. Lee* (W.W. Norton & Co., 1995) at 67-69.

[179] Tragle at 65, 77-78; Robert V. Remini, *The Legacy of Andrew Jackson* (Louisiana State University Press, 1988) at 90.

[180] Tragle at 62.

[181] Tragle at 16, 252, 266.

[182] Tragle at 54; Parramore, "Covenant in Jerusalem" at 70; Oates at 100.

[183] Tragle at 7, 71, 165.

[184] Tragle at 173-174, 253, 268, 270, 272.

[185] Tragle at 70-72, 98-101, 174.

[186] William H. Hening, *Hening's Statutes at Large*, Vol. 4, at 127; Guild at 153, 160; Ballagh at 83; Thomas D. Morris, "Slaves and the Rules of Evidence in Criminal Trials" at 213.

[187] Tragle at 57; Crofts at 15, 25, 45-46, 115, 130, 186, 189-190; Oates at 124; Drewry at 62-63, 95; Parramore, *Southampton County*, at 51.

[188] Tragle at 229-245.

[189] Crofts at 100.

[190] Parramore, *Southampton County*, at 107-109; Oates, at 102.

[191] Tragle at 201.

[192]   Tragle at 75.

[193]   Tragle at 229-230.

[194]   Tragle at 99.

[195]   Tragle at 176, 217, 242.

[196]   Guild at 161; Catteral at 140-141; Thomas D. Morris, *Southern Slavery and the Law 1619-1860* (University of North Carolina Press, 1996) at 265; Mark V. Tushnet, *Slave Law in the American South* (University Press of Kansas, 2003) at 23-24; Daniel S. Fabricant, "Thomas R. Gray and William Styron: Finally, A Critical Look at the 1831 *Confessions Nat Turner," The American Journal of Legal History,* Vol. 37 (1993) at 347.

[197]   Tragle at 69-70; Ballagh at 85; Schwarz, *Twice Condemned,* Table 4 at 41-42.

[198]   Tragle at 74-75.

[199]   Tragle at 72-73; David F. Allmendinger, Jr., "The Construction of *The Confessions of Nat Turner"* at 28.

[200]   Tragle at 62, 75, 77, 80, 229-237.

[201]   Tragle at xvii, 49-50, 62, 188; Oates at 95, 98; David F. Allmendinger, Jr., "The Construction of *The Confessions of Nat Turner"* at 26-27.

[202]   Tragle at 58, 191-192, 231, 452.

[203]   Tragle at 192-193, 231-232, 452; Oates at 104.

[204]   Tragle at 193-194, 232; Oates at 53, 103.

[205]   Tragle at 94; David F. Allmendinger, "The Construction of *The Confessions of Nat Turner"* at 31-33.

[206]   Tragle at 195-198, 233.

[207]   Tragle at 253-254, 427-428; David F. Allmendinger, "The Construction of *The Confessions of Nat Turner"* at 29; Phillip D. Morgan, "The Significance of Kin," Gad Heuman and James Walvin, Editors, *The Slavery Reader* (Routledge, 2003) at 332.

[208]   Tragle at 197-198, 273, 453.

[209]   Tragle at 77, 85, 200-201, 234, 453.

[210]   Tragle at 200-201, 234-235.

[211]   Tragle at 251-252, 255.

[212]   Tragle at 220-221.

[213] Tragle at 208-209, 237-238; Mary Kemp Davis, "What Happened in This Place?" at 163-164.

[214] Tragle at 99, 213-216, 240-241, 452; Scot French, *The Rebellious Slave* (Houghton Mifflin Co., 2004) at 38-40; Schwarz, *Twice Condemned* at 277-278.

[215] Schwarz, *Slave Laws in Virginia*, at 81; French at 38-41; Tragle at 252-256, 260, 432, 452.

[216] Tragle at 99, 101; French at 61-63.

[217] Tragle at 85-87, 99, 452-453.

[218] Tragle at 98.

[219] Tragle at 101, Schwarz, *Slave Laws in Virginia*, at 118, footnote 43 at 227.

[220] In 1830, Southampton had a total population of 16,074, composed of 6,573 whites, 7,756 slaves and 1,745 free blacks. Tragle at 15; Drewry at 108-109.

[221] Crofts at 16-17.

[222] Hinks, *To Awaken My Afflicted Brethren* at 134-137, 160; Oates at 47-49; Freehling, *Drift Toward Dissolution* at 82-83; Peter P. Hinks, Editor, *David Walker's Appeal to the Coloured Citizens Of The World* (The Pennsylvania State University Press, 2000) at 22, 95-97.

[223] *Aldridge v. the Commonwealth*. Catteral at 140-141, on Habeas at 207; John H. Russell, *The Free Nego in Virginia* (Dover Publications, Inc., 1969) at 103-104; Tragle at 175.

[224] Tragle at 199, 234.

[225] Parramore, *Southampton County* at 116, footnote 45 at 253; Tragle at 180, 206-207, 209, 237-238.

[226] Tragle at 202-203.

[227] Tragle at 203-204.

[228] Tragle at 227.

[229] Tragle at 180.

[230] Tragle at 211-212, 220, 239-240, 243.

[232] Tragle at 211, 239; Oates at 53; Drewry at 158.

[233] Tragle at 239; Luther Porter Jackson, *Free Negro Labor and Property Holding in Virginia, 1830-1860* (Russell & Russell,

1971) at 70-73; Guild at 103-106; Berlin, *Slaves Without Masters* at 226-227.

234   Tragle at 202-203; Oates at 125.

235   Parramore, *Southampton County* at 116; Tragle at 175; Drewry stated that three of the four free blacks bound over for trial were executed. Drewry at 101.

236   Tragle at 315.

237   Tragle at 46, 54.

238   Tragle at xiii, 73, 75, 80, 229.

239   Tragle at 76-77, 274.

240   Tragle at 420-423.

241   Tragle at 92.

242   Tragle at 315.

243   Tragle at 116-118, 123, 131, 139-140.

244   Tragle at 316.

245   Tragle at 134-135, 138.

246   Tragle at 260.

247   Tragle at 134-136, 138-139, 316; Charles L. Perdue, Jr., Thomas E. Barden, & Robert K. Phillips, Editors, *Weevils in the Wheat* (University Press of Virginia, 1976) at 76.

248   Tragle at 132-137. There is a dispute about who authored the November 1, 1831 letter in the November 8, 1831 edition of the Richmond Enquirer. The letter is found in Tragle at 136-137. David F. Allmendinger, "The Construction of *The Confessions of Nat Turner*" contends that William C. Parker wrote it. At 35, 256-257. He notes in a footnote that the letter is attributed to Thomas R. Gray by Daniel S. Fabricant, "Thomas R. Gray and William Styron: Finally, A Critical Look at the 1831 *Confessions of Nat Turner*," *American Journal of Legal History* 37 (1993).

249   Tragle at 137-138.

250   Tragle at 317; Parramore, *Southampton County* at 106-107.

251   Tragle at 316-317; Rhys Issac, *The Transformation of Virginia 1740-1790* (University of North Carolina Press, 1982) at 122-123.

252   Tragle at 310.

[253] For the biblical citations see: "The Confession of Nat Turner," in William L. Andrews, and Henry Louis Gates, Jr., *Slave Narratives* (The Library of America, 2000) at 1026; See also Raymond E. Brown, *The Death of the Messiah* (Doubleday, 1998) Vol. 1, at 4.

[254] Tragle at 307-308; See Luke 12:31, 49, 51-53. Luke 12:31 reads "But rather seek ye the kingdom of God; and all these things shall be added unto you." See also Luke 6:27-35, 9:22 and 13:33.

[255] Tragle at 221, 244, 318; Kenneth S. Greenberg, "Name, Face, Body" at 3-14.

[256] Tragle at 221-223.

[257] Tragle at 135, 222.

[258] Wyndham B. Blanton, M.D., *Medicine in Virginia* (Arno Press & The New York Times, 1972) at 131; Ida Macalpine & Richard Hunter, *George III and the Mad-Business* (Pantheon Books, 1969) at 310-321; Thomas Maeder, *Crime and Madness* (Harper & Row, 1985) at 12-14; Schwarz, *Twice Condemned* at 24.

[259] Tragle at 308-310, 420-421; Am. Psychiatric Ass'n, *Diagnostic and Statistical Manual of Mental Disorders* (4th ed., 1994) at 273-315; Dorothy O. Lewis, M.D., *Guilty By Reason of Insanity* (Ballantine Publishing Group 1st ed., 1998) at 10-11, 255. "From a medical point of view, whipping inflicted cruel and often permanent injuries upon its victims." Todd L. Savitt, *Medicine and Slavery: The Diseases and Health Care of Blacks in Antebellum Virginia* (University of Illinois Press, 1978) at 111-115.

[260] For a review of the cases after the 1800 Hadfield decision, which moved away from an emphasis on delusion to the modern "right-wrong" test see: Kathleen Jones, *Lunacy, Law and Conscience 1744-1845* (Routledge & Kegan Paul Limited, 1995) at 203-213; Richard Moran, *Knowing Right from Wrong* (The Free Press, 1981) tells the history of the McNaughten case.

[261] Tragle at 140, 427.

[262] Parramore, *Southampton County* at 112, 119-121.

[263] Tragle at 140; Drewry at 102; Greenberg, "Name, Face, Body" at 18-23; Franny Nudelman, *John Brown's Body* (The University of North Carolina Press, 2004) at 40-70.

264 Andrew Jackson, "Third Annual Message, December 6, 1831," in James D. Richardson, *A Compilation of the Messages and Papers of the Presidents,* Vol. II (Bureau of National Literature, 1911) at 1117-1118; Ronald N. Satz, *American Indian Policy in the Jacksonian Era* (University of Oklahoma Press, 2002); Leonard L. Richards, "The Jacksonians And Slavery," in Lewis Perry and Michael Fellman, Editors, *Antislavery Reconsidered: New Perspectives on the Abolitionists* (Louisiana State University Press, 1979) at 109-111.

265 Tragle at 250, 276.

266 Tragle at 261.

267 Tragle at 430-433.

268 Tragle at 432-433.

269 Tragle at 433-434.

270 Tragle at 262, 436-438, 442-444.

271 Tragle at 455-462; Guild at 106-108; *Anderson v. Commonwealth,* 5 Leigh 740, July 1835, in Catteral, Vol. 1, at 177-178.

272 Tragle at 15; Crofts at 293; Parramore, *Southampton County* at 114-116; Philip J. Schwarz, *Migrants against Slavery* (University Press of Virginia, 2001) at 13-14, 72.

273 Tragle at 15; Crofts, Table 1.1 at 293.

274 Tragle at 15; Crofts at 16-17.

275 Tragle at 262; Wolf, *Race And Liberty In The New Nation* at 196-234.

276 Freehling, *Drift Toward Dissolution,* at 6-7, 129-135; Tragle at 263. Jefferson, as he did in so many other areas, set the parameters for the racist ideology. He started with color, which he said was the foundation of beauty. He found that "immoveable veil of black" was unattractive when compared to white, and blacks preferred the "flowing hair, a more elegant symmetry of form" of whites "as is the preference of the Oranootan for the black woman over those of his own species." Jefferson noted that blacks had "a very strong and disagreeable odour," had a "difference in the pulmonary apparatus," were more tolerant of heat and less of cold than whites, required less sleep, and were more "ardent after their female… In general, their existence appears to participate more of sensation than reflection." Jefferson concluded: "I advance it therefore as a

suspicion only, that the blacks, whether originally a distinct race, or made distinct by time and circumstances, are inferior to the whites in the endowments both of body and mind." While the Romans required only one act to free their slaves, "The slave, when made free, might mix with, without staining the blood of his master. But with us a second is necessary, unknown to history. When freed, he is to be removed beyond the reach of mixture." Jefferson, *Writings* at 264-265, 270; In the North these sentiments had support. In the middle of the Civil War, Abraham Lincoln told Congress and a group of free blacks that it was better for both blacks and whites if blacks were colonized outside the United States. In 1862, Congress, with Lincoln's support, appropriated $600,000 to colonize free blacks in Haiti, and funded one effort, which failed. Abraham Lincoln, *Speeches and Writings 1859-1865* (The Library of America, 1989) at 291-292, 353-357. Rayford W. Logan, *The Diplomatic Relations of the United States With Haiti, 1776-1891* (University of North Carolina Press, 1941) at 308-310. There were other whites, however, like Benjamin Rush, a signer of the Declaration of Independence, who believed slavery should end and former slaves should be accepted as full citizens. Dagobert D. Runes, Editor, *The Selected Writings of Benjamin Rush*, (Philosophical Library, 1947) at vi, 3-18, 24-25.

[277] Freehling, *Drift Toward Dissolution*, at 148, 162-169, 182-195; Masur, *1831*, at 48-62; Tragle at 264.

[278] Thomas Roderick Dew, "Abolition of Negro Slavery" in Drew Gilpin Faust, *The Ideology of Slavery* (Louisiana State University Press, 1981) at 51; Tragle at 250-251; Freehling, *Drift Toward Dissolution* at 202-203; Larry E. Tise, *Proslavery: a history of the defense of slavery in America, 1701-1840* (The University of Georgia Press, 1987) at 70-74.

[279] Dew at 33.

[280] Id. at 30.

[281] Id. at 42-57.

[282] Id. at 71-77; Midori Takagi, *"Rearing Wolves to Our Own Destruction"* (University Press of Virginia, 1999) at 81-82.

[283] Parramore, *Southampton County* at 72-74; Lincoln, *Speeches and Writings 1859-1865* at 50-58; Don E. Fehrenbacher, *Slavery, Law, & Politics* (Oxford University Press, 1981) at 183-213.

[284] Frederick Douglass, *Autobiographies* (The Library of America,

1994) at 746; David S. Reynolds, *John Brown, Abolitionist* (Alfred A. Knopf, 2005) at 54-56; 167-168; Schwarz, *Twice Condemned* at 282-283; Phillip J. Schwarz, "Forging the Shackles: The Development of Virginia's Criminal Code for Slaves," in David J. Bodenhamer & James W. Ely, Jr., Editors, *Ambivalent Legacy: A Legal History of the South* (University Press of Mississippi, 1984) 138.

285   David DeVillers, *The John Brown Slavery Revolt Trial* (Enslow Publishers, Inc, 2000) at 29-33; Work Projects Administration, *The Negro in Virginia* (John F. Blair, Publisher, 1994) at 202-205.

286   Louis Ruchames, Editor, *A John Brown Reader* (Abelard-Schuman, 1959) at 159, also 125-158; Daniel Aaron, "The Trial of John Brown," in Robert S. Brumbaugh, *Six Trials* (Thomas Y. Crowell Co., 1969) at 42-59; Allan Nevins, *The Emergence of Lincoln* (Charles Scribners Sons, 1950) Vol. 2, at 5-11.

287   Brian Steel Wills, *The War Hits Home* (University Press of Virginia, 2001); Crofts at 193-217; Parramore, *Southampton County* at 157-177.

288   Freeman Cleaves, *Rock of Chickamauga* (University of Oklahoma Press, 1948) at 3-9, 62, 158-176, 201-217; Steven E. Woodworth, *Chickamauga* (University of Nebraska Press, 1999) at 72-82; R.J.M. Blackett, Editor, *Thomas Morris Chester, Black Civil War Correspondent* (Louisiana State University Press, 1989) at 212; Joseph T. Wilson, *The Black Phalanx* (Da Capo Press, 1994) at 286-305; Parramore, *Southampton County* at 152-153, 170-173; Lincoln, *Speeches And Writings 1859-1865* at 481, 490.

289   United States, War Department, *The War of the Rebellion* (Government Printing Office, 1891), "Report of Brig. Gen Charles A Heckman," U.S. Army, Mar. 12, 1864 in Series 1, Vol. XXXIII at 238; Richard S. West, Jr. *Lincoln's Scapegoat General: A Life of Benjamin F. Butler 1818-1893* (Houghton Mifflin Co., 1965) at 168-169, 221-226, 248; Both free blacks and slaves from Southampton also were members of the 1st U.S. Cavalry, and several colored infantry and artillery units. Daniel T. Balfour, *Franklin and Southampton County in the Civil War* (H.E. Howard, Inc., 2002) at 110-116. The black troops were paid seven dollars a month, whereas white troops received thirteen. In July 1864 free black troops were granted equal pay retroactive to the day of enlistment, while those who were slaves at the start of the war did not get retroactive equal pay until

1865. Nudelman, *John Brown's Body*, at 207; Clayton Charles Marlow, *Matt W. Ransom* (McFarland & Company, Inc., 1996) at 84-87.

[290] Wills, *The War Hits Home* at 213-220; Ervin J. Jordan, Jr. *Black Confederates And Afro-Yankees in Civil War Virginia* (University Press of Virginia, 1995) at 279; *The War of Rebellion* at 237-239, 1270; LaSalle C. Pickett, *Pickett And His Men* (J.B. Lippincott Co., 1913) at 179-221; *The Black Phalanx* at 315-374; T.H. Pearce, Editor, *Diary of Captain Henry A. Chambers* (Broadfoot's Bookmark, 1983) at 179-184; Noah Andre Trudeau, "Proven Themselves in Every Respect to Be Men: Black Cavalry in the Civil War," in John David Smith, Editor, *Black Soldiers in Blue* (The University of North Carolina Press, 2002) at 277-305; George S. Burkhardt, *Confederate Rage, Yankee Wrath* (Southern Illinois University Press, 2007) at 99-100.

[291] Clifford Dowdey and Louis H. Manarin, Editors, *The Wartime Papers of R.E. Lee* (Little, Brown and Company, 1961) at 914; James D. Richardson, Editor, *The Messages and Papers of Jefferson Davis and the Confederacy including Diplomatic Correspondence 1861-1865* (Chelsea House Publishers, 1966) Vol. 1 at 547; Jordan, *Black Confederates And Afro-Yankees in Civil War Virginia* at 246, notes that several companies of black Virginia troops volunteered and served as Confederate troops in March and April 1865.

[292] Blackett, *Thomas Morris Chester, Black Civil War Correspondent* at 288-294; Dowdey and Manarin, *The Wartime Papers of R.E. Lee* at 934-935; Michael B. Chesson & Leslie J. Roberts, Editors, *Exile in Richmond* (The University Press of Virginia, 2001) at 367.

[293] Karen J. Greenberg and Joshua L. Dratel, *The Torture Papers* (Cambridge University Press, 2005) at 26, 3-24 (The Woo Memorandum on Presidential Authority); On the Congressional resolution see *Hamdi v. Rumsfeld* (2004) 542 U.S. 507. See also: Mark Danner, *Torture and Truth* (The New York Review of Books, 2004) at 78-79; "Plan to Keep Detainees in Jail for Life Criticized by Senators," *L.A. Times*, January 3, 2005, A11; Douglas Jehl and Neil A. Lewis, "U.S. Said to Hold More Foreigners in Iraq Fighting," *N.Y. Times*, Jan. 8, 2005, A1.

[294] See the discussion of *Hamdi v. Runsfeld* and *Rumsfeld v. Padilla* (2004) 542 U.S. 426.

[295]   Greenberg & Dratel, *The Torture Papers* at 134-135, 910-912; Seymour M. Hersh, *Chain of Command* (Harper Collins Publisher, 2004) at 1-72; Mark Danner, "We Are All Torturers Now," *N.Y. Times*, Jan. 6, 2005, A27.

[296]   "CIA: No Comment on report 11 Qaida suspects held in Jordan", Haaretz.com, October 13, 2004; Chris Mullin, "Why Condi roiled Europe," *L.A. Times*, Dec. 9, 2005, at B15; Sarah Lyall, "Britain's Top Court Rules Information Gotten by Torture Is Never Admissible Evidence," *N.Y. Times*, Dec. 9, 2005 at A6; Joseph Margulies, *Guantanamo And The Abuse of Presidential Power* (Simon & Schuster, 2006).

[297]   Mark Danner, *Torture and Truth* at 22, 78-82, 105-106; Anthony Lewis, "The US Case for Torture," *The New York Review of Books*, July 15, 2004, at 6-8. As of October 2005, U.S. military documents indicated 44 prisoners had died in U.S. custody, 21 of whom were homicides, including 8 who were fatally abused. John Hendren, "Autopsies Support Abuse Allegations," *L.A. Times*, Oct. 25, 2005 at A4. For the origin of the torture techniques see: Alfred W. McCoy, *A Question of Torture: CIA Interrogation From the Cold War to the War on Terror* (Henry Holt and Company, 2006) and Jane Mayer, *The Dark Side* (Doubleday, 2008).

[298]   Greenberg & Dratel, *The Torture Papers* at 223.

[299]   Greenberg & Dratel, *The Torture Papers* at 227-366; Tim Golden, "After Terror, a Secret Rewriting of Military Law," *N.Y. Times*, Oct. 24, 2004, 1, 12-13; Danner, 16-17, 22-24, 33-36, 42-45, 251-275; Neil A. Lewis, "Red Cross President Plans Visit to Washington on Question of Detainees' Treatment," *N.Y. Times*, December 1, 2004, A23; Richard A. Serrano, "FBI Agents Complained of Prisoner Abuse, Records Say," *L.A. Times*, Dec. 21, 2004, at 1; Neil A. Lewis, "Broad Use of Harsh Tactics Is Described at Cuba Base," *N.Y. Times*, Oct. 17, 2004, A1; Neil A. Lewis, "Red Cross Finds Detainee Abuse in Guantanamo," *N.Y. Times*, Nov. 30, 2004, A1; Editorial, "Abu Ghraib, Caribbean Style," *N.Y. Times*, Dec. 1, 2004, A30.

[300]   Sam Roberts, *Who We Are Now* (Times Books, 2004) 142-175; Douglas C. McDonald and Kenneth E. Carlson, *Sentencing in the Federal Courts: Does Race Matter?* (U.S. Department of Justice, December 1993).

[301]   Jack Goldsmith, *The Terror Presidency* (W.W. Norton & Co., 2007) at 109; Greenberg & Dratel, *The Torture Papers* at 27;

Jonathan Mahler, "The Bush Administration vs. Salim Hamdan," *The New York Times Magazine*, Jan. 8, 2006 at 47, 51 and 81.

[302] Kevin Phillips, *The Politics of Rich and Poor* (Harper Perennial, 1991) at 8-14, 241; *Wealth and Democracy* (Broadway Books 2002) 108-138; Edward N. Wolff, *Top Heavy* (The New Press, 2002) 8-16; Robert Frank, "The Rich Really Are Like Everyone-in Debt," *The Wall Street Journal*, May 5, 2005, C1.

[303] *N.Y. Times*, Sept. 19, 2004, Sec. 4, at 2; Phillips, *Wealth and Democracy* at 293-346.

[304] *Rumsfeld v. Padilla* (2004) 542 U.S. 426; *Rasul v. Bush* (2004) 542 U.S. 466; and *Hamdi v. Rumsfeld* (2004) 542 U.S. 507. Rasul held that Federal courts have jurisdiction to hear habeas petitions of foreign nationals held at Guantanamo Bay Naval Base. In addition the detainees could file suits under the federal question statute and the Alien Tort Claim Statute. They also have the right to counsel. Neil A. Lewis, "Guantanamo Detainees Make Their Case," *N.Y. Times*, March 24, 2005, at A17.

[305] *Rumsfeld v. Padilla* at 465.

[306] *Padilla v. C.T. Hanft*, 126 S.Ct. 978 (2006); Richard B. Schmitt, "Sidestepping Courts in the War on Terrorism," *L.A. Times*, Nov. 30, 2005, A18; Jose Padilla (prisoner), en.wikipedia.org.

[307] *Hamdi v. Rumsfeld* at 518-519, 533-534; See also: Ronald Dworkin, "The Supreme Court & Guantanamo," *The New York Review of Books*, Aug. 12, 2004 at 26; Serrano, "FBI Agents Complained of Prisoner Abuse, Records Say," supra at A19.

[308] "Rules Could Allow Guantanamo Executions," *N.Y. Times*, Jan. 25, 2006, A14.

[309] *Hamdan v. Rumsfeld*, 126 S.Ct. 2749 (2006); David G. Savage, "High Court Rejects Bush's Claim That He Alone Sets Detainee Rules," *L.A. Times*, Jun. 30, 2006 at A1.

[310] Jan Crawford Greenburg, *Supreme Conflict* (The Penguin Press, 2007); On 6/16/08 a copy of the Boumediene opinion was downloaded from accesslaw.com.

[311] John W. Brockenbrough, Editor, *Cases Decided by the Honorable John Marshall* (1837) Vol. 1 at 423; John P. Roche, Editor, *John Marshall Major Opinions and Other Writings* (Bobbs-Merrill Co., Inc. 1967) at 197. On privateers see: Edgar S. Maclay, *A History of American Privateers* (Burt Franklin,

1968). On Buenos Aires see: Jeremy Adelman, *Republic of Capital* (Stanford University Press, 1999) at 119; Bryan A. Garner, Editor, *Black's Law Dictionary* 7th Edition (West Group, 1999) at 1214.

[312] Roche at 202-203; Wolf, *Race And Liberty In The New Nation* at 157-161.

[313] T.H. Breen and Stephen Innes, *Myne Owne Ground* (Oxford University Press, 2005) at 19; Morgan, *Slave Counterpoint*, Table 11 at 63.

[314] Michael A. Gomez, *Exchanging Our Country Marks* (The University of North Carolina Press, 1998) at 38, 107, and 116.

[315] Allan Kulikoff, *Tobacco and Slaves* (University of North Carolina Press, 1986) at 319-322, 335-345.

[316] Ira Berlin, *Many Thousands Gone* (Belknap Press, 1998) at 126-128; Morgan, *Slave Counterpoint* Table 19 at 81.

[317] Michael Mullin, *Africa in America* (University of Illinois Press, 1994) at 175-177; Morgan, *Slave Counterpoint* at 617, 620.

[318] Morgan, *Slave Counterpoint* at 395-396; Schwarz, *Slave Laws in Virginia* at 7.

[319] Schwarz, *Twice Condemned* at 92.

[320] Schwarz, *Twice Condemned* at 97; a convicted person could escape death if there was no ill intent or medicine was given with the owner's consent. Guild at 159.

[321] Morgan, *Slave Counterpoint* Table 10 at 61; Schwarz, *Twice Condemned*, Table 10 at 96.

[322] Schwarz, *Twice Condemned* at 323-335.

[323] Schwarz, *Twice Condemned* Table 5 at 43-44, 108-110.

[324] For details on Bush's military commissions see Chapter 10 infra. Michael A. Gomez, at 20-21; Guild, at 151; Schwarz, *Twice Condemned*, at 16-17.

[325] Charles M. Andrews, Ed., *Narratives of the Insurrection 1675-1690* (Charles Saiber Sons, 1915) at 94-95; Edmund S. Morgan, *American Slavery American Freedom* (W.W. Norton & Co., 1975) at 250-270; Ira Berlin, *Generations of Captivity* (The Belknap Press, 2003) 36-39, 55-67; Breen and Innes, *"Myne Owne Ground"*.

[326] Anthony S. Parent, Jr., *Foul Means* (University of North Carolina Press, 2003) at 105-134, 143-148; A. Leon

Higginbotham, Jr. *In the Matter of Color* (Oxford University Press, 1978) at 19-60.

[327] Hening, Vol. 3, 102-103 (1823).

[328] Catteral, Vol. 1 at 177; Thad W. Tate, *The Negro in Eighteenth-Century Williamsburg* (The University Press of Virginia, 1965) at 164-169; Schwarz, *Twice Condemned* at 50. Guild at 152; Goodell, *The American Slave Code*, Pt. II, Ch. V at 313, found at http://www.dinsdoc.com/goodell-1-2-5.htm, last visited 4/24/2004; Schwarz, *Slaves Laws in Virginia*, at 64, 71-73.

[329] Schwarz, *Slaves Laws in Virginia*, at 95, 97-Table 4.1 at 105, 117-119; Catteral at 137.

[330] Thomas D. Morris, "Slaves and the Rules of Evidence in Criminal Trials," in Paul Finkelman, Editor, *Slavery & The Law* (Rowan & Littlefield Publishers, Inc, 1997) at 212-215; Tate, at 168-169; Schwarz, *Twice Condemned*, at 19-20; Hening, Vol. 4 at 127.

[331] Edmund S. Morgan notes that the lesson the elite learned from the Bacon rebellion was, "Resentment of an alien race might be more powerful than resentment of an upper class." Morgan, at 269-270.

[332] Edward Pessen, *Riches, Class And Power: America Before the Civil War* (Transaction Publishers, 1990); on the concentration of wealth in the U.S. today see Chapter 9 supra.

[333] "Aristocracy and Democracy in the Southern Tradition," in George M. Fredrickson, *The Arrogance of Race* (Wesleyan University Press, 1988) at 134,140-141.

[334] Oates, at 2.

[335] Crofts, at 165, 303, 317. The figures are from 1840 and 1843, but are suggestive of the situation in 1831.

[336] Tragle, footnote 4 at 175.

[337] See: The November 21, 1831 unanimous recommendation for Sheriff by the Southampton Court sent to Governor Floyd. *The Executive Papers of Governor John Floyd*, 1831, Box 5, Folder 2, The Library of Virginia, Richmond, Virginia; and Crofts at 164; Herbert S. Klein, *Slavery in the Americas* (First Elephant Paperback, 1989) at 29-30.

[338] Crofts at 108, 130; Oates at 124.

[339] Crofts at 45-46, 50-51, 92-93, 189-90; Parramore, *Southampton County, Virginia* (University Press of Virginia, 1978) at 58.

[340] Crofts at 115, 186; Parramore, *Southampton County*, at 58; Tragle at 191-192.

[341] Parramore, *Southampton County* at 51; Oates 88-90.

[342] Tragle at 35-36, 251-252; Parramore, *Southampton County* at 98; Crofts at 15.

[343] Crofts at 25, 107.

[344] Five free blacks were also examined by the magistrates. See infra Chapter 6 on Slave Trials.

[345] Schwarz, *Twice Condemned*, Table 1 at 15, Table 3 at 39. See Appendix II for a Note on African Virginian Crime.

[346] Schwarz, id., Table 27 at 248.

[347] Schwarz, *Slave Laws In Virginia*, at 74, 80-82, 94-95,103-106, 117-119, 206; the decline in slave executions was an aspect of the national reform movement to eliminate public executions in the antebellum period. Louis P. Masur, *Rites of Execution* (Oxford University Press, 1989) and Edward L. Ayers, *Vengeance and Justice* (Oxford University Press, 1984).

[348] Schwarz, *Slave Laws in Virginia* at 206; Schwarz, *Twice Condemned* Table 27 at 248, 282, 297-299.

Bibliography

The Library of Virginia Archivist refers a scholar interested in the Nat Turner insurrection to Henry Irving Tragle's *The Southampton Slave Revolt of 1831: A Compilation of Source Material* (The University of Massachusetts Press, 1971) as a source of the first impression. Tragle collected, in a single volume, most of the primary source materials, i.e., newspaper articles, government records, the diary and letters of the Governor, as well as the 50 transcripts of the insurrection trials. Tragle is cited directly by page in the text, without specification of the title of the primary source. Those interested in the citations should have a copy of Tragle available. In addition, there are several excellent studies of Southampton and the Turner insurrection also cited frequently in the text. None of them, however, have focused on the trials. Throughout the preparation of the book an effort was made to carefully document the factual assertions as well as to use the voice of Nat Turner himself. He is the only American slave rebel to leave a written testament behind.

Aaron, Daniel, "The Trial of John Brown" in Robert S. Brumbaugh, *Six Trials* (Thomas Y. Crowell, Co, 1969).

Adams, Charles Francis, *Memoirs of John Quincy Adams* (J.P. Lippincott & Co., 1876).

Adelman, Jeremy, *Republic of Capital* (Stanford University Press, 1999).

Allmendinger, David F., Jr., "The Construction of the *Confessions* of Nat Turner" in Kenneth S. Greenberg, Ed. *Nat Turner* (Oxford University Press, 2003).

Ambler, Charles H., *The Life and Diary of John Floyd* (Richmond Press, Inc., 1918); and *Thomas Ritchie* (Bell Books and Stationary Co., 1913).

American Psychiatric Association, *Diagnostic and Statistical Manual of Mental Disorders* (4th Edition, 1994).

Andrews, Charles M., Editor, *Narratives of the Insurrection 1675-1690* (Charles Saiber Sons, 1915).

Andrews, William L. And Gates, Henry Louis, Jr., *Slave Narratives* (The Library of America, 1994).

Aptheker, Herbert, *American Negro Slave Revolts* (Sixth Edition, International Publishers, 1993);

Ayers, Edward L., *Vengeance and Justice* (Oxford University Press, 1984).

Balfour, Daniel T., *Franklin and Southampton County in the Civil War* (H.E. Howard, Inc., 2002).

Ballagh, James C. *History of Slavery in Virginia* (Johnson Reprints, 1968).

Berlin, Ira, *Slaves Without Masters* (The New Press, 1974); *Generations of Captivity* (The Belknap Press, 2003); and *Many Thousands Gone* (Belknap Press, 1998).

Blackett, R.J.M., Editor, *Thomas Morris Chester, Black Civil War Correspondent* (Louisiana State University Press, 1989).

Blanton, Wyndham, B., M.D., *Medicine in Virginia* (Arno Press and the New York Times, 1972).

Bogga, Thomas L., *Free Blacks in Norfolk, Virginia 1790-1860* (University Press of Virginia, 1997).

Breen, Patrick H., "A Prophet in His Own Land," in Kenneth S. Greenberg, Editor, *Nat Turner* (Oxford University Press, 2003).

Breen T.H. and Innes, Stephen, *Mine Own Ground* (Oxford University Press, 2005).

Brockenbrough, John W., Editor, *Cases Decided by the Honorable John Marshall*, Vol.1 (1837).

Brown, Raymond E., *The Death of the Messiah* (Doubleday, 1998).

Burkhardt, George S., *Confederate Rage, Yankee Wrath* (Southern Illinois University Press, 2007).

Catteral, Helen Tunnicliff, *Judicial Cases Concerning American Slavery and the Negro* (Negro University Press, 1968).

Chesson, Michael B. & Roberts, Leslie J., *Exile in Richmond* (The University Press of Virginia, 2001).

Cleaves, Freeman, *Rock of Chickamauga* (University of Oklahoma Press, 1948).

Crofts, Daniel W., *Old Southampton* (University Press of Virginia, 1992).

Danner, Mark *Torture and Truth* (The New York Review of Books, 2004).

Davis, Mary Kemp, "What Happened in This Place?" in Kenneth S. Greenberg, Editor, *Nat Turner* (Oxford University Press, 2003).

De Villers, David, *The John Brown Slavery Revolt Trial* (Enslow Publishers, Inc., 2000).

Dew, Thomas Roderick, "Abolition of Negro Slavery" in Faust, Drew Galpin, *The Ideology of Slavery* (Louisiana State University Press, 1981).

Douglass, Frederick, *Life and Times of Frederick Douglass* (Macmillan Publishing Company, 1962).

Dowdey, Clifford and Manarin, Louis H., *The Wartime Papers of R.E. Lee* (Little, Brown and Company, 1961).

Drewry, William Sidney, *The Southampton Insurrection* (Johnson Publishing Co., 1968).

Du Bois, W.E.B., "The Suppression of the African Slave-Trade" in *Writings* (The Library of America, 1986).

Duke, Maurice, Editor, *Don't Carry Me Back!* (The Dietz Press, 1995).

Egerton, Douglas R., *Gabriel's Rebellion* (The University of North Carolina Press, 1993).

Fabricant, Daniel S., "Thomas R. Gray and William Styron: Finally, A Critical Look at the 1831 Confessions of Nat Turner," *The American Journal of Legal History*, Vol. 37 (1993).

Fehrenbacker, Don E., *Slavery, Law & Politics* (Oxford University Press, 1981).

Flournoy, H.W., *Calender of Virginia State Papers and Other Manuscripts from January 1, 1799 to December 31, 1807* (Richmond, 1890).

Fogel, Robert William, *Without Consent or Contract* (W.W. Norton & Company, Inc., 1989).

Fogel, Robert W. and Engerman, Stanley L., *Time on the Cross* (W.W. Norton & Company, Inc., 1989).

Foner, Eric, Editor, "Recollections of James L. Smith" in *Nat*

Turner (Prentice-Hall, Inc., 1971).

Frazier, E. Franklin, *The Negro Church in America* (Schocken Books, Inc., 1974).

Fredrickson, George M., "Aristocracy and Democracy in the Southern Tradition" in *The Arrogrance of Race* (Wesleyan University Press, 1988).

Freehling, Alison Goodyear, *Drift Toward Dissolution* (Louisiana State University Press, 1982).

Freehling, William W., *The Road to Disunion, Vol 1, Secessionists at Bay 1776-1854* (Oxford University Press, 1990).

French, Scot, *The Rebellious Slave* (Houghton, Mifflin Co., 2004).

Garner, Bryan A., Editor, *Black's Law Dictionary* 7th Edition, (West Group, 1999).

Goldman, Martin S., *Nat Turner and the Southampton Revolt of 1831* (Franklin Watts, 1992).

Goldsmith, Jack, *The Terror Presidency* (W.W. Norton & Company, 2007).

Gomez, Michael A., *Exchanging Our Country Marks* (The University of North Carolina Press, 1998).

Goodell, William, *The American Slave Code in Theory and Practice* (American and Foreign Anti-Slavery Society, 1853).

Greenberg, Karen J. and Dratel, Joshua L., *The Torture Papers* (Cambridge University Press, 2005).

Greenberg, Kenneth S., "Name, Face, Body," in Kenneth S. Greenberg, Editor, *Nat Turner* (Oxford University Press, 2003).

Greenburg, Jan Crawford, *Supreme Conflict* (The Penguin Press, 2007).

Guild, June P., *Black Laws in Virginia* (Negro Universities Press, 1969).

Hamilton, Stanislaus M., *The Writings of James Monroe* (G.P. Putnam's Sons, 1900).

Heckman Charles A., "Report of Brig. Gen. Charles A. Heckman," U.S. Army, Mar. 12 1864, in United States, War Department *The War of the Rebellion: a compilation* of the official records of the Union and Confederate armies, (Government Printing Office, 1891).

Hening, William H., *Hening's Statutes at Large* Vol. 3, (1823).

Hersh, Seymour M., *Chain of Command* (Harper Collins Publisher, 2004).

Hickey, Donald R., *The War of 1812* (University of Illinois Press, 1990).

Higginbotham, Leon, Jr., *In the Matter of Color* (Oxford University Press, 1978).

Hinks, Peter P., *To Awaken My Afflicted Brethren* (The Pennsylvania State University Press, 1997); Editor, *David Walker's Appeal to the Coloured Citizens of the World* (The Pennsylvania State University Press, 2000).

Issac, Rhys, *The Transformation of Virginia 1740-1790* (University of North Carolina Press, 1982).

Jackson, Andrew, "Third Annual Message, December 1831", in James D. Richardson, *A Compilation of the Messages and Papers of the Presidents*, Vol. 11, (Bureau of National Literature, 1911).

Jackson, Luther P., *Free Negro Labor and Property Holding in Virginia 1830-1860* (Russell & Russell, 1971).

James, C.L.R., *The Black Jacobins* (Vintage Books, 1989).

Jefferson, Thomas, *Writings* (The Library of America, 1984).

Johnson, F. Roy, *The Nat Turner Slave Insurrection* (Johnson Publishing Co., 1966); *The Nat Turner Story* (Johnson Publishing Co., 1970).

Johnston, James H., *Race Relations in Virginia & Miscegenation in the South, 1776-1860* (University of Massachusetts Press, 1970).

Jones, Kathleen, *Lunacy Law and Conscience 1744-1845* (Routledge & Kegan Paul United, 1995).

Jordan, Ervin J., *Black Confederates And Afro-Yankees in Civil War Virginia* (University Press of Virginia, 1995).

Kennedy, Roger G., *Mr. Jefferson's Lost Cause* (Oxford University Press, 2003).

King, B.B. and Ritz, David, *Blues All Around Me* (Aron Books, 1996).

163

Klein, Herbert S., *Slavery in the Americas* (First Elephant Paperback, 1989).

Kulikoff, Allan, *Tobacco & Slaves* (University of North Carolina Press, 1986).

Lakwete, Angela, *Inventing the Cotton Gin* (The John Hopkins University Press, 2003).

Lewis, Dorothy O., M.D., *Guilty by Reason of Insanity* (Ballantine Publishing Group, 1998).

Lincoln, Abraham, *Speeches and Writings 1859-1865* (The Library of America, 1989).

Logan, Rayford W., *The Diplomatic Relations of the United States With Haiti, 1776-1891* (University of North Carolina Press, 1941).

Macalpine, Ida & Hunter, Richard, *George III and the Mad-Business* (Pantheon Books, 1969).

Maclay, Edgar S., *A History of American Privateers* (Burt Franklin, 1968).

Maeder, Thomas, *Crime and Madness* (Harper & Row, 1985).

Margulies, Joseph, *Guantanamo And The Abuse of Presidential Power* (Simon & Schuster, 2006).

Masur, Louis P., *Rites of Execution* (Oxford University Press, 1989); *1831* (Hill and Wang, 2001).

Marlow, Clayton Charles, *Matt W. Ransom* (McFarland & Company, Inc., 1996).

Mayer, Jane, *The Dark Side* (Doubleday, 2008).

McCoy, Alfred W., *A Question of Torture: CIA Interrogation from the Cold War to the War on Terror* (Henry Holt & Co., 2006).

McDonald, Douglas C., and Carlson, Kenneth E., *Sentencing in the Federal Courts: Does Race Matter?* (U.S. Department of Justice, 1993).

Miller, John C., *The Wolf by the Ears* (The University Press of Virginia, 1991).

Moran, Richard, *Knowing Right From Wrong* (The Free Press, 1981).

Morgan, Edmund S., *American Slavery American Freedom* (W.W. Norton & Co., 1975).

Morgan, Phillip D., "The Significance of Kin," in Heuman,

Gad and Walvin, James, Editors, *The Slavery Reader* (Routledge, 2003).

Morris, Thomas D., *Southern Slavery and the Law 1419-1860* (University of North Carolina Press, 1996); "Slaves and the Rules of Evidence in Criminal Trials," in Finkelman, Paul, Editor, *Slavery and the Law* (Rowan & Littlefield Publishers, Inc., 1997).

Mullin, Gerald W., *Flight and Rebellion* (Oxford University Press, 1972).

Mullin, Michael, *Africa in America* (University of Illinois Press, 1994).

Nevins, Allan, *The Emergence of Lincoln* (Charles Scribners Sons, 1950).

North, Douglas C., *The Economic Growth of the United States 1790-1860* (W.W. Norton and Co., Inc., 1966).

Nudelman, Franny, *John Brown's Body* (The University of North Carolina Press, 2004).

Oates, Stephen B., *The Fires of Jubilee* (Harper Perennial, 1975).

Parent, Anthony S., Jr., *Foul Means* (University of North Carolina Press, 2003).

Parramore, Thomas C., *Southampton County Virginia* (University Press of Virginia, 1978); *Norfolk* (University Press of Virginia, 1994); "A Covenant in Jerusalem," in Greenberg, Kenneth S., *Nat Turner* (Oxford University Press, 2003).

Pearce, T. H., Editor, *Diary of Captain Henry A. Chambers* (Broadfoot's Bookmark, 1983).

Perdue, Charles L., Jr., Barden, Thomas F., and Phillips, Robert K., Editors, *Weevils in the Wheat* (University Press of Virginia, 1976).

Pessen, Edward, *Riches, Class and Power: America Before the Civil War* (Tranciting Publishers, 1990).

Phillips, Kevin, *The Politics of Rich and Poor* (Harper Perennial, 1991).

Phillips, Ulrich B., Edited by Eugene Genovise, *The Slave Economy of the Old South* (Louisiana State University Press, 1968).

Pickett, LaSalle C., *Pickett And His Men* (J.B. Lippincott, Co., 1913).

Remini, Robert V., *The Legacy of Andrew Jackson* (Louisiana State University Press, 1988).

Reynolds, David S., *John Brown, Abolitionist* (Alfred A. Knopf, 2005).

Richards, Leonard L., "The Jacksonians and Slavery," in Perry, Lewis and Fellman, Michael, Editors, *Antislavery Reconsidered: New Perspectives on the Abolitionists* (Louisiana State University Press, 1979).

Richardson, James D., Editor, *The Messages and Papers of Jefferson Davis and the Confederacy including Diplomatic Correspondence 1861-1865* (Chelsea House Publishers, 1966).

Roberts, Sam, *Who We Are Now* (Times Books, 2004).

Roche, John P, Editor, *John Marshall Major Opinions and Other Writings* (Bobbs-Merrill Co., Inc., 1967).

Ruchames, Louis, Editor, *A John Brown Reader* (Abelard-Schuman, 1959).

Runes, Dagobert D., *The Selected Writings of Benjamin Rush* (Philosophical Library, 1947).

Russell, John A., *The Free Negro in Virginia* (Dover Publications, Inc., 1969).

Satz, Ronald N., *American Indian Policy in the Jacksonian Era* (University of Oklahoma Press, 2002).

Savitt, Todd L., *Medicine and Slavery: The Diseases and Health Care of Blacks in Antebellum Virginia* (University of Illinois Press, 1978).

Schlotterbeck, John T., *Plantation and Farm: Social and Economic Change in Orange and Greene Counties, Virginia 1716 to 1860* (University Microfilms, 1980).

Schwarz, Phillip J., *Twice Condemned* (Louisiana State University Press, 1988); *Slave Laws in Virginia* (The University of Georgia Press, 1996); *Migrants Against Slavery* (University Press of Virginia, 2001); "Forging the Shackles: The Development of Virginia Criminal Code for Slaves," in Boderhamer, David J. and Ely, James N., Jr., Editors, *Ambivalent Legacy: A legal History of the*

South (University Press of Mississippi, 1984).

Scully, Randolph Ferguson, *Religion and the Making of Nat Turner's Virginia* (University of Virginia Press, 2008).

Sidbury, James, *Ploughshares into Swords* (Cambridge University Press, 1997); "Thomas Jefferson in Gabriel's Virginia," in Horn, James, Ellen Jan, and Onuf, Peter S., Editors, *The Revolution of 1800* (University of Virginia Press, 2002).

Sobel, Mechal, *Trabelin' On* (Greenwood Press, Inc., 1979).

Tadman, Michael, *Speculators and Slaves* (The University of Wisconsin Press, 1989, 1996).

Takagi, Midori, *Rearing Wolves to Our own Destruction* (University Press of Virginia, 1999).

Tate, Thad W., *The Negro in Eighteenth-Century Williamsburg* (University Press of Virginia, 1965).

Thomas, Emory M., *Robert E. Lee* (W.W. Norton & Co., 1995).

Tise, Larry E., *Proslavery: A History of the Defense of Slavery in America* (The University of Georgia Press, 1987).

Tragle, Henry I., *The Southampton Slave Revolt of 1831: A Compilation of Source Material* (University of Massachusetts Press, 1971).

Trudeau, Noah Andre, "Proven Themselves in Every Respect to Be Men: Black Cavalry in the Civil War," in Smith, John David, *Black Soldiers in Blue* (The University of North Carolina Press, 2002).

Tushnet, Mark, *The American Law of Slavery 1810-1860* (Princeton University Press, 1981); *Slave Law in the American South* (University of Kansas Press, 2003).

West, Richard S., Jr., *Lincoln's Scapegoat General: A Life of Benjamin F. Butler, 1818-1893* (Houghton Mifflin Co., 1965).

Wills, Brian S., *The War Hits Home* (University Press of Virginia, 2001).

Wills, Garry, *"Negro President"* (Houghton Mifflin Co., 2003); *Mr. Jefferson's University* (National Geographic Society, 2002).

Wilson, Joseph T., *The Black Phalanx* (Da Capo Press, 1994).

Wolf, Edward N., *Top Heavy* (The New Press, 2002).

Wolf, Eva Sheppard, *Race And Liberty In The New Nation* (Louisiana State University Press, 2006).

Woodworth, Steven E., *Chickamauga* (University of Nebraska Press, 1999).

Works Projects Administration, *The Negro in Virginia* (John F. Blair, Publisher, 1994).

Index

Walter L. Gordon, III is an attorney who has practiced law in California for over 30 years. He received his law degree from UCLA Law School, where he was a member of the law review. Attorney Gordon also has a Masters in Public Administration and a Ph.D. in Political Science from UCLA. Associated Faculty Press, Inc. published his Ph.D. dissertation *Crime And Criminal Law: The California Experience 1960-1975*. Over the years he has kept a foot in both the academic and real worlds. In addition to pursuing an active private law practice, he served as a Lecturer in advance criminal procedure at UCLA Law School from 1978 to 1982. He has also taught in the Pan African Studies Department at California State University at Los Angeles. A chapter of *The Nat Turner Insurrection Trials: A Mystic Chord Resonates Today* was published by Black Renaissance/Renaissance Noire, a magazine of the Africana Studies Program and the Institute of African American Affairs at NYU.

Breinigsville, PA USA
13 November 2010
249296BV00006B/7/P

JOHN HENRY
NEWMAN

JOHN HENRY NEWMAN

Heart Speaks to Heart

selected spiritual writings

introduced and edited by
Lawrence S. Cunningham

New City Press

Published in the United States by New City Press
202 Cardinal Rd., Hyde Park, NY 12538
www.newcitypress.com

© 2004, New City Press

Cover design by Nick Cianfarani

Cover picture: a portrait by an unknown author of John Henry Newman (1879), San Giorgio
in Velabro, Newman's diaconal church in Rome.

Library of Congress Cataloging-in-Publication Data:
A catalog record for this book is available from the Library of Congress

ISBN: 1-56548-193-3

Printed in the United States of America

Contents

Introduction

Newman's Life

John Henry Newman's life spanned nearly the whole of the nineteenth century. He was born in London in 1801 and died at the Oratory that he had founded near Birmingham in 1890. He lived from the time of Napoleon into the waning days of the reign of Queen Victoria. As a young boy he came to some deep religious convictions (despite passing temptations during his adolescent years to skepticism after reading a bit of David Hume and Voltaire) under the influence of pious school masters who provided him with both evangelical and Calvinist ideas. In some famous words in the opening pages of the *Apologia Pro Vita Sua* Newman said that in his youth he came to rest upon "two and two only absolute and luminously self-evident beings—myself and my creator." If there is one thing that can be said abut John Henry Newman with certainty it is that from the time of his late adolescence, he was a deeply committed Christian who had a luminous sense of the presence of God in his life. Newman's life was, in fact, a series of conversions within the Christian tradition as his mind and heart matured. He passed through various understandings of the nature of the Church of England in which he had been born until he entered the Roman Catholic Church in 1845.

Newman entered Oxford in 1817, while still in his adolescent years. Four years later was elected a fellow of Oriel College. In 1824 he was ordained a deacon in the Church of England and a year later a priest. It should be noted that from the time of Newman's ordination as a deacon until his death decades later he almost always engaged in some form of pastoral ministry.

Two years after his priestly ordination Newman was appointed a tutor at Oxford's Oriel College and in 1828 he became vicar of Saint Mary's Church in Oxford with additional responsibility for the chaplaincy of the village of Littlemore some fifteen miles outside Oxford. By 1832 he had already been named a select preacher to the university, which meant that he alternated preaching with another priest on Sundays (at the Church of Saint Mary the Virgin). As a select preacher he was also honored to give "select" sermons to the university. Newman gave his first "select" sermon in 1826. The fifteen that he finally delivered make up the *University Sermons.* Newman, thinking that those sermons (more like a series of lectures) stood the test of time, reissued them in 1872 in a third edition. As Mary Katherine Tillman, the most recent editor of that volume has noted, these sermons were a crucial proving ground for his mature theological thinking and, as such, need be read as a whole. Those sermons contain, in embryo, ideas that would appear both in his essay on the development of doctrine and his later work on the relationship between reason and faith. As sermons they are far more cerebral than the *Parochial and Plain Sermons* that we will discuss in their proper place.

In 1832, in Sicily, while on a continental tour with his friend Richard Hurrell Froude, Newman fell ill. In his illness he became convinced that he was destined to do important work in England. It was on the voyage home, in a becalmed

(1832)

sea, that he wrote his most famous hymn, "Lead, Kindly Light." He returned to England as some momentous events were beginning to unfold. Between 1833 and 1841 Newman was a central figure in what was to become known as the Oxford Movement. Triggered by his friend John Keble's famous sermon, "National Apostasy" or the Assize Sermon, a group of high-minded ecclesiastics reacted strongly to what they saw in the Church of England as a betrayal of its religious foundations that they held to be articulated in the creedal phrase "one, holy, catholic, and apostolic Church." Keble's sermon insisted on the supernatural origin of the Church and the tradition of apostolic succession. It equally rejected state interference in the doctrinal, canonical, and ethical workings of the Church. Those who rallied to Keble's denunciation of civil interference with matters pertaining to the Church were passionate in their opposition to those who saw the Church as a simple department of the State; they were equally opposed to the corrosive effects of rationalism on church doctrine and the indifference of many to the tradition and spirituality of the English church. They further resisted the state acting as if the Church were simply an outpost of the state, especially when the state acted in ways that infringed on the life of doctrine and practice.

Their ire focused on the parliamentary decision to suppress some Anglican dioceses in Ireland. Those ecclesiastical jurisdictions may well have been redundant but their continued existence or their suppression, according to the mind of Newman, Keble, and others, should have been the province of the Church and not the decision of politicians. Their preferred weapon of attack against these dangers was the publication of a series of pamphlets ranging from a few pages to substantial monographs. They collectively called these publications the *Tracts for the Times*. The Oxford Movement, in short, began as a pamphlet war in defense of a certain understanding of the nature of the Church. Their nemesis within the Church was the tendency within certain strands of Anglicanism to erase the catholic character of the Church either by a kind of semi-rationalism that veered toward Unitarianism or an emotional evangelical spirit that downplayed liturgy and apostolic succession, which is to say, the "catholic" character of the established Church. Outside the Church, their enemy was "liberalism," which was a catchphrase encompassing all of the worst fallout of the Enlightenment suspicion of revealed religion in general and the power of the historic Church in particular.

Years later Newman would append a note on liberalism to his *Apologia Pro Vita Sua* describing it as "the mistake of subjecting to human judgment those revealed doctrines which are in their nature beyond and independent of it, and of claiming to determine on intrinsic grounds the truth and values of propositions which rest for their reception simply on the external authority of the divine Word." Newman played a central role in this struggle against the corrosive effects of religious liberalism on the Church and its message. He was a highly sought after and much admired preacher who not only contributed to the tracts but oversaw their publication. In the midst of this battle Newman worked out a theory of church doctrine known as the *via media* in which he argued that the Church of England steered a third way—a middle way—between the corruptions of the Church of Rome and the reductionist errors of the Protestant Reformation.

The *via media* was a theological (or, more precisely, an ecclesiological) concept that had already been worked out in its main lines in the seventeenth century by a series of Anglican theologians (the "Caroline Divines") who did so in the midst of the Puritan revolution of the times. The seventeenth century English poet, George Herbert, himself sympathetic to the catholic character of the established church, put it vividly: the Church of England stood between the gaudiness of Rome and the sluttishness of dissent. Newman was to reformulate this theory and describe its character in two works which argued for the *via media*. They are the *Lectures on the Prophetical Office of the Church* (1837) and the *Lectures on Justification* (1838).

In the frantic period of the Oxford Movement Newman found time to work systematically on a close reading of the patristic authors both out of his own interest and as a vehicle to insist on the catholicity of the Church. He oversaw publication of English language editions of the Fathers in English as part of his campaign to underscore the ancient roots of the Church. The work of Newman and others would result in a series of publications under the generic title of *The Library of the Fathers of the Holy Catholic Church Anterior to the Division of East and West*. Forty-eight volumes would be published in this series between 1838 and 1885.

Newman also gained great prominence as a preacher. People flocked to his Sunday afternoon sermons (delivered in the context of the liturgical celebration of Evensong) at Saint Mary's Church. His ordinary parishioners were less impressed than the university community who would fill the chapel when he spoke. Years later, the poet and critic, Matthew Arnold, would reminisce about his youthful attendance to hear Newman: "Who could resist the charm of that spiritual apparition, gliding in the dim afternoon light through the aisles of St. Mary's, rising into the pulpit, and then, in the most entrancing of voices, breaking the silence with words and thoughts which were a religious music—subtle, sweet, mournful."

Since the custom of the day required that priests read their sermons it was easy enough for Newman to publish them periodically, which he did under the title *Parochial and Plain Sermons*. Eventually those sermons would appear in eight volumes and, in their day, be bestsellers. Some scholars have argued that the sermons were even more important than the tracts themselves for the success of the Oxford Movement. In

1879 William Gladstone said that in his opinion it would be
the sermons that would be read a hundred years in the future.
This was still a time, after all, when the well-preached sermon
and its publication were still a highly regarded part of the
national culture. It was just over a generation before
Newman's birth that the great doctor Johnson remarked to
James Boswell: "Sir, you are to consider that sermons make a
considerable branch of English literature; so that a library
must be very imperfect if it has not a numerous collection of
sermons."

In 1841 Newman published the (in)famous *Tract 90,* where
he tested the essential Catholic doctrines as articulated by
Rome at the Council of Trent (whose decrees he had earlier
detested) against the Church of England's Articles of Religion, also called the Thirty-nine Articles (enshrined in its official *Book of Common Prayer*). He asserted that the anti-Catholic
parts of the articles militated against common exaggerations
and popular errors but not official Catholic doctrine. Newman
argued, in other words, for the essential catholicity of the
Thirty-nine Articles. His intention was not to "Romanize" his
church but to show the deep continuous historical roots of the
Church of England as he understood it. What he sought, in a
word, was historic and apostolic Tradition. Unfortunately, he
had to reckon with the deep-seated suspicion of "Romanism"
that was profoundly embedded in the fabric of English life in
general and the life of the established church in particular.
The tract caused such a storm of protest that Newman
stopped publication of the tracts and withdrew from public
life after having been silenced by the bishop of Oxford.

In the Spring of 1842, in the wake of the fallout from the
Tract 90 controversy, Newman retired with a small group of
friends to the village of Littlemore where he set up a
quasi-monastic community (although he always resisted the
imputation that he was creating an Anglican monastery). He
set for himself and his confreres a rigorous program of study,

prayer, exercises of piety, and a rather rigorous ascetic lifestyle. Newman also studied works of piety coming from continental Europe, making himself acquainted with the works of
such early modern Catholic writers as Ignatius of Loyola,
Alphonsus Liguori, Lorenzo Scupoli, and Charles Borromeo.
Newman even attempted to make the spiritual exercises of
Saint Ignatius without the help of a director. He especially
found his scholarly interests centered on the patristic
period—a period in which he became an acknowledged
authority. In 1843 he resigned his position as vicar of St.
Mary's Church in Oxford.

While in Littlemore he wrote one of his most famous and
influential works, *An Essay on the Development of Christian
Doctrine* (finished in 1844; published in 1845). In 1843, the
same year that Newman gave up his parish responsibilities, he
published a retraction of all his negative writings about the
Roman Catholic church. On 9 October 1845 he was received
into the Catholic church by an Italian Passionist missionary
priest, Domenico Barberi, who was himself later beatified by
Pope Paul VI and then canonized a saint by Pope John Paul II.
Within a year after his reception into the Roman Catholic
church he was ordained a Catholic priest in Rome and in 1847
settled, after some fits and starts, into an oratorian house just
outside Birmingham, England.

The next decade and a half found Newman, the new
convert clergyman, involved in a series of projects that came
to grief. In 1851 he lost a libel suit (in an egregious miscarriage
of justice that even the London *Times,* no friend of the Roman
Catholic church, deplored) brought by an ex-Dominican friar
whom Newman had accused of immorality. Between 1852
and 1856, encouraged by members of the Irish hierarchy, he
attempted to found a Catholic University in Dublin with scant
success (he had to give up the rectorship) apart from the stunning lectures he gave that later became the seminal volume
The Idea of a University. The university would survive, but

without Newman's guiding participation. A scheme to translate the Bible into English in 1857 failed to gain the unqualified support of the English hierarchy. His desire to open an Oratory at Oxford was thwarted by Archbishop Henry Edward Manning (1808–1892), himself a prominent convert, who was suspicious of Newman (and not a little jealous). Manning's total opposition to Catholic students attending Oxford was an element in the estrangement of the two prominent converts who once had been collaborators in their Anglican days. At the First Vatican Council Manning was an unyielding proponent of papal infallibility. He is most remembered today as a staunch champion of social justice and a spokesperson for the rights of laboring people. In fact, he was once described as the "lonely pioneer of social Catholicism in England" for his unstinting concern for the poor and disenfranchised of England.

Newman's editorship of a journal of opinion called *The Rambler* ended when his essay on consulting the faithful on matters of doctrine was sent to Rome and found wanting (Newman was a century ahead of his time on this topic of what today would be called "reception theory"). An English prelate in the Vatican gleefully reported to Cardinal Manning, some years after *The Rambler* incident, that a cloud hung over Newman's head in Rome, with the monsignor further adding that Doctor Newman "was the most dangerous man in England."

Newman's response to printed slurs about priestly truthfulness by the Protestant Charles Kingsley occasioned Newman's *Apologia Pro Vita Sua* that began publication in 1864. The work was an international success bringing an end to Newman's obscurity and the string of frustrations that up to then had haunted his Catholic life. Now recognized as a classic autobiographical work, it brought Newman fame even though that was not enough to permit him to fulfill his dream

of opening an Oratory at Oxford—a plan still opposed both by
Manning and the Roman authorities.

In the years 1867–1870 Newman was part of a party of
Catholic thinkers and writers in the British Isles and continental Europe who thought the definition of papal infallibility was an untimely truth to define (such folk are
commonly known as the "inopportunists"). However, when
the dogma was defined at the First Vatican Council, Newman
accepted the doctrine; he never gave serious thought, as some
did, of moving into schism. His famous *Letter to the Duke of
Norfolk* (1875) expressed his own understanding of the
doctrine of papal infallibility. In 1870 he had published *The
Grammar of Assent*, his most subtle and sophisticated theological work. It was a work whose seeds were already to be found
in his university sermons where he took up the relationship of
faith and reason; the role of conscience; the possibility of
certainty in making judgments on religious matters. Then,
four years later his *Letter to the Duke of Norfolk* answered
William Gladstone's public charge that Catholics who
accepted papal infallibility could not be good British citizens
since their loyalties were divided. It was his last great apologetic work recognized in its own day as a brilliant work.

In his last years, now venerated both in the Church and
without, honors began to roll in. In 1878 he was made an
honorable fellow of Trinity College at Oxford. A year later he
was raised to the college of cardinals, given the title of cardinal
deacon of the Roman Church of San Giorgio in Velabro, by
Pope Leo XIII. On that occasion he chose as his motto a phrase
that certainly said much of what he understood as his own
style of discipleship: *cor ad cor loquitur*: "heart speaks to heart."
Given his advanced age there was no expectation that he
would live in Rome as a residential cardinal, even though that
was the custom for cardinals who were not bishops of a local
diocese. In 1880 he returned, for the first time, to his beloved
Oxford where he preached at the Jesuit church in the city.

A decade later, on 11 August 1890, full of years, he died at the Oratory near Birmingham surrounded by members of his community. Buried in the same grave as his beloved friend and fellow priest, Ambrose St. John, his headstone reads: *Ex umbris et imaginibus in Veritatem*: "From the shadows and images into the Truth." At the Brompton Oratory in London, on 20 August there was a Requiem Mass at which Cardinal Manning, his sometime rival, preached in a spirit of genuine admiration for Newman: "The history of our land will hereafter record the name of John Henry Newman among the greatest of our people, as a confessor for the faith, a great teacher of men, a preacher of justice, of piety, and of compassion."

The process of canonization for Newman, introduced in 1958, is in progress but has not yet come to pass. In 1991 he was declared "venerable"—the first step in the canonization process. Shortly before his death, his sister's grandson asked if it were greater to be a cardinal or a saint. Newman replied, "Cardinals belong to this world and saints to heaven."

In this long life of controversy, aborted schemes, stunning publication, zealous pastoral work, and public honors it must be kept in mind that Newman worked as a simple priest in the community of priests who made up the Oratory community. He preached, taught catechism, administered the sacraments, visited the sick and elderly, taught in the Oratory school, handed out school prizes even in his last days, gave spiritual direction and advice to numerous persons, carried on an enormous correspondence, and contributed to the intellectual life of his time. He never lived the life of an academic scholar even in his younger days in Oxford. He was what we would term today a public intellectual, yet still carried on as a simple parish priest. His regular entries into his diaries and the care with which he preserved his letters have allowed his biographers to map out his life almost on a day-by-day basis.

The above notes are a thumbnail sketch of a long and complicated life. Newman has been more than well served by his biographers and more than passingly commented on by scholars, critics, historians, and belletrists; indeed, the bibliography of works about Newman is enormous. It is now commonplace to note that he was a prescient thinker whose profound study of church doctrine and ecclesiological structures would not bear fruit until well after his death. His study of the dynamics of faith has been seminal and his reflections on the character of university life still bring forth comment. More than one person has called the Second Vatican Council "Newman's Council" since so many of the things that he stood for (and for which he suffered in his own day) came to fruition only in the second half of the twentieth century. His studies and reflections on how the mind of a person moves toward faith and the certitude that faith affords, a topic that engaged him from his university days down to the end of his life, have been a source of inspiration for contemporary theologians and philosophers. Pope John Paul II mentioned him by name in his encyclical *Fides et Ratio* as one of those figures who brilliantly reconciled a life of reason and a life of faith. His writings, further, are part of the canon of any course on nineteenth century prose since he was, as anyone who even reads bits of Newman knows, a supreme and supple stylist.

Newman's Spirituality

This brief anthology of Newman's spiritual texts will not deal with either Newman's theology or his epistemological reflections into the life of faith. Nor will it concern itself with the many controversies that exercised his talent over his long public life. In short, there is much of Newman about which this volume will not comment. It is Newman the preacher, priest, and spiritual writer that will be the main interest of this collection. There is something quite unique about his spiritual writings even though he never dedicated his skills to any systematic spiritual treatise as did, for example, such masters

as Saint John of the Cross or Saint Francis de Sales. It is in his
sermons, devotional reflections, occasional prayers,
hymnody, letters of direction, and meditations that we must
look to glean his attitude toward spirituality.

The above paragraph contains two words that demand a
word of explication: spirituality and unique.

Spirituality, notoriously difficult to define, will simply
mean, in this work, Newman's expression of the Christian life
found in his public utterances (mainly his sermons), in his
occasional writings, in the sources to which he gravitated, and
in his own works of prayer and devotion. A broad examination of those sources will reveal not so much a coherent
doctrine as a certain way of thinking and being, which I have
judged to be unique when set against much spiritual writing
coming from his contemporaries, especially his fellow Catholics in England and those in continental Europe.

In one sense, his spiritual doctrine is not unique if we think
that we will find in Newman what is odd, peculiar, or overly
refined. In fact, the opposite is true. More than once Newman
insists that a Christian be like every person on the outside, but
with a radically different interior life. In an early Christmas
sermon in his Anglican days Newman preached that a Christian possesses a deep inner peace that is silent and hidden
"like some well in a retired and shady place, difficult of
access." That inner peace brings, in Newman's vocabulary, a
range of changes in a person that makes such a person sober,
kind, gentle, courteous, candid, without pretense or affectation or ambition. Such a person is not to be simply mistaken
for a person of mere refinement or gentlemanly virtues even
though Newman was both refined and a gentleman. Such a
person lives with the constant sense of being under God's eye.
Such a person, to borrow from the old monastic vocabulary,
possesses "purity of heart."

In a wonderful conference he gave to his Oratorian
community in Birmingham on the character of the Christian

life ("A Short Road to Perfection") Newman, with the kind of blunt common sense one detects in some English writing, says simply that the secret of Christian perfection is to get up each morning after a decent night's sleep, start the day with prayer and worship, put in a good day's work at one's appointed tasks, and get to bed on time with a serene faith in God. That text is reprinted in this anthology. It is a text that I often use when speaking to my students about the Christian life. His description of the Christian life is not unlike the spirituality of the Little Flower, Saint Thérèse of the Child Jesus: do the ordinary in an extraordinary fashion.

The advice he gave on the occasion when he spoke to his Oratorian confreres was not so different from what he preached from his pulpit in his Anglican days at Oxford. His message was that one advanced in the Christian life by doing the ordinary in an extraordinary fashion. That view explains the repeated use of such words as fidelity, obedience, faith, regularity, steadfastness, etc., which occur over and over in his writings and sermons. This regularity of life had deep roots in Newman's early life. When he was still an adolescent, soon after a conversion experience when he was sixteen, Newman mapped out a regular program of spiritual observance centered on the reading of Scripture, daily prayer, self-examination, and, at least later, regular reception of Holy Communion. By the time he got to Oxford he devoted at least an hour a day to the reading (and memorizing) of Scripture. He also showed an early desire to lead an ascetic life, sometimes to the detriment to his physical health. Newman was sparing in the taking of food, spent little time on idle activities, and was severely disciplined in his habits of work. Every evidence support the judgment that as a parish priest, both as an Anglican and later as a Catholic, he was conscientious to a fault.

That Newman lived the ordinary life of a priest but in an extraordinary fashion is not only evident from a study of his

life but from the testimony of others. One clear example
might suffice. Father Joseph Bacchus who lived in Newman's
community during the last years of Newman's life made this
striking observation about him: "[Newman] carried the art of
being ordinary to perfection. He was singular in nothing. He
took his food, his recreation, went about his ordinary duties,
conversed without any mannerisms whatsoever. He had no
foibles, no crotchets. The best testimony to this is the absence
of good stories about him."

Nonetheless, I judge his approach to the spiritual life
"unique" mainly because of the ways in which he both
possessed and, simultaneously, lacked the training and
temperament of most of his Roman Catholic contemporaries.
First, he was a great and original theologian but his theology
was not much touched (if touched at all) by the reigning
methodology of scholasticism. He was no logic chopper—
indeed, he is famous for his remark that nobody ever died for a
conclusion. He did encounter that kind of arid syllogistic
theology during his brief Roman sojourn but it did not shape
him much and for that deficiency we must be grateful.
Indeed, he had a distaste for any kind of rationalism by which
one "proved" the faith by clever argument. He loved Saint
Ambrose's *mot* that God was not pleased to save his people by
dialectics. Believe, he once said in a sermon, and clear
evidence will come. How that process worked was the subject
of his sophisticated *Grammar of Assent*—a book that to this day
attracts commentators.

He never considered himself a theologian or a philosopher
because he did not fit the profile of those who carried out such
responsibilities—he never taught those subjects as an
academic. He never held a post in a seminary or faculty of
theology that was the normal home for a theologian in that
period. Nonetheless, he was perhaps the most original theologian of his age; he certainly was the only noteworthy theologian writing in the English language. If Newman did not

consider himself a theologian, others did. It should be remembered that the French Bishop Felix Dupanloup, a central figure at the First Vatican Council, wanted him to be a theologian at his side during the proceedings of the Council but Newman declined just as he declined to be a member of the preparatory commissions organized before the opening of the Council proper and the invitation of one English bishop (Brown of Newport) to serve as a theological advisor.

His thinking was profoundly marked by his intense engagement with the early Fathers of the Church and his assiduous meditation on, and explication of, the Scriptures. In that sense, his whole approach to the Christian life in general and his theology in particular drew from the most authentic wellsprings of the tradition. His instinct was to turn to the witness of the apostolic church and the great defenders of orthodoxy. Indeed, it was his study of that early period in the life of the Church that finally set him on the course to Rome.

If one were to look for the wellsprings of his piety, it would be to the life of prayer within the Church. Newman was, from his earliest days, a man of the Church. Long before he became a Catholic, he revered the Church as the guardian of faith. As he put it succinctly in the *Apologia,* a truth he learned from an early mentor: ". . . the sacred text was never intended to teach doctrine but only to prove it, and that, if we would learn doctrine we must have recourse to the formularies of the Church, for instance, to the catechism and to the creeds."

The same approach held true for the sources of his piety. He treasured the devotions, sacramental usages, the readings, and the hymns of the Anglican *Book of Common Prayer.* In his book on the prophetical office of the Church he remarked that to follow the Church was "to follow the prayer book, instead of following preachers, who are but individuals. Its words are not the accidental outpourings of this or that age or country but the joint and accordant testimony of that innumerable company of the saints, whom we are bound to follow. They are the accents of the church catholic and apostolic as it manifests itself in England." He also made a lifelong habit of composing prayers for private devotion. Some of these prayers—for morning and evening use—were written in a small book that he assembled before he was out of his teen years.

Newman also early came to recognize the same source of inspiration in the Roman Catholic tradition, even before he became a Catholic. When his friend Richard Hurrell Froude died prematurely of consumption in 1836, Newman chose Froude's set of Roman breviaries as a memento. He loved the sobriety of the Latin and the centrality of the Psalms for the hours. One of the *Tracts for the Times* (#75) was a study of the Roman breviary that Newman wrote. Newman not only used the breviaries for his own prayers but translated many of the hymns of the breviary into English. When Newman retired to Littlemore he recited the hours of the breviary every day, in addition to his fidelity to the Anglican practice of morning and evening song. It is to such sources as the Anglican *Book of Common Prayer* and the Roman breviary and the prayer life of the seventeenth century Caroline Divines that one must turn to understand the shape of Newman's spiritual vocabulary.

It should come as no surprise that Newman put a high value on the devotional writings of the polymath Bishop Lancelot Andrewes (+1626). He translated Andrewes's *Preces Privatae* (written mainly in Greek) into English and made it a part of his own prayer life. Those devotional prayers, organized for each day of the week, were taken mainly from the liturgy, the Fathers, and the Bible. They had a structure (six sections: introduction, confession, prayer for grace, profession of faith, intercessions, and praise) that appealed strongly to Newman, whose own devotional life was nourished by the same sources.

Second, and more important, Newman the Catholic did not find himself naturally drawn to the exuberant piety of baroque Catholicism. Both by temperament (fastidious) and training (patristic) he never found any natural sympathy for the flamboyant piety that derived from the Counter-Reformation. As an Anglican, indeed, he had a certain antipathy for the exuberant devotional practices oriented toward Mary and the saints. He was not an "aesthetic" Catholic if one understands "aesthetic" to be the flamboyant baroque rediscovered in the nineteenth century. He most certainly did not take an obsessive interest in church ornament, vestments, and the other ecclesiastical ephemera that so beguiled the more aesthetic "ritualists" of the day. While Newman loved the liturgy he was no slave to the precious details of rubrics or liturgical ephemera.

In this instance, one may contrast his writing and sensibility with that of his fellow convert oratorian Frederick William Faber (1814–1863) who entered the Roman Catholic church only a few weeks after Newman. Faber's rococo enthusiasms were never fully congenial to Newman—a lack of sympathy that caused strained relations between the two Oratories, Faber's in London and Newman's in Birmingham. Faber's books, redolent of the florid piety of the baroque age, are largely and justifiably unread today even though some of his hymns remain in the repertoire. The Italianate exuberance of the London Oratory's architecture and decoration reflects Faber's taste. His desire to translate into English a series of continental hagiographies of the more credulous sort reflected a taste which Newman could not find congenial.

During the years leading up to the First Vatican Council Archbishop Manning wrote disdainfully of Newman's "style" describing it in a personal letter as "old Anglican, patristic, literary, Oxford tone translated into the Church. It takes the line of deprecating exaggerations, foreign devotions, ultramontanism, anti-national sympathies." While Manning saw

that style as "dangerous," in many ways, from our vantage
point in history, while surely the use of the adjective "Oxford"
is striking, it is the most attractive side of Newman. It offers
an attractiveness that we may well better appreciate from the
spiritual tastes we shaped after the Second Vatican Council
with its emphasis on biblical and patristic piety. We would be
inclined to say that his style was biblical, patristic, traditional,
centered in the liturgy—all of those hallmarks so prized after
the Second Vatican Council. Newman, in a certain sense,
predated the cry for going back to the sources (*ressourcement*)
which was so much part of the Catholic revival of the twentieth century.

That Newman's spirituality was restrained is in no way to
say that he held in low esteem the devotional life of Catholic
piety. As some selections in this anthology will show, he had a
strong devotion to our Lady and to the saints. His meditations
on the titles of the Blessed Mother written for the students of
the Oratory school are notable both for their feeling and their
solid roots in Scripture and Tradition. His devotion to (as well
as his desire to emulate) Saint Philip Neri was both passionate
and well articulated.

Furthermore, to point out the more restrained nature of
Newman's piety is not to say that it was either overly cerebral
or lacking in passion; quite the contrary as any brief examination of his prayers or hymns will testify. He never denied the
possibility of the miraculous in the post apostolic age. He grew
to accept, as we have said, the veneration of the saints and he
had well thought out devotion to the Virgin Mary. His piety,
however, was intensely christocentric and his love for Christ
was passionately stated. When one reads his sermons, especially those collected under the title *Parochial and Plain
Sermons,* Newman clearly preaches directly to the mind but
with the ever ready desire to stir and convert his hearers to a
greater love of God. That desire to stir up and convert is not
only to be seen as some evangelical impulse (Newman's

flirtation with Evangelical tendencies was temporary but made its mark on him). It was a deeply felt conviction that in the Christian life growth is not merely a desideratum but essential to arrive at its full meaning.

In this regard I find myself in complete sympathy with the observation of Father Ian Ker, the best Newman scholar of this generation. Reflecting on Newman's early collected sermons (those from his Anglican days) Ker writes that the dominant theme of those sermons is the call to *holiness*. Ker observes that "the idea that the whole Church, the whole people of God, are called to be holy was not in Newman's day the truism that it is now in the Catholic church; until the Second Vatican Council there was a widespread feeling that holiness was a condition that pertained principally to priests and religious. Certainly, as an Anglican preacher, Newman entertained no such restricted view."

When one goes back over those sermons it is helpful to remember that he preached them in an age, as he himself admitted, when the aristocracy of intellect went over to unbelief. His sermons, to a largely university audience, were not exercises in mere rhetorical expression. They are reflections of a person who was a transparent believer who wished to share that belief with a congregation that was intellectually and morally under siege. His approach however was not apologetic but, rather, a conviction that the holiness in the gospel spoke its own truth. He put the matter succinctly in one of his early sermons: ". . . faith is to love as religion is to holiness; for religion is the divine law as coming to us from without, as holiness is the acquiescence in the same law written within."

What is most striking about Newman's early sermons is not that they hewed so closely to the scriptural reading appointed by the liturgy for the day on which he preached—one expects that—but that he rarely ventures away from the Scriptures themselves. In the eight volumes of those sermons one could count on one hand the number of times he refers to a book outside the canon of Scripture. There is only one direct quotation from a patristic author in the entire series and it is not even acknowledged as such. By contrast, in one sermon on Epiphany Sunday (1840), he cites the Scriptures sixty-four times. If there ever was a corpus of sermons and homilies that bear justly the title of "scriptural," it is in the eight volumes of the *Parochial and Plain Sermons*. They remind us of nothing more than those homilies that have come down to us from the age of the Fathers. The similarity is not accidental for Newman was a first class, if selftaught, patristics scholar, as both his essay on development and his justly praised *The Arians of the Fourth Century* (published in 1833) so amply attest.

Further, of course, is the quality of the prose. There is something profoundly satisfying in reading again those long periodic sentences, perfectly balanced in their construction, free from any overblown ciceronianism (but, nonetheless, a product of a superb classical education), which seem just right on rereading. It is no wonder that in their day—at a time when there was a keen appreciation for the preached word—the published sermons went through various editions and easily were the bestsellers in the homiletic field. Newman's care for language, as Father Louis Bouyer, himself an Oratorian and a convert, has pointed out in more than one place, that makes us think of those brilliant Christian humanists who lived at the dawn of the sixteenth century—Thomas More, Erasmus of Rotterdam, John Colet—who combined serious scholarship, deep piety, a predilection for the ancient classics of the tradition, a love for language and a disdain for scholastic pedantry.

Nevertheless, it is not for the elegance of the language that one feels free to take out parts of these homilies as meditative texts. It is, rather, a matter of lucid exposition, deeply felt religious sentiment, and solid doctrine that makes them a resource for anyone who wishes to meditate (which is to say, ruminate) on scriptural reflection that leads to prayer. For that reason one of the more pleasant tasks undertaken for the compilation of this anthology was to go back and reread all of the parochial and plain sermons (now available in an elegant one-volume version published by Ignatius Press in 1997) straight through while annotating those places where, by a purely personal judgment, portions would lend themselves to reflection and prayer.

My selection criterion also included a desire to produce rather short discrete selections from the sermons rather than reproduce whole ones. It struck me that the meditative reader might find useful a meaty paragraph or two that could form the basis for a brief devotional reading or self-examination. Newman's prose lends itself well to such exercises, especially in those sermons where he ends with a kind of recapitulation. Typically, he will provide such a summary in a catena of exhortations or questions. Each of those invites pause and reflection.

Those sermon selections were prefaced by some pages that reproduce some of Newman's better known classic hymns and prayers. Deciding what to put there was made quite simple because many who have compiled anthologies of prayers in general or devotional anthologies of Newman's works in particular have reached a consensus, now nearly a century in the making, about what has and still endures of Newman's prayers and hymns.

My selection strategy for this volume was simple enough: a careful perusal of many manuals of prayers that are part of my own library looking for Newman selections: *The Oxford Book of Prayer* (1985); *The New Book of Christian Prayers* (1986); *The HarpeR/Collins Book of Prayers* (1993); the *Doubleday Prayer Collection* (1996); and *2000 Years of Classic Christian Prayers* (1999). I also found some early prayers in an appendix of Vincent Blehl's recent study of the early Newman (see the bibliography), which I have reprinted.

From those general collections I cross-checked several standard anthologies containing the spiritual writings of Newman to see if my collection of prayers should be amplified. In that search I made ample use of some more recent collections especially those published with the last decade or so like *John Henry Newman: Prayers-Poems-Meditations*, edited by A. N. Wilson (1990) and *Selected Sermons, Prayers, and Devotions: John Henry Newman*, edited by John F. Thornton and Susan B. Verenne (1999). Those anthologies supplement older standards like the two volumes of *Kindly Light: A Cardinal Newman Prayer Book*, edited by Daniel O'Connell, S.J. (1940). I have slightly modified archaisms throughout the text, including capitalization, to bring it in line with the New City Press "Spirituality throughout the Ages" series.

I was particularly anxious to do justice in the section on the prayers to provide a generous selection of works by Newman that represent his spirituality after 1845, where his attention was given more fully to Catholic piety. His prayers in honor of the Blessed Mother and the saints reflect faithfully his tremendously deep roots in the tradition of historical Christianity now nourished by the stream of Catholic piety to which he had been drawn. His love for Mary and the saints derive from his capacious understanding of the Church by which he understood not only the earthly church but the "cloud of witnesses" who stand both on earth and before the heavenly throne. That understanding was further strengthened by his consideration of the place of Mary in the scheme of salvation and the witness of the saints—especially the martyrs—who give witness to the holiness within the Church. His translations of the hymns from the Roman breviary deserve their place at least in a selected form although their poetic style may not be to the contemporary taste, and his translations from Bishop Lancelot Andrewes, the prince of the seventeenth century Caroline Divines, will receive fair attention since Newman kept those prayers on his *prie dieu* until the day he died. From the recently reprinted *John Henry Newman: Prayers, Verses, and Devotions* (San Francisco, CA: Ignatius, 2000) I have culled some representative examples of his Catholic piety, especially his prayers to the Blessed Virgin.

Newman the Oratorian

When Newman became a Catholic, he did not join any of the traditional religious orders. Had he done so his spirituality would have borne more markedly the influence of the schools of spirituality that derive from those orders. Hence, it is hard to say that his spirituality can be categorized as "Ignatian" or "Franciscan." With the little band of brethren who joined him in going over to Rome he formed an Oratory modeled on the one founded by Saint Philip Neri (1515–1595) in Rome. The Oratory consists of a community of diocesan priests who take no special vows but who live in community with the express purpose of administering the sacraments, preaching, teaching catechism, and ministering to the surrounding community. Each Oratory has its own elected superior and operates more or less independently depending on the circumstances and the times (the seventeenth century French Oratory was more centralized than the earlier Italian model). Their presence in Great Britain is due to the founding of the first Oratory there in 1848 by Newman himself. He had already spent some five months with the Roman oratorians (serving a truncated novitiate with them at the Church of Santa Croce) during his sojourn in Rome for his ordination.

The oratorian model was congenial to Newman since it bore a small similarity to Oxford College life and to the community he set up at Littlemore in the 1840s. More important, it permitted a good deal of flexibility in developing forms of spiritual practice appealing to its members and consonant with the actual circumstances of their work. The spirit of the Oratory prizes community without a rigid monastic rule, space for intellectual work as well as pastoral functions, and adaptation to the needs and requirements of a given geographical location. Each Oratory prides itself on a being a home for all members of the community. There is no uniform customary for all oratorian houses; each shapes itself according to the needs and dictates of the place and the apostolate in which it finds itself.

In addition to his love for the oratorian style of life, Newman found Saint Philip Neri, the founder of the first Oratory in Rome, a kindred spirit and the kind of model he wanted to emulate himself. He paid high tribute to him in a classic passage in *The Idea of a University*, praising Saint Philip as an "ordinary individual priest as others: and his weapons should be but unaffected humility and unpretending love. All he did was to be done by the light and fervor and convincing eloquence of his personal character and his easy conversation." The adjectives that Newman chose to describe Saint Philip should not be skipped over lightly: "ordinary," "unaffected," "unpretending," "easy." They are some of the hallmarks of Newman's own approach to spirituality.

Philip Neri (1515–1595) was a simple Florentine-born priest who spent the better part of his life in Rome with a small community of priests who lived in community but not under religious vows. Philip Neri himself was widely sought after as a confessor, spiritual director, counselor to popes and prelates, teacher, servant of the poor, and guide for pilgrims. His openness to culture, his friendliness, and his burning love for God attracted Newman in a powerful way. At his own Oratory in Birmingham Newman honored his feast day (26 May). We have, from Newman's pen, a litany in honor of the saint: a collection of prayers that was to be a novena in the saint's honor (unfinished), and other acts of devotion some of which are reproduced in this volume.

In a sense, Philip Neri saw a "new way" of being of service to the Church as a simple priest. As Newman said in a song he composed in the saint's honor in 1850: "Yet there is one I more affect/ Than Jesuit, hermit, monk, or friar/ 'Tis an old man of sweet aspect/ I love him more, I more admire." Newman saw Philip Neri as a model of contrasts: urbane and simple; profoundly spiritual but lighthearted; open to the cultured discourse of his day but direct in his piety; a lover of place who took a keen interest in the worldwide church. It was in Philip and his model of the Oratory that Newman found a way of duplicating a field of intense pastoral ministry that was not alien to the life that he knew at Oxford in his days as an Anglican priest.

The Venerable John Henry Newman

On 22 January 1991, the Congregation for the Causes of the Saints, in the presence of Pope John Paul II, promulgated a decree stating that John Henry Newman lived a life of heroic piety. They took cognizance of the local process investigating the claims of Newman's sanctity that extended over the years 1958–1986 at the local level (the diocese of Birmingham in England) and the subsequent investigations on his life, virtues, and activities done in Rome. Those two investigations were published for the Sacred Congregation for the Causes of Saints in two hefty red-bound volumes known as the *Positio Super Virtutibus,* with one volume summarizing the material developed at the local level and the other at the Roman level. Much of the material came from Newman's own writings and pertinent statements from contemporaries who knew him well. His case was then accepted for the next stage in the canonization process, that of beatification. The congregation took note of the fact that his reputation for holiness, widely accepted in his own time, had only increased over the decades.

Those who admire the life of Newman and consider him an apt intercessor in heaven frequently use a prayer that hopes for the beatification of Newman. That prayer composed for that purpose reads:

Prayer to Obtain the Beatification of John Henry Cardinal Newman

God, our Father,
Your servant John Henry Newman
upheld the faith by his teaching and his example.
May his loyalty to Christ and the Church,
his love of the immaculate Mother of God,
and his compassion for the perplexed
give guide to the Christian people of today.

We beg you to grant the favors we ask
through his intercession
so that his holiness may be recognized by all
and the Church may proclaim him a saint.
We ask this through Christ our Lord.
Amen.

A Final Word

This volume was put together in those odd moments stolen from the ordinary duties of an academic: teaching, grading papers, committee assignments, writing obligations, and so on. It was, of course, a pleasure to turn from those tasks to read Newman when leisure afforded the chance. That it is possible to find such moments is largely due to the congenial atmosphere that one finds here at the University of Notre Dame in general and the Department of Theology in particular. I am deeply grateful to the university and its president, Reverend Edward Malloy, CSC, for appointing me to one of the endowed professorships honoring the late John A. O'Brien, which allows for time and resources to do research. I am equally in debt to my colleagues in the department and especially to John Cavadini, the chair, whose generosity and friendship contribute so much to our common life. The University of Notre Dame has long been a center for Newman scholarship. The University of Notre Dame Press has been zealous in publishing both books by Newman and studies about him. For all of those interests I am grateful. My thanks also goes to the editors of New City Press who encouraged me to work on this book. New City Press is exemplary in its labors of putting before the public excellent works in the tradition of Catholic theology and spirituality.

Finally, a word of profound gratitude to my wife Cecilia and my daughters Sarah and Julia who make coming home each evening such a joy.

Hymns and Prayers

The selections below are taken from Newman's *Meditations and Devotions* unless otherwise noted.

"LEAD, KINDLY LIGHT"
Lead, kindly light, amid the circling gloom,
Lead thou me on;
The night is dark and I am far from home;
Lead thou me on.
Keep thou at my feet; I do not ask to see
The distant scene; one step enough for me.
I was not ever thus, nor prayed that thou
Shouldst lead me on;
I loved to choose and see my path; but now
Lead thou me on.
I loved the garish day, and spite of fears,
Pride ruled my will: remember not past years.
So long thy power hath blest me, sure it still
Will lead me on.
O'er moor and fen, o'er crag and torrent, till
The night is gone,
And with the morn those angel faces smile
Which I have loved long since, and lost awhile.

Praise to the holiest in the height,
And in the depth be praise;
In all his words most wonderful,
Most sure in all his ways.
O loving wisdom of our God!
When all was in sin and shame,
A second Adam to the fight
and to the rescue came.
O wisest love! That flesh and blood,
Which did in Adam fail,
Should strive afresh against the foe,
Should strive and should prevail.
And that a higher gift than grace
Should flesh and blood refine,
God's presence and his very self,
And essence all-divine.
O generous love! That he who smote
In Man, for man, the foe
The double agony in Man,
For man, should undergo.
And in the garden secretly,
and on the cross on high,
Should teach his brethren and inspire
to suffer and to die.
Praise to the holiest in the height,
And in the depth be praise;
In all his words most wonderful,
Most sure in all his ways.

Guard me, should the foe assail me;
Call me when my life shall fail me,
Bid me come to thee above,

With thy saints to sing thy love,
World without end. Amen.

(Translation of the *Anima Christi*)

God Almighty! Keep me through this day! Let me grow in grace! Thou, O God! Have graciously brought me to the beginning of this day, defend me in the same by thy mighty power! Grant, O Lord, that as I now rise this morning after sleep, fresh, healthful, and rejoicing, so my body, after the sleep of death, may rise, spiritualised and blessed to dwell with thee for evermore!

(A morning prayer—written at age sixteen)

Glory be to thee, O Lord, glory to thee.
Glory to thee who gives me sleep to recruit my
       weakness,
and to remit the toils of this fretful flesh.
To this day and all days,
a perfect, holy, peaceful, healthy, sinless course,
Grant, O Lord.
Teach me to the thing that pleases thee,
for thou art my loving God;
Let thy loving Spirit lead me forth into the land of
       righteousness.
Quicken me, O Lord, for thy name's sake,
and for thy righteousness sake bring my soul out
       of trouble;
remove from me foolish imaginations,
inspire those which are good and pleasing in thy
       sight.
Turn my eyes away lest they behold vanity;
let my eyes look right on,
and let my eyelids look straight before me.

Hedge up my ears with thorns lest they incline to
undisciplined words.
Give me early the ears to hear,
and open my ears to the instruction of thy oracles.
Set a watch, O Lord, before my mouth,
and keep the doors of my lips.
Let my word be seasoned with salt,
that it may minister grace to the hearers.

(A morning prayer of Bishop Lancelot Andrewes
translated by Newman)

The day is done and I give thanks to thee, O Lord.
Evening is at hand, make it bright unto us.
As day has its evening, so also has life;
the evening of life is age,
age has overtaken me, make it bright unto us.
Cast me not away in the time of age;
forsake me not when my strength fails me . . .
Abide with me, Lord,
for it is evening,
and the day is far spent of this fretful life.
Let thy strength be made perfect in my weakness.

(An evening prayer of Bishop Lancelot Andrewes
translated by Newman)

Let us arise and watch by night,
      and meditate always;
And chant, as in our maker's sight,
United hymns of praise.
So, singing with the saints in bliss,
      With them we might attain

Life everlasting after this,
   And heaven for earthly pain.

         (Translation of *Nocte surgentes*
              for Sunday matins)

Who madest all and dost control,
   Lord, with thy touch divine,
Cast out the slumber of the soul,
   The rest that is not thine.
Look down, eternal holiness,
   And wash the sins away,
Of those, who, rising to confess,
   Outstrip the lingering day.
Our hearts and hands by night, O Lord,
   We lift them in our need;
As holy psalmists give the word,
And holy Paul the deed.
Each sin to thee of years gone by,
   Each hidden stain lies bare;
We shrink not from thine awful eye,
   But pray that thou would spare.

         (Translation of *Rerum Creator Optime*
             for Wednesday matins)

See, the golden dawn is glowing
While the paly shades are going,
Which have led us far and long,
In a labyrinth of wrong.
May it bring us peace serene;
May it cleanse, as it is clean;
Plain and clear our words be spoke,
And our thoughts without a cloak;
So the day's account, shall stand.

Guileless tongue and holy hand,
Steadfast eyes and unbeguiled,
"Flesh as of a little child."
There is One who from above
Watches how the still hours move
Of our day of service done,
From the dawn to setting sun.
To the Father and the Son,
And the Spirit, three and one,
As of old and as in heaven,
Now and here be glory given.

(Translation of *Lux ecce surgit aurea*
for Thursday lauds)

Now that the day-star glimmers bright,
　　　　We suppliantly pray,
That he, the uncreated light,
　　　　May guide us on our way.
No sinful word, no deed of wrong,
　　　　Nor thoughts that idly rove;
But simple truth be on our tongue,
　　　　And in our hearts be love.
And while the hours in order flow,
　　　　O Christ, securely fence
Our gates, beleaguer'd by the foe—
　　　　The gate of every sense.
And grant that to thine honor, Lord,
　　　　Our daily toil may tend;
That we begin it at thy word,
　　　　And in thy blessing end.
And, lest the flesh in its excess,
　　　　Should lord it o'er the soul,
Let taming abstinence repress
　　　　The rebel and control.

To God the Father glory be,
 And to his only Son,
And to the Spirit, one and three,
 While endless ages run.

    (Translation of *Jam lucis orto sidere*
        for the hour of prime)

Come Holy Ghost, who ever one
Reigns with the Father and with Son,
It is the hour our souls possess
With thy full flood of holiness.
Let flesh and heart and lips and mind,
Sound forth our witness to mankind;
And love light up our mortal frame,
Till others catch the living flame.
Now to the Father, to the Son,
And the Spirit, three in one,
Be praise and thanks and glory given
By men on earth, by saints in heaven.

    (Translation of *Nunc Sancte Nobis Spiritus,*
        a hymn for tierce)

O God who cannot change nor fail,
 Guiding the hours, as they roll by,
Bright'ning with beams the morning pale,
 And burning in the mid-day sky.
Quench thou the fires of hate and strife,
 The wasting fever of the heart;
From perils guard our feeble life,
 And to our souls thy peace impart.
Grant this, O Father, only Son,
 And Holy Spirit, God of grace,

To whom all glory, three in one,
  Be given in every time and space.
(Translation of *Rector potens, verax Deus,* a hymn for sext)

O God, unchangeable and true,
  Of all the life and power,
Dispensing light in silence through
  Every successive hour.
Lord, brighten our declining day,
  That it may never wane,
Till death, when all things round decay,
  Bring back the morn again.
This grace on thy redeem'd confer,
  Father, co-equal Son,
And Holy Ghost, the comforter,
  Eternal three in one.
      (Translation of *Rerum Deus tenax vigor,*
          a hymn for none)

Father of lights, by whom each day
  Is kindled out of night,
Who, when the heavens were made, did lay
  Their rudiments in light.
Thou, who did bind and blend in one
  The glistening morn and evening pale,
Hear thou our plaint, when light is gone,
  And lawlessness and strife prevail.
Hear, lest the whelming weight of crime
  Wreck us with life in view;
Lest thoughts and schemes of sense and time
  Earn us a sinner's due.
So may we knock at heaven's door,

And strive the immortal prize to win,
Continually and evermore
    Guarded without and within.
Grant this, O Father, Only Son,
    And Spirit, God of grace,
To whom all worship shall be done
    In every time and place.

(Translation of *Lucis Creator optime,*
a hymn Sunday vespers)

Now that the day-light dies away,
    By all thy grace and love,
Thee, maker of the world, we pray,
    To watch our bed above.
Let dreams depart and phantoms fly,
    The offspring of the night,
Keep us, like shrines, beneath thine eye,
    Pure in our foe's respite.
This grace on thy redeem'd confer,
    Father, co-equal Son,
And Holy Ghost, the comforter,
    Eternal three in one.

(Translation of *Te lucis ante terminum,*
a hymn for compline)

O Almighty God and Father of our Lord Jesus Christ, who
day by day renews thy mercies to sinful man, accept, I pray
thee, this morning sacrifice of praise and thanksgiving, and
give me grace to offer it reverently, and in humble faith, and
with a willing mind.

I praise thee for my birth from kind and anxious parents,
and in a Christian land; for the gifts of health and reason; for
sound body and perfect senses; for thy continued care of me;

for my baptism in thy holy Church and the early knowledge given me of thee, my creator and redeemer, through the affection of dear relatives; for all the prayers offered for me, and every measure of thy grace granted to me from my youth up; for the blessing of a good education; for the gifts of mind thou has entrusted to me and the means of their cultivation; for all known and unknown escapes, vouchsafed to me, from bodily and spiritual evil; for the gracious forgiveness of all my aggravated sins, and for the victory thou gives me in my youth over my rebellious passions and misguided reason.

I thank thee for thy bountiful providence in opening on me prospects of life beyond my birthright, and for the temper of mind and principles of conduct with which I come to this place; for the friends thou has given me here, and the success with which, amid many trials, thou has blessed my toil; for thy great condescension and abundant mercy in putting me in the ministry of thy Church, and in setting me on high and fitting me in a measure for my office, and giving me opportunities in various ways of being useful to thy redeemed people.

Also, I praise and magnify thy name for every affliction and anxiety thou has laid or now lay upon me and I acknowledge thankfully that hitherto all has worked for good.

Lord, I am abashed before thee and abhor myself in thy sight, I am not worthy of the least of thy mercies; thou has given me good gifts, and I have dishonored them by my neglect or corrupt use of them. I sinned before thou has given them and I have sinned since thou has given them. Yet thou renews thy goodness to me every morning. Praise the Lord, O my soul, and all that is within me praise his holy name.

(Morning prayer composed in 1828)

Lord, I thank thee, that thou hast safely brought me to the end of this day. Protect me from the perils and dangers of the night. Let me rest in peace. Let me lay myself down piously and gratefully, as if in death, knowing my spirit may this night be required of me; give me grace that whenever that time comes I may be prepared for it and that when my soul parts from this body, it may hear the grateful words "Well done, good and faithful servant, enter into the joy of the Lord."

(Night Prayer)

O God, give me grace at this time duly to confess my sins before thee and truly repent of them, as I review them.

O Lord I am not in myself fit to lift up my face to thee. I acknowledge my utter unworthiness in thy sight, the perverseness of my heart, my wilful ignorance and blindness, and my habitual sinfulness. Thou gives me a sense of right and wrong and a moral nature and the aid of the Holy Spirit; but I have dishonored thy gifts and rebelled against thee. I have no plea for pardon but thy mercy offered to us all in thy son, Jesus Christ.

Blot out of thy book, O gracious Lord God, all my manifold acts of sin committed against thee in former years, remembered or forgotten, every impulse of anger, jealousy, hatred, pride, ill temper, uncleanness, covetousness, self-conceit; every unkind deceitful, quarrelsome, intemperate, irreverent, or corrupting word, which has passed my lips; and every deed of cowardice, malice, injustice, cruelty, meanness, sullenness, obstinacy, gluttony, lewdness, and self-indulgence, which I have ever committed—impute them not to me for the Savior's sake. Forgive me, Lord, every act of ingratitude towards thee, and unwillingness to think of thee and to do thy will, every act of disobedience to my loving parents, and to my superiors, every rudeness and want of humility and of inconsiderate love in my dealings with my friends or with the world. Forgive me all my wanderings in prayer, my unbelief, my sins of omission, my deliberate and repeated sins against conscience and conviction.

O Lord, I need deliverance also from my sinful heart, as well as from its actual bad fruits—as in baptism thou forgave me Adam's sin so now pardon all of evil habit that thou see in me, since my new birth—pride, self-esteem, blameful error, selfishness, sloth, hardness of heart, fear of man, love of the world, and all the other marks of evil in me such as are hid from my own view.

And, O holy Lord, while thou saves me from the imputation of sin, save me also from its power within me. Give me eyes to see what is right, and a heart to follow it, and strength to perform it; and grant that I may in all things press forward in the work of sanctification and verily do thy will, and at length through thy mercy attain to the glories of thy everlasting kingdom through Jesus Christ our Lord.

(Evening Prayer, 1828? 1831?; revised 1851)

O Lord, how wonderful in depth and height,
But most in man, how wonderful thou art!
With what a love, what soft persuasive might
Victorious o'er the stubborn fleshly heart;
The tale complete, of saints thou dost provide
To fill the throne with angels lost through pride!

I need thee to teach me day by day, according to each day's opportunities and needs.
Give me, O My Lord, that purity of conscience which alone can receive, which alone can improve thy inspirations.
My ears are dull, so that I cannot hear thy voice.
My eyes are dim, so that I cannot see thy tokens.
Thou alone can quicken my hearing and purge my sight and cleanse and renew my heart.
Teach me to sit at thy feet and hear thy word.

Give me grace, O My Father, to be utterly ashamed of my own reluctance.
Rouse me from my sloth and coldness and make me desire thee with my whole heart.
Teach me to love meditation, sacred reading, and prayer.
Teach me to love that which must engage my mind for all eternity.

O Lord, I give myself to thee, I trust thee wholly.
Thou art wiser than I, more loving to me than I myself.
Deign to fulfil thy high purpose in me whatever they be;
Work in me and through thee.
I am born to serve thee, to be thine, to be thy instrument.
Let me be thy blind instrument, I ask not to see, I ask not to know,
I ask simply to be used. Amen.

Lord, you are the living flame, burning ceaselessly with love for man.
Enter into me and inflame me with your fire so that I might be like you.

Help me to spread your fragrance everywhere I go—
Let me preach you without preaching, not by words but by example—
By catching force, the sympathetic influence of what I do,
The evident fullness of the love my heart bears to you.

Dear Jesus, help us to spread your fragrance everywhere we go.
Flood our souls with your spirit and life.

Penetrate and possess our whole being so utterly
that our lives may be a radiance of yours.
Shine through us and be so in us that every soul
we come in contact with may feel your
presence in our soul.

Let them look upon us and see no longer us but Jesus. Stay
with us and then we shall begin to shine as you shine; so to
share as to be a light to others; the light, O Jesus, will be all
from you, none of it will be ours, it will be shining on others
through us.

(Recited daily by Mother Teresa's
Missionaries of Charity)

O best and first and truest of teachers!
Thou art the truth!
I know and believe with my whole heart, that this very flesh
of mine will rise again.
I know, base and odious as it is at present, that it will one day,
if I be worthy,
be raised incorruptible and altogether beautiful and glorious.
This I know, and this, by thy grace, I will keep ever before me.

The more, O Lord, I meditate on thy words, works, actions
and sufferings in the gospel, the more wonderfully glorious
and beautiful I perceive them to be. And therefore, O my dear
Lord, since I perceive thee to be so beautiful I love thee, and
desire to love thee more and more. Since thou art the one
goodness, beautifulness, gloriousness, in the whole world of
being and there is nothing like thee, but thou art infinitely
more glorious and good than even the most beautiful of creatures, therefore I love thee with a singular love, a one, only,

sovereign love. . . . And I would lose everything whatever rather than lose thee. For thou, O my Lord, are my supreme and only Lord and love.

My Lord, give me to know thee, to believe in thee, to love thee, to serve thee,
to live to and for thee.
Give me to die just at that time and in that way which is most for thy glory.

O my God, give me thy grace so that the things of this earth and things more naturally pleasing to me, may not be as close as thou art to me.
Keep thou my eyes, my ears, my heart from clinging to the
        things of this world.
Break my bonds, raise my heart. Keep my whole being fixed
        on thee.
Let me never lose sight of thee; and while I gaze on thee,
let my love of thee grow more and more every day.

Godhead, paternal love, power,
providence:
salvation, anointing, adoption,
lordship;
conception, birth, passion,
cross, death burial,
descent, resurrection, ascent,
sitting, return, judgment;
breath and holiness,
calling from the universal,
hallowing in the universal,
communion of saints, and of saintly things,

resurrection,
life eternal.

(Profession of faith of Bishop Lancelot Andrewes,
translated by Newman)

Hedge up my way with thorns,
that I may not find the path for following vanity.
Hold thou me in bit and bridle,
lest I fall from thee.
O Lord, compel me to come to thee.

Two things I require of thee, O Lord,
deny thou me not before I die;
remove from me vanity and lies;
give me neither poverty or riches,
feed me with food convenient for me;
lest I be full and deny thee and say, who is the Lord?
O lest I be poor and steal,
and take the name of my Lord in vain.
Let me learn to abound, let me learn to suffer need,
in whatsoever state I am, therewith be content.
For nothing earthly, temporal, mortal, to long not
to wait.
Grant me a happy life, in piety, gravity, purity,
in all things good and fair,
in cheerfulness, in health, in credit,
in competency, in safety, in gentle estate, in quiet;
a happy death,
a deathless happiness.

May thy strong hand, O Lord, be ever my defense;
thy mercy in Christ, my salvation;

thy all-veritable word, my instructor;
the grace of thy life-bringing Spirit, my consolation
all along and at last. Amen.

("Prayer for Grace" by Bishop Lancelot Andrewes,
translated by Newman)

Up with our hearts;
we lift them to the Lord.
O how very meet and right and fitting and due,
in all, and for all,
at all times, places, manners,
in every season, every spot,
everywhere, always, altogether,
to remember thee, to worship thee,
to confess to thee, to praise thee,
to bless thee, to hymn thee,
to give thanks to thee,
maker, nourisher, guardian, governor,
preserver, worker, perfecter of all,
Lord and Father—king and God,
fountain of life and immortality,
treasure of everlasting goods,
whom the heavens hymn,
and the heaven of heavens,
the angels and all the heavenly powers,
one to one, crying continually—
and we the while, weak and unworthy,
under their feet—
Holy, holy, holy
Lord the God of hosts;
full is the heaven,
and the whole earth,
of the majesty of thy glory.

Blessed be the glory of the Lord out of this place,
for his Godhead, his mysteriousness,
his height, his sovereignty, his almightiness,
his eternity, his providence.
The Lord is my strength, my stony rock, and my
defense,
my deliverer, my succor, my buckler,
my horn also of my salvation and my refuge.

Wherefore day by day
for these thy benefits towards me, which I
remember—
wherefore also for others very many which I have
let slip
from their number, from my forgetfulness—
for those which I wished, knew and asked,
and those I asked not, knew not, wished not—
I confess and give thanks to thee,
I bless thee and praise thee, as is fit, and every day,
and I pray with my whole soul,
and with my whole mind, I pray. . . .
Now, in this day and hour,
and every day until my last breath,
and till the end of the world,
and for ages and ages.

O Lord, my Lord,
for my being, life, reason,
for nurture, protection, guidance,
for education, civil rights, religion,
for the gifts of grace, nature, fortune,
for redemption, regeneration, catechising,

for my call, recall, yea, many calls besides;
for my forbearance, long-suffering, long long
     suffering to me-ward
many seasons, many years, up to this time;
for all good things received, successes granted me,
good things done;
for the use of things present,
for thy promise, and my hope of the enjoyment of
     good things to come;
for my parents honest and good,
teachers kind,
benefactors never to be forgotten,
religious intimates congenial,
hearers thoughtful, friends sincere, domestics
     faithful,
for all who have advantaged me,
by writings, homilies, conversations, prayers,
patterns, rebukes, injuries,
for all these and all others
which I know and which I know not,
open, hidden, remembered, forgotten,
done when I wished and when I wished not,
I confess to thee and will confess,
I bless thee and will bless,
I give thanks to thee and will give thanks,
all the days of my life.

                ("Praise" of Bishop Lancelot Andrewes,
                            translated by Newman)

O most tender and gentle Lord Jesus, when will my heart
have a portion of thy perfections? When will my cold and
stony heart, my proud heart, my unbelieving, my impure

heart, my narrow and selfish heart, be melted and conformed to thine?
O teach me so to contemplate thee sincerely and simply as thou hast loved me.

My God, thou know infinitely better than I, how little I love thee. I should not love thee at all, except for thy grace.
It is thy grace which has opened the eyes of my mind and enabled them to see thy glory.
It is thy grace that has touched my heart and brought upon it the influence of what is so wonderfully beautiful and fair.
O my God, whatever is nearer to me than thou, things of this earth, and things more naturally pleasing to me, will be sure to interrupt the sight of thee, unless thy grace interfere.
Keep thou my eyes, my ears, my heart, from any miserable
      tyranny.
Break my bonds—raise my heart. Keep my whole being fixed
      on thee.
Let me never lose sight of thee; and while I gaze on thee,
let my love of thee grow more and more every day.

O my God, I confess that you can enlighten my darkness. I confess that you alone can. I wish my darkness to be enlightened. I do not know whether thou will but that you can and that I wish are sufficient reasons for me to ask what you have at least not forbidden my asking. I hereby promise by thy grace which I am asking, I will embrace whatever I at length feel certain is the truth, if ever I come to be certain. And by thy grace I will guard against all self-deceit which may lead me to take what nature would have, rather than what reason approves.

(Prayer for the light of truth)

My God, I will put myself in your hands without reserve. What have I in heaven and apart from you what do I want upon this earth? My heart and my flesh fail, but God is the God of my heart, and my portion forever.

Teach us, dear Lord, frequently and attentively to consider this truth: that if I gain the whole world and lose you, in the end I have lost everything; whereas if I lose the world and gain you, in the end I have lost nothing.

O my Lord Jesus, I believe, and by thy grace will ever believe and hold and I know that it is true, and will be true to the end of the world, and that nothing great is done, without suffering, without humiliation, and that all things are possible by means of it.

My Dear Lord, though I am so very weak that I have not the strength to ask you for suffering as a gift, at least I will beg from you grace to meet suffering well when you in your love and wisdom bring it on to me. Let me bear pain, reproach, disappointment, slander, anxiety, suspense, as you want me to, O my Jesus, and as you by your own suffering have taught me, when it comes.

Thou, O my God, are ever new, though thou art the most ancient—thou alone are the food for eternity. I am to live for ever, not for a time and I have no power over my being. I cannot destroy myself even though I were so wicked as to wish to do so. I must live on, with intellect and consciousness for ever, in spite of my self. Without thee eternity would be another name for eternal misery. In thee alone have I that which can stay me up for ever: thou alone are food for my soul. Thou alone are inexhaustible, and ever offers to me

something new to know, something new to love—and so on
for eternity. I shall ever be a little child beginning to be taught
the rudiments of thy infinite divine nature. For thou art the
seat and center of all good, and the only substance in this
universe of shadows, and the heaven in which blessed spirits
live and rejoice. Amen.

O my God, shall I one day see thee? What sight can compare
to that great sight? Shall I see the source of that grace which
enlightens me, strengthens me, and consoles me? As I came
from thee, as I am made through thee, so, My God, may I at
last return to thee, and be with thee for ever and ever.

May he support us all the day long, till the shades lengthen,
and the evening comes, and the busy world is hushed, and the
fever of life is over and our work is done. Then in his mercy
may he give us a safe lodging, and a holy rest, and peace at
last.

Then, O Lord, in thy mercy, grant us a safe lodging, and a
holy rest, and peace at last; through Jesus Christ our Lord.

(Often attributed to Newman,
this prayer goes back to the sixteenth century)

O God of the spirits of all flesh, O Jesus, lover of souls, we
recommend unto thee the souls of all those thy servants, who
have departed with the sign of faith and who sleep the sleep of
peace. We beseech thee, O Lord and Savior, that, as in thy
mercy to them thou became man, so now thou would hasten
the time, and admit them to thy presence above. Remember,

O Lord, that they are thy creatures, not made by strange gods, but by God, the only true and living God; for there is no other God but thou, and none that can equal thy works. Let their souls rejoice in thy light, and impute not to them their former iniquities, which they committed through the violence of passion or the corrupt habits of their fallen nature. For, although they have sinned, yet they always firmly believed in the Father, Son, and Holy Ghost; and before they died, they reconciled themselves to thee by firm contrition and the sacraments of thy Church.

O gracious Lord, we beseech thee, remember not against them the sins of their youth and their ignorance but according to thy great mercy be mindful of them in thy heavenly glory.

May the heavens be opened to them and the angels rejoice with them.

May the archangel Saint Michael conduct them to thee.

May thy holy angels come forth to meet them and carry them to the city of the heavenly Jerusalem,

May Saint Peter, to whom you gave the keys of the kingdom of heaven, receive them.

May Saint Paul, the vessel of election, stand by them.

May Saint John, the beloved disciple, who had the revelation of the secrets of heaven, intercede for them.

May all the holy apostles, who received from thee the power of binding and loosing, pray for them.

May all the saints and elect of God, who in this world suffered torments for thy name, befriend them that, being freed from the prison beneath, they may be admitted to the glories of that kingdom, where with the Father and the Holy Ghost thou lives and reigns one God, world without end.

Come to their assistance, all ye saints of God; gain for them deliverance from the place of punishment; meet them all ye angels: receive these holy souls, and present them before the Lord,

Eternal rest give to them, O Lord.

And may perpetual light shine upon them.
May they rest in peace.
Amen.

(Prayer for the faithful departed)

Oh, my Lord and Savior, support me in that hour in the strong arms of thy sacraments, and by the fresh fragrance of thy consolations. Let the absolving words be said over me and the holy oil sign and seal me, and thy own body be my food, and thy blood my sprinkling; and let my sweet mother, Mary, breathe on me and my angel whisper peace to me and my glorious saints_____ smile upon me; that in them all, and through them all, I may receive the gift of perseverance, and die, as I desire to love, in thy faith, in thy Church, in thy service, and in thy love. Amen.

(Prayer for a happy death)

I know, O Lord, thou will do thy part towards me, as I, through thy grace, desire to do my part towards thee. I know well thou can never forsake those who seek thee, nor disappoint those who trust in thee. Yet I know too, the more I pray for thy protection, the more surely and fully I shall have it. And therefore now I cry out to thee and entreat thee, first that thou would keep me from myself, and from following any will but thine. Next, I beg of thee that, in thine infinite compassion, thou would temper thy will to me. Visit me not, O my loving Lord, if it be not wrong so to pray, visit me not with those trying visitations which saints alone can bear! Pity my weakness and lead me heavenwards in a safe and tranquil course. Still I leave it all in thy hands, only, if thou shall bring heavier trials on me, give me more grace, flood me with the fulness of thy strength and consolation. Amen.

From the Litany of the Passion

R/   Have mercy on us.

Jesus, the eternal wisdom, *R/*
The Word made flesh, *R/*
Hated by the world, *R/*
Sold for thirty pieces of silver, *R/*
Sweating blood in thy agony, *R/*
Betrayed by Judas, *R/*
Forsaken by thy disciples, *R/*

Struck upon the cheek, *R/*
Accused by false witnesses, *R/*
Spit upon thy face, *R/*
Denied by Peter, *R/*
Mocked by Herod, *R/*
Scourged by Pilate, *R/*
Rejected for Barabbas, *R/*
Loaded with the cross, *R/*
Crowned with thorns, *R/*
Stripped of thy garments, *R/*
Nailed to the tree, *R/*
Reviled by the Jews, *R/*
Scoffed at by the malefactor, *R/*
Wounded in the side, *R/*
Shedding thy last drop of blood, *R/*
Forsaken by the Father, *R/*
Dying for our sins, *R/*
Taken down from the cross, *R/*
Laid in the sepulchre, *R/*
Rising gloriously, *R/*
Ascending into heaven, *R/*
Sending down the Paraclete, *R/*
Jesus our sacrifice, *R/*

Jesus our mediator, R/
Jesus our judge, R/

R/   Lord Jesus, deliver us.

From all sin, R/
From all evil, R/
From anger and hatred, R/
From malice and revenge, R/
From unbelief and hardness of heart, R/
From blasphemy and sacrilege, R/
From hypocrisy and covetousness, R/
From blindness of the understanding, R/
From contempt of thy warnings, R/
From relapse of thy judgments, R/
From dangers of soul and body, R/
From everlasting death, R/

R/   Beseech thee, hear us.

We sinners, R/
That thou would spare us, R/
That thou would pardon us, R/
That thou would defend thy Church, R/
That thou would bless thy own, R/
That thou would convert thy foes, R/
That thou would spread thy truth, R/
That thou would destroy error, R/
That thou would break to pieces false gods, R/
That thou would increase thy elect, R/
That thou would let loose the holy souls in purgatory, R/
That thou would unite us to the thy saints above, R/

Let us pray.
O God, who for the redemption of the world was pleased to
be born; to be circumcised; to be rejected; to be betrayed; to be

bound with thongs; to be led to the slaughter; to be shame-
fully gazed at; to be falsely accused; to be scourged and torn; to
be spit upon; to be crowned with thorns; to be mocked and
reviled; to be buffeted and struck with rods; to be stripped; to
be nailed to the cross; to be hoisted up thereon; to be reckoned
among thieves; to have gall and vinegar to drink; to be pierced
with a lance: through thy holy passion which we, thy sinful
servants, call to mind and by thy holy cross and gracious
death, delivers us from the pains of hell, and leads us whither
thou did lead the good thief who was crucified with thee, who
with the Father and the Holy Ghost lives and reigns, God,
world without end. Amen.

Meditations on the Stations of the Cross

[Each station is prefaced by the invocation, "We adore thee of Christ
and we bless thee/Because by the holy cross thou has redeemed the
world." After each meditation a Lord's Prayer and a Hail Mary are
recited. These meditations were adapted for use in the Roman
Colosseum for Good Friday in the year 2001 with Pope John Paul II
in attendance. Newman wrote these meditations in 1860 and used
them again in 1885.]

Station one: Jesus is condemned to death

Leaving the house of Caiphas, and dragged before Pilate
and Herod, mocked, beaten, and spit upon, his back torn with
scourges, his head crowned with thorns, Jesus. Who on the
last day will judge the world, is himself condemned by unjust
judges to a death of ignominy and torture.

Jesus is condemned to *death*. His death warrant is signed
and who signed it but I, when I committed my first mortal
sins. My first mortal sins, when I fell away from the state of

grace into which thou did place me by baptism; these it was that were thy death warrant, O Lord. The innocent suffered for the guilty. Those sins of mine were the voices which cried out "Let him be crucified." That willingness and delight of heart with which I committed them was the consent which Pilate gave to this clamorous multitude. And the hardness of heart which followed upon them, my disgust, my despair, my proud impatience, my obstinate resolve to sin on, the love of sin which took possession of me—what were these contrary and impetuous feelings but the blows and the blasphemies with which the fierce soldiers and the populace received thee, thus carrying out the sentence which Pilate had pronounced?

Station two: Jesus receives his cross

A strong, and therefore heavy cross, for it is strong enough to bear him upon it when he arrives at Calvary, is placed upon his torn shoulders, he receives it gently and meekly, nay, with gladness of heart, for it is to the salvation of mankind.

True; but recollect, that heavy cross is the weight of our sins. As it fell upon his neck and shoulders, it came down with a shock. Alas! What a sudden, heavy weight have I laid upon thee, O Jesus. And though in the calm and clear foresight of thy mind—for thou sees all things—thou was fully prepared for it, yet thy feeble frame tottered under it when it dropped down on thee. Ah! How great a misery is it that I have lifted up my hands against my God. How could I ever fancy he would forgive me! unless he had himself told us that he underwent his bitter passion in order that he might forgive us. I acknowledge, O Jesus, in the anguish and agony of my heart, that it was my sins that struck thee in the face, that bruised thy sacred arms, that tore thy flesh with iron rods, that nailed thee to the cross, and let thee slowly die upon it.

Station three: Jesus falls the first time

Jesus, bowed down under the weight and length of the unwieldy cross, which trailed after him, slowly sets forth on his way, amid the mockeries and insults of the crowd. His agony in the garden, itself was sufficient to exhaust him; but it was only the first of a multitude of sufferings. He sets off with his whole heart, but his limbs fail him, and he falls.

Yes, it is as I feared. Jesus, the strong and mighty Lord, has found for the moment our sins stronger than himself. He falls—yet he bore the load for a while; he tottered but he bore up and walked onward. What, then, made him give way? I say, I repeat, it is an intimation and memory to thee, O my soul, of thy falling back into mortal sin. I repented of the sins of my youth, and went on well for a time; but at length a new temptation came when I was off my guard, and I suddenly fell away. Then all my good habits seemed to go at once; they were like a garment which is stripped off, so quickly and so utterly did grace depart from me. And at that moment I looked at my Lord, and lo! He had fallen down, and I covered my face with my hands and remained in a state of great confusion.

Station four: Jesus meets his mother

Jesus rises, though wounded by his fall, journeys on, with his cross still on his shoulders. He is bent down, but at one place, looking up, he sees his mother. For an instant they just see each other and he goes forward.

Mary would rather have had all his sufferings herself could that have been, that not have known what they were by ceasing to be near him. He too, gained a refreshment, as from some soothing and grateful breath of air, to see her sad smile amid the sights and the noises which were about him. She had known him beautiful and glorious, with the freshness of divine innocence and peace upon his countenance; *now* she saw him so changed and deformed that she could scarce have recognized him, save for the piercing, thrilling, peace-inspired look he gave her. Still, he was now carrying the load of the world's sins, and all-holy though he was, he carried the image of them on his very face. He looked like some outcast or outlaw who had frightful guilt upon him. He has been made sin for us, who knew no sin; not a feature, not a limb, but spoke of guilt, of a curse, of punishment, of agony.

Oh, what a meeting of Son and mother! Yet there was a mutual comfort, for there was a mutual sympathy. Jesus and Mary—do they forget that passion-tide through all eternity?

Station five: Simon of Cyrene helps Jesus carry his cross

At length his strength fails utterly and he is unable to proceed. The executioners stand perplexed. What are they to do? How is he to get to Calvary? Soon they see a stranger who seems strong and active—Simon of Cyrene. They seize on him, and compel him to carry the cross with Jesus. The sight of the sufferer pierces the man's heart. Oh, what a privilege! O happy soul, elect of God! He takes the part assigned to him with joy.

This came of Mary's intercession. *He* prayed, not for himself, except that he might drink the full chalice of suffering and do his Father's will; but *she* showed herself a mother by following him with her prayers, since she could help him in no other way. She then sent this stranger to help him. It was she who led the soldiers to see that they might be too fierce with him. Sweet Mother, even *do* the like for us. Pray for us, whatever be our cross, as we pass along on our way. Pray for us and we shall rise again though we have fallen. Pray for us when sorrow, anxiety, or sickness comes upon us. Pray for us when we are prostrate under the power of temptation and send some faithful servant of thine to succour us. And in the world to come, if found worthy to expiate our sins in the fiery prison, send some good angel to give us a season of refreshment. Pray for us, holy Mother of God.

Station six: Jesus and Veronica

As Jesus toils along the hill, covered with the sweat of death, a woman makes her way through the crowd, and wipes his face with a napkin. In reward for her piety the cloth retains the impression of the sacred countenance upon it.

The relief which a mother's tenderness secured is not yet all she did. Her prayers sent Veronica as well as Simon; Simon to do a man's work, Veronica to do the work of a woman. The devout servant of Jesus did what she could. As Magdalen had poured the ointment at the feast, so Veronica now offered him this napkin in his passion. "Ah," She said, "Would I could do more. Why have I not the strength of Simon, to take part of the burden of the cross? But men only can serve the great high priest, now that he is celebrating the solemn act of sacrifice." O Jesus! Let us one and all minister to thee according to our places and powers. And as thou did accept from thy followers refreshment in thy hour of trial, so give us the support of thy grace when we are hard pressed by our foe. I feel I cannot bear up against temptations, weariness, despondency, and sin. I say to myself, what is the good of being religious? I shall fall, O my dear Savior, I shall certainly fall, unless thou do renew for me my vigor like the eagle's and breathe life into me by the soothing application and the touch of the holy sacraments which thou have appointed.

Station seven: Jesus falls a second time

The pains of his wounds and the loss of blood increasing at every step of his way, again his limbs fail him, and he falls to the ground.

What has he done to deserve all this? This is the reward received by the long-awaited Messiah from the chosen people, the children of Israel. I know what to answer. He falls because I have fallen. I have fallen again. I know well that without thy grace, O Lord, I could not stand; and I fancied that I had kept close to thy sacraments; yet in spite of my going to Mass and to my duties, I am out of grace again. Why is it but because I have lost my devotional spirit, and have come to thy holy ordinances in a cold, formal way, without inward affection. I became lukewarm, tepid. I thought the battle of life was over, and became secure. I had no lively faith, no sight of spiritual things. I came to church from habit, and because I thought others would observe it. I ought to be a new creature, I ought to live by faith, hope, and charity; but I thought more of this world than of the world to come—and at last I forgot that I was a servant of God, and followed the broad way that leads to destruction, not the narrow way which leads to life. And thus I fell from thee.

Station eight: Jesus comforts the women of Jerusalem

At the sight of the sufferings of Jesus the holy women are so pierced with grief that they cry out and bewail him, careless about what happens to them by so doing. Jesus turning to them said: "Daughters of Jerusalem, weep not over me, but weep for yourselves and for your children."

Ah! Can it be, O Lord, that I shall prove one of those sinful children for whom thou bids theirs mothers to weep. "Weep not for me," he said, "For I am the lamb of God and am making atonement at my own will for the sins of the world. I am suffering now, but I shall triumph; and when I triumph, those souls for whom I am dying will either be my dearest friends or my deadliest enemies." Is it possible? O my Lord, can I grasp the terrible thought that thou did weep over Jerusalem? Is it possible that I am one of the reprobate? Possible that I shall lose by thy passion and death, not gain by it? Oh, withdraw not from me. I am in a very bad way, I have so much evil in me. I have so little of an earnest, brave spirit to set against that evil. O Lord, what will become of me? It is so difficult to drive away the evil spirit from my heart. Thou alone can effectually cast him out.

Station nine: Again, a third time Jesus falls

Jesus had now reached almost to the top of Calvary; but, before he had gained the very spot where he was to be crucified, again he fell, and is again dragged up and goaded onwards by the brutal soldiery.

We are told in Scripture of three falls of Satan, the evil spirit. The first was in the beginning; the second when the gospel and the kingdom of heaven were preached to the world; the third will be at the end of all things. The first is told by Saint John the Evangelist; he says: "There was a great battle in heaven. Michael and his angels fought with the dragon and the dragon fought with his angels. And they prevailed not, neither was their place found any more in heaven. And that great dragon was cast out, the old serpent, who is called the devil and Satan" (see Rv 12:7). The second fall, at the time of the gospel, is spoken of by our Lord when he says "I saw Satan, like lightening, falling from heaven." And the third by the same Saint John "There came down fire from God out of heaven . . . and the devil—was cast into the pool of fire and brimstone."

These three falls—the past, present, and future—the evil spirit had in mind when he moved Judas to betray our Lord. This was just his hour. Our Lord, when he was seized, said to his enemies—"This is your hour and the power of darkness." Satan knew his time was short, and thought he might use it to good effect. But little dreaming that he would be acting in behalf of the redemption of the world, which our Lord's passion and death were to work out, in revenge, and, as he thought, in triumph, he smote him once, he smote him twice, and he smote him a third time, each a heavier blow. The weight of the cross, the barbarity of the soldiers, and the crowd were his instruments. O Jesus, the only begotten Son of God, the Word Incarnate, we praise, adore and love thee for thy ineffable condescension, even to allow thy self thus for a time to fall into the hands and under the power of the enemy of God and man, in order thereby to save us from being his servants and companions for eternity.

Or this:

This is the worst fall of the three. His strength for a while has utterly failed him and it is some time before the barbarous soldiers can bring him to. Ah! It was his anticipation of what was to happen to me. I get worse and worse. He sees the end from the beginning. He was thinking of me all the time he dragged himself along, up the hill of Calvary. He saw that I should fall again in spite of all former warnings and former assistance. He saw that I should become secure and self-confident, and that my enemy would then assail me with some new temptation, to which I never thought I should be exposed. I thought my weakness lay all on one particular side which I knew. I had not a dream that I was not strong on another side. And so Satan came down on my unguarded-side, and the better of me from my self-trust and self-satisfaction. I was wanting in humility. I thought no harm would come on me. I thought I had outlived the danger of sinning. I thought it was an easy thing to go to heaven, and I was not watchful. It was my pride, and so I fell a third time.

Station ten: Jesus is stripped of his garments

At length he has arrived at the place of sacrifice, and they begin to prepare him for the cross. His garments are torn from his bleeding body, and he, the holy of holiest, stands exposed to the gaze of the coarse and scoffing multitude. O thou who in thy passion was stripped of all thy clothes, and held up to the curiosity and mockery of the rabble, strip me of myself here and now, that in the last day I come not in shame before men and angels. Thou did endure the shame on Calvary that I might be spared the shame of the Judgment. Thou had nothing to be ashamed of personally, and the shame which thou did feel was because thou have taken on man's nature. When they took from thee the garments, those innocent limbs of thine were but objects of humble and loving adoration to the highest seraphim. They stood around in speechless awe, wondering at thy beauty, and they trembled at thy divine self-abasement. But I, O Lord, how shall I appear if thou shall hold me up hereafter to be gazed upon, stripped of that robe of grace which is thine, and seen in my own personal life and nature? O how hideous I am in myself, even in my best estate. Even when I am cleansed from my mortal sins, what disease and corruption is seen even in my venial sins. How shall I be fit for the society of angels, how for thy presence, until thou burn this foul leprosy in the fires of purgatory?

Station eleven: Jesus is nailed to the cross

The cross is laid upon the ground, and Jesus is stretched upon it, and then, swaying heavily to and fro, it is, after much exertion, jerked into the hole ready to receive it. Or, as others think, it is set upright and Jesus is raised and fastened to it. As the savage executioners drive in the huge nails, he offers himself to the Eternal Father, as a ransom for the world. The blows are struck—the blood gushes forth.

Yes, they set the cross on high, and they placed a ladder against it, and having stripped him of his garments, made him mount. With his hands feebly grasping its sides and cross-woods, and his feet slowly, uncertainly, with much effort, with many slips, mounting up, the soldiers propped him on each side, or he would have fallen. When he reached the projection where his sacred feet were to be, he turned around with sweet modesty and gentleness towards the fierce rabble, stretching out his arms, as if he would embrace them. Then he lovingly placed the backs of his hands close against the traverse beam, waiting for the executioners to come with their sharp nails and heavy hammers to dig into the palms of his hands and to fasten them securely to the wood. There he hung, a perplexity to the multitude, a terror to the evil spirit, the wonder, the awe, yet the joy, the adoration of holy angels.

Station twelve: Jesus dies upon the cross

Jesus hung for three hours. During this time he prayed for his murderers, promised paradise to the penitent robber, and committed his blessed mother to the guardianship of Saint John. Then all was finished, and he bowed his head and gave up the Spirit.

The worst is over. The holiest is dead and departed. The most tender, the most affectionate, the holiest of the sons of men is gone. Jesus is dead, and with his death my sin shall die. I protest once for all, before men and angels, that sin shall no more have dominion over me. This Lent I make myself God's own for ever. The salvation of my soul shall be my first concern. With the aid of his grace I will create in me a deep hatred and sorrow for my past sin. I will try hard to detest sins, as much as I have ever loved it. Into God's hands I put myself, not by halves, but unreservedly. I promise thee, O Lord, with the help of thy grace, to keep out of the way of temptation, to avoid all occasions of sin, to turn at once from the voice of the evil one, to be regular in my prayers, so to die to sin that thou may not have died for me on the cross in vain.

Station thirteen: Jesus is taken from the cross and laid on Mary's bosom

The multitude have gone home. Calvary is left solitary and still, except that Saint John and the holy women are there. Then come Joseph of Arimathea and Nicodemus, and take down from the cross the body of Jesus and place it in the arms of Mary.

O Mary, at last you have possession of thy son. Now, when his enemies can do no more, they leave him in contempt of thee. As his unexpected friends perform their difficult work, you look on with unspeakable thoughts. Your heart is pierced with the sword of which Simeon spoke. O Mother most sorrowful; yet in your sorrow there is still a greater joy. The joy in prospect nerved you to stand by him as he hung upon the cross; much more now, without swooning, without trembling, you receive him to your arms and on your lap. Now you are supremely happy at having him, though he comes to you not as he went from you. He went from your home, O Mother of God, in the strength and beauty of his manhood and he comes back to you dislocated, torn to pieces, mangled, dead. Yet, O blessed Mary, you are happier in this hour of woe than on the day of the marriage feast, for then he was leaving you, and now in the future, as a risen Savior, he will be separated from you no more.

Station fourteen: Jesus is laid in the tomb

But for a short three days, for a day and a half—Mary then must give him up. He is not yet risen. His friends and servants take him from thee and place him in an honorable tomb. They close it safely, till the hour comes for his resurrection.

Lie down and sleep in peace in the calm grave for a little while, dear Lord, and then wake up for an everlasting reign. We, like the faithful women, will watch around thee, for all our treasure, all our life, is lodged with thee. And when our turn comes to die, grant, sweet Lord, that we may sleep calmly too, the sleep of the just. Let us sleep peacefully for the brief interval between death and the general resurrection. Guard us from the enemy; save us from the pit. Let our friends remember us and pray for us, O dear Lord. Let Masses be said for us, so that the pains of purgatory, so much deserved by us, and therefore so truly welcomed by us, may be over with little delay. Give us seasons of refreshment there; wrap us round with holy dreams and soothing contemplations, while we gather strength to ascend let our faithful guardian angels help us up the glorious ladder, reaching from earth to heaven, which Jacob saw in vision. And when we reach the everlasting gates, let them open upon us with the music of angels, and let Saint Peter receive us, and our Lady, the glorious queen of saints, embrace us and bring us to thee and to thy eternal Father, and to thy co-equal Spirit, Three Persons, one God, to reign with them for ever and ever.

Let us Pray.

God, who by the precious blood of thy only begotten Son did sanctify the standard of the cross, grant, we beseech thee, that we who rejoice in the glory of that same holy cross, may at all times and places, rejoice in thy protection. Through the same Christ, our Lord. Amen.

Prayers and Meditations on the Blessed Virgin Mary

The heart of Mary
Holy the womb that bore him,
Holy the breasts that fed,
But holier still the royal heart
That in his passion bled.

(Written to be put under a picture of the heart of Mary)

Ave Maris Stella [Hail, Star of the Sea].

Truly thou art a star, O Mary! Our Lord indeed himself, Jesus Christ, he is the truest and chief star, the bright and morning star, as Saint John calls him; that star which was foretold from the beginning as destined to rise out of Israel, and which was displayed in figure by the star which appeared to the wise men in the East. But if the wise and learned and they who teach men in justice shall shine as stars for ever and ever; if the angels of the churches are called stars in the hands of Christ; if he honored the apostles even in the days of their flesh by a title, calling them the lights of the world; if even those angels who fell from heaven are called by the beloved disciple stars; if lastly all the saints in bliss are called stars, in that they are like stars differing from stars in glory; therefore most assuredly, without any derogation from the honor of our Lord, is Mary his mother called the Star of the Sea, and the more so because even on her head she wears a crown of twelve stars. Jesus is the light of the world, illuminating every man, who comes into it, opening our eyes with the gift of faith, making souls luminous by his almighty grace; and Mary is the star, shining with the light of Jesus, fair as the moon, and special as the sun, the star of the heavens, which it is good to look upon, the star of the sea, which is welcome to the tempest-tossed, at whose smile the evil spirits flies, the passions are hushed, and peace is poured upon the soul.

Hail, then, Star of the Sea, we joy in the recollection of thee. Pray for us ever at the throne of grace; plead our cause, pray with us, present our prayers to thy Son and Lord—now and in the hour of death, Mary be thou our help. Amen.

In Jesus Christ is the fullness of Godhead with all its infinite sanctity. In Mary is reflected the sanctity of Jesus, as by his grace it could be found in a creature.

Mary, as the pattern both of maidenhood and maternity, has exalted woman's state and nature, and made the Christian virgin and the Christian mother understand the sacredness of their duties in the sight of God.

Her very image is as a book in which we may read at a glance the mystery of the Incarnation and the mercy of the Redemption; and withal her own gracious perfection also, who was made by her divine Son the very type of humility, gentleness, fortitude, purity, patience, and love.

What Christian mother can look upon her image and not be moved to pray for gentleness, watchfulness, and obedience like Mary's? What Christian maiden can look upon her without praying for the gifts of simplicity, modesty, purity, recollection, gentleness such as hers?

Who can repeat her very name without finding in it a music which goes to the heart and brings before him thoughts of God and Jesus Christ, and heavens above, and fills him with the desire of those graces by which heaven is gained?

Hail then, great Mother of God, Queen of Saints, Royal Lady clothed with the sun and crowned with the stars of heaven, whom all generations have called and shall call blessed. We will take our part in praising thee in our own time and place with all the redeemed of our Lord, and will exalt thee in the full assembly of the saints and glorify thee in the heavenly Jerusalem.

(A prayer composed for a service
on Rosary Sunday)

Titles Attributed to Mary

[The selections in this part are a sample of some of the meditations Newman wrote on the titles of the Virgin Mary found in the Litany of Loreto.]

Mary is the "Domus Aurea"—The House of Gold

Why is she called a *house*? And why is she called *golden*? Gold is the most beautiful, the most valuable, of all the metals. Silver, copper, and steel may in their way be made good to the eye but nothing is so rich, so splendid, as gold. We have few opportunities of seeing it in any quantity, but anyone who has seen a large number of bright gold coins knows how magnificent is the look of gold. Hence it is in Scripture the holy city, is, by a figure of speech called golden. "The city," says Saint John, "was pure gold, as it were transparent glass." He means of course to give us a notion of the wondrous beautifulness of heaven, by comparing it with what is the most beautiful substances which we see on earth.

Therefore, it is that Mary too is called *golden*; because her graces, her virtues, her innocence, her purity, are of that transcendent brilliancy and dazzling perfection, so costly, so exquisite, that the angels cannot, so to say, keep their eyes off her any more than we could help gazing upon any great works of gold.

But observe further, that she is a *golden house* or, I will rather say, a *golden palace*. Let us imagine we saw a whole palace of a large church all made of gold, from foundation to roof; such, in regard to the number, the variety, the extent of her spiritual excellence, is Mary.

But why called a *house* or palace? And *whose* palace? She is the house and palace of the great king, of God himself. Our Lord, the co-equal Son of God, once dwelt in her. He was her guest; nay, more than guest, for a guest comes into a house as well as leaves it. But our Lord was actually *born* in this house. He took his flesh and blood from this house, from the flesh, from the veins of Mary. Rightly then was she made of pure gold, because she was to give of that gold to form the body of the Son of God. She was *golden* in her conception, *golden* in her birth. She went through the fires of her suffering like gold in the furnace, and when she ascended on high she was, in the words of the hymn: Above all the angels in glory untold/Standing next to the king in a vesture of gold. (Newman's emphasis)

Mary is the "Speculum Justitiae"—the Mirror of Justice

Here first we must consider what is meant by *justice*, for the word used by the Church has not that sense which it bears in ordinary English. By "justice" is not meant the virtue of fairness, equity, uprightness in our dealings; but it is a word denoting all virtues at once, a perfect, virtuous state of soul—righteousness, or moral perfection; so that it answers very nearly to what is meant by *sanctity*. Therefore, when our Lady is called the "mirror of justice" it is meant to say that she is the mirror of sanctity, holiness, supernatural goodness.

Next, what is meant by calling her a *mirror*? A mirror is a surface which reflects, as still water, polished steel, or a looking glass. What did Mary reflect? She reflected our Lord—but he is infinite *sanctity*. She, then, as far as a creature could, reflected his divine sanctity, and therefore she is the mirror of sanctity, or, as the litany says, of *justice*.

Do we ask how she came to reflect his sanctity? It was by living with him. We see every day how like people get to each other who live with those they love. When they live with those whom they don't love, as for, instance, the members of a family who quarrel with each other, then the longer they live with each other the more unlike each other they become; but when they love each other, as husband and wife, parents and children, brothers with brothers, sisters, friends with friends, then in the course of time they become surprisingly like each other All of us perceive this; we are witnesses to it with our own eyes and ears—in the expression of their features, in their voice, in their walk, in their language, even in their hand-writing, they become like each other; and so with regard to their minds, in their opinions, their tastes, their pursuits. And again, doubtless in the state of their souls, which we do not see, whether for good or bad.

Now, consider that Mary loved her divine Son with unutterable love; and consider too that she had him to herself for thirty years. Do we not see that, as she was full of grace *before* she conceived him in her womb, she must have had a vast incomprehensible sanctity when she had lived close to God for thirty years—a sanctity of an angelical order, reflecting back the attributes of God with a fullness and an exactness of which no saint upon earth or hermit or holy virgin, can even remind us. Truly then she is the *speculum justitiae*, the *mirror* of divine *perfection*. (Newman's emphasis)

Mary is the "Janua Coeli"—The Gate of Heaven

Mary is called the *gate* of heaven because it was through her that our Lord passed from heaven to earth. The prophet Ezechiel, prophesying of Mary, says, the gate shall be closed, it shall not be opened and no man shall pass through it, since the Lord God of Israel has entered through it—and it shall be closed for the prince, the prince himself, shall sit in it (see Ez 44: 1–3).

Now this is fulfilled not only in our Lord taking flesh from her, and being her son, but, moreover, in that she had a place in the economy of redemption; it is fulfilled in her spirit and her will, as well as in her body. Eve had a part in the fall of man, though it was Adam who was our representative, and whose sin made us sinners. It was Eve who began, and tempted Adam. Scripture says: "The woman saw that the tree was good to eat and fair to the eyes, and delightful to behold; and she took of the fruit thereof and did eat, and gave it to her husband, and he did eat" (Gn 3:6). It was fitting then in God's mercy that, as the woman began the *destruction* of the world, so woman also began its *recovery*, and that, as Eve opened the way for the fatal deed of the first Adam, so Mary should open the way for the great achievement of the second Adam, even our Lord Jesus Christ, who came to save the world by dying on the cross for it. Hence Mary is called by the holy fathers a second and better Eve, as having taken that first step in the salvation of mankind which Eve took in its ruin.

How, and when, did Mary take part, and the initial part, in the world's restoration? It was when the Angel Gabriel came to her to announce to her the great dignity which was to be her portion. Saint Paul bids us to present our bodies to God as a reasonable service. We must not pray only with our lips and fast, and do outward penance, and be chaste in our bodies; but we must be obedient and pure in our minds. And so, regarding the Blessed Virgin, it was God's will that she should undertake *willingly* and with *full understanding* to be the mother of our Lord and not be a mere passive instrument whose maternity would have no merit and no reward. The higher our gifts, the heavier our duties. It was no light lot to be so intimately near to the redeemer of men, as she experiences afterwards when she suffered with him. Therefore, weighing well the angel's words before giving her answer to them—first she asked whether so great an office would be a forfeiture of that virginity which she had vowed. When the angel told her no, then, with the full consent of a full heart, full of God's love to her and her own lowliness, she said "Behold the handmaid of the Lord; be it done unto me according to thy word" (Lk 1:38). It was by this consent that she became the *gate of heaven*.

Mary is the "Mater Creatoris"—The Mother of the Creator

This is the title which, of all others, we should have thought it impossible for any creature to possess. At first sight we might be tempted to say that it throws into confusion our primary ideas of the creator and the creature, the eternal and the temporal, the self-subsisting and the dependent; and yet on further consideration we shall see that we cannot refuse the title to Mary without denying the divine incarnation—that is, the great and fundamental truth of revelation, that God became man.

And this was seen from the first age of the Church. Christians were accustomed from the first to call the Blessed Virgin "the Mother of God" because they saw that it was impossible to deny her that title without denying John's words, "The Word (that is, God the Son) was made flesh" (Jn 1:14).

And in no long time it was found necessary to proclaim this truth by the voice of the Ecumenical Council of the Church [The Council of Ephesus]. For, in consequence of the dislike which men have of mystery, the error sprang up that our Lord was not really God, but a man, differing from us in this merely—that God dwelt in him, as God dwells in all good men, only in a higher measure, as in a sort of temple; or again, as our Lord now dwells in the tabernacle in church. And then the bishops and faithful people found there was no other way of hindering this false, bad view being taught but by declaring distinctly, and making it a point of faith, that Mary was the mother, not of man only but of God. And since that time the title of Mary, as *Mother of God*, has become what is called a dogma, or article of faith, in the Church.

But this leads us to a larger view of the subject. Is this title as given to Mary more wonderful than the doctrine that God, without ceasing to be God, should become man? Is it more mysterious that Mary should be Mother of God than that *God* should become *man*? Yet the latter, as I have said, is the elementary truth of revelation, witnessed by prophets, evangelists, and apostles, all through Scripture. And what can be more consoling and joyful than that Mary is the Mother of God—the great wonder, namely, that we become the brethren of our God; that, if we live well, and die in the grace of God, we shall all of us hereafter be taken up by our incarnate God to that place where angels dwell; that our bodies shall be raised from the dust and be taken to heaven; that we shall be really united to God; that we shall be partakers of the divine nature; that each of us, soul and body, shall be plunged into the abyss of glory which surrounds the Almighty; that we shall see him and share his blessedness, according to the text "Whosoever shall do the will of my father that is in heaven the same is my brother and sister and mother" (Mt 12:50).

From the Litany of the Seven Dolours of the Blessed Virgin Mary

R/   Pray for us.

Mother of sorrows, *R/*
Mother, whose soul was pierced by a sword, *R/*
Mother who did flee with Jesus into Egypt, *R/*
Mother, who did seek him sorrowing for three days, *R/*
Mother who saw him scourged and crowned with thorns, *R/*
Mother who did stand with him while he hung on the cross, *R/*
Mother who did receive him into thine arms when he was dead, *R/*
Mother who did see him buried in the tomb, *R/*
O Mary, queen of martyrs, *R/*
O Mary, comfort of the sorrowful, *R/*
O Mary, help of the weak, *R/*
O Mary, strength of the fearful, *R/*
O Mary, light of the desponding, *R/*
O Mary, nursing-mother of the sick, *R/*
O Mary, refuge of sinners, *R/*

R/   Save us by thy prayers.

Through the bitter passion of thy son, *R/*
Through the piercing anguish of thy heart, *R/*
Through the heavy weight of woe, *R/*
Through thy sadness and desolation, *R/*
Through thy maternal pity, *R/*
Through thy perfect resignation, *R/*
Through thy meritorious prayers, *R/*

From immoderate sadness, *R/*
From a cowardly spirit, *R/*
From an impatient temper, *R/*
From fretfulness and discontent, *R/*
From sullenness and gloom, *R/*
From despair and unbelief, *R/*
From final impenitence, *R/*

R/   Beseech thee, hear us.

We sinners, *R/*
Preserve us from a sudden death, *R/*
Teach us how to die, *R/*
Succour us in our last agony, *R/*
Guard us from the enemy, *R/*
Bring us to a happy end, *R/*
Gain for the gift of perseverance, *R/*
Aid us before the judgment seat, *R/*
Mother of God, *R/*
Mother most sorrowful, *R/*
Mother most desolate, *R/*

From the Litany of the Immaculate Heart of Mary

R/   Have mercy on us.

Heart of Mary, *R/*
Heart, after God's own heart, *R/*
Heart, in union with the heart of Jesus, *R/*
Heart, vessel of the Holy Spirit, *R/*
Heart of Mary, shrine of the Holy Trinity, *R/*
Heart of Mary, home of the Word, *R/*
Heart of Mary, immaculate in thy creation, *R/*

Heart of Mary, flooded with grace, *R/*
Heart of Mary, blessed of all hearts, *R/*
Heart of Mary, throne of glory, *R/*
Heart of Mary, abyss of humbleness, *R/*
Heart of Mary, victim of love, *R/*
Heart of Mary, nailed to the cross, *R/*
Heart of Mary, comfort of the sad, *R/*
Heart of Mary, refuge of the sinner, *R/*
Heart of Mary, hope of the dying, *R/*
Heart of Mary, seat of mercy, *R/*

From the Litany of the Holy Name of Mary

R/   Have mercy on us.

Heavenly Father, who has Mary for thy daughter, *R/*
Eternal Son, who has Mary for thy mother, *R/*
Holy Spirit, who has Mary for thy spouse, *R/*
Glorious Trinity, who has Mary for thy handmaid, *R/*

R/   Pray for us.

Mary, Mother of the Living God, *R/*
Mary, daughter of the Light Unapproachable, *R/*
Mary, our light, *R/*
Mary, our sister, *R/*
Mary, stem of Jesse, *R/*
Mary, offspring of kings, *R/*
Mary, best work of God, *R/*
Mary, immaculate, *R/*
Mary, all fair, *R/*
Mary, virgin mother, *R/*
Mary, suffering with Jesus, *R/*
Mary, pierced with a sword, *R/*

Mary, bereft of consolation, R/
Mary, standing by the cross, R/
Mary, ocean of bitterness, R/
Mary, rejoicing in God's will, R/
Mary, our lady, R/
Mary, our queen, R/
Mary, bright as the sun, R/
Mary, fair as the moon, R/
Mary, crowned with twelve stars, R/
Mary, seated at the right hand of Jesus, R/
Mary, our sweetness, R/
Mary, our hope, R/
Mary, glory of Jerusalem, R/
Mary, joy of Israel, R/
Mary, honor of thy people, R/

Jesus Son of Mary

When our Lord came upon the earth, he might have created a fresh body for himself out of nothing—or he might have formed a body for himself out of the earth, as he formed Adam. But he preferred to be born as other men are born, of a human mother. Why did he do so? He did so to put honor on all those human relations and connections which are ours by nature; and to teach us that, though he has begun a new creation, he does not wish to cast off the old creation as far as it is not sinful. Hence it is our duty to love and honor our parents, to be affectionate to our brothers and sisters, friends, husbands, wives, not only not less, but even more, than it was man's duty before our Lord came on earth. As we become better Christians, more consistent and zealous servants of Jesus, we shall become only more and more anxious for the good of all around us— our kindred, our friends, our acquaintances, our neighbors, our superiors, our inferiors, our masters, our employers. And this we shall do from the

ing at our doors at night implies the presence of one
outside in the dark who asks for admittance, so this
Word within us not only instructs us up to a certain
point, but necessarily raises our minds to the idea of
a Teacher, an unseen Teacher: and in proportion as
we listen to that Word, and use it, not only do we
learn more from, it, not only do its dictates become
clearer, and its lessons broader, and its principles
more consistent, but its very tone is louder and more
authoritative and constraining. And thus it is, that to
those who use what they have, more is given; for,
beginning with obedience, they go on to the intimate
perception and belief of one God. His voice within
them witnesses to him, and they believe his own witness about himself.

Venerable John Henry Newman

*Venerable John Henry Newman († 1890) established the
Oratory in Birmingham, England, and was a preacher of
great eloquence.*

Prayer for the Evening

The reign of God is at hand: come, let us rejoice!

Glory to the Father... Alleluia!

Hymn   Meter: 76 76 D
This hymn can be sung to the tune used for
I Sing the Mighty Power of God

Look up, O drooping hearts, today,
The King is very near;
O cast your griefs and fears away,
For, lo, your help is here!
Hope on, O broken hearts, at last
The King comes in his might;
He loved us in the ages past
When we lay wrapped in night.

Newman

MEDITATION OF THE DAY

John Believed Jesus' Witness about Himself

The Holy Baptist was sent before our Lord to prepare his way; that is, to be his instrument in rousing,
warning, humbling, and inflaming the hearts of men,
so that, when he came, they might believe in him...
When then he was about to appear on earth among
his chosen people, and to claim for himself their faith,
he made use of Saint John first to create in them
these necessary dispositions; and therefore it is that, at
this season, when we are about to celebrate his birth,
we commemorate again and again the great Saint
who was his forerunner,... lest we should forget, that,
without a due preparation of heart, we cannot hope
to obtain and keep the all-important gift of faith...

What is the main guide of the soul, given to the
whole race of Adam, outside the true fold of Christ as
well as within it, given from the first dawn of reason,
given to it in spite of that grievous penalty of ignorance, which is one of the chief miseries of our fallen
state? It is the light of conscience, "the true Light," as
the same Evangelist says, in the same passage,
"which enlightens every man that cometh into this
world."...

This is Conscience; and, from the nature of the
case, its very existence carries on our minds to
a Being exterior to ourselves; for else whence did it
come and to a Being superior to ourselves; else
whence its strange, troublesome peremptoriness?
I say, without going on to the question of what it says,
and whether its particular dictates are always as clear
and consistent as they might be, its very existence
throws us out of ourselves, and beyond ourselves, to
go and seek for him in the height and depth, whose
Voice it is. As the sunshine implies that the sun is in
the heavens, though we may see it not, as a knock-

recollection of how our Lord loved his mother. He loves her still in heaven with a special love. He refuses her nothing. We must then on earth feel a tender solicitude for all our relations, all our friends, all we know and have dealings with. And moreover, we must love not only those who love us, but those who hate us or injure us, that we may imitate him, who not only was loving to his mother, but even suffered Judas, the traitor, to kiss him, and prayed for his murderers on the cross.

Let us pray God for our relations, friends, well wishers, and enemies, living and dead.

O Jesus, son of Mary, whom Mary followed to the cross when thy disciples fled, and who did bear her tenderly in mind in the midst of thy sufferings, even in thy last words, who did commit her to thy best beloved disciple, saying to her, "Woman, behold thy son," and to him, "Behold thy mother" we, after thy pattern, would pray for all who are near and dear to us, and we beg thy grace to do so continually. We beg thee to bring them all into the light of thy truth or to keep them in the truth if they already know it, and to keep them in a state of grace, and to give them the gift of perseverance. We thus pray for our parents, for our fathers, and our mothers, for our children, for every one of them, for every one of our brothers and every one of our sisters, for our cousins, and all our kindred, for our friends, and our father's friends, for all our old friends, for our dear and intimate friends, for teachers, for our pupils, for our masters and employers, for our servants or our subordinates, for our associates and fellow-workers, for our neighbors, for our superiors, and rulers; for those who wish us well, for those who wish us ill; for our enemies, for our rivals; for our injurers and for our slanderers. And not only for the living, but for the dead, who have died in the grace of God, that he may shorten the time of their expiation, and admit them into his presence above. Amen.

(A meditation and prayer for Good Friday)

Texts for Meditation

The texts taken from the *Plain and Parochial Sermons,* as published by Ignatius Press in 1997, are marked as *PPS* followed by the volume in Roman numerals and the sermon number in arabic numerals. The other selections, unless noted, come from his own *Meditations and Devotions*. The final selection is from Sermon XV of the *University Sermons* from the recent reprinting by the University of Notre Dame Press, 1997.

In a very few places I have broken up Newman's very long paragraphs into shorter ones for the sake of readability.

It is the saying of holy men that, if we wish to be perfect, we have nothing more to do that to perform the ordinary duties of the day well. A short road to perfection—short, not because easy, but because pertinent and intelligible. There are no short ways to perfection, but there are sure ones.

I think this is an instruction which may be of great practical use to persons like ourselves. It is easy to have vague ideas of what perfection is, which serve well enough to talk about, when we do not intend to aim at it; but as soon as a person really desires and sets about seeking it himself, he is dissatisfied with anything but what is tangible and clear and constitutes some sort of direction towards the practice of it.

We must bear in mind what is meant by perfection. It does not mean any extraordinary service, anything out of the way and especially heroic—not all have the way of heroic acts, of suffering—but it means what the word perfection ordinarily means. By perfect we mean that which has no flaws in it, that which is complete, that which is consistent, that which is sound—we mean the opposite of imperfect. As we know well what *im*perfection in religious service means, we know by the contrast what is meant by perfection.

He, then, is perfect who does the work of the day perfectly, and we need not go beyond this to seek for perfection. You need not go out of the *round* of the day.

I insist on this because I think it will simplify our views, and fix our exertions on a definite aim. If you ask me what you are to do in order to be perfect, I say, first—Do not lie in bed beyond the due time of rising; give your first thoughts to God; make a good visit to the Blessed Sacrament; say the Angelus devoutly; eat and drink to God's glory; say the rosary well; be recollected; keep out bad thoughts; make your evening meditation well; examine yourself daily; go to bed in good time, and you are already perfect.

(Conference of 27 September 1865; Newman's emphasis)

God has created me to do for him some definite service. He has committed some work to me which he has not committed to another. I have my mission. I am a link in a chain, a connection between people. God has not created me for nothing. I shall do good. I shall do his work. I shall be a preacher of truth in my own place, while not intending it, if I do but keep his commandments and serve him in my calling.

Love is the gentle, tranquil, satisfied acquiescence and adherence of the soul in the contemplation of God; not only a preference of God before all things, but a delight in him because he is God, and because his commandments are good; not only violent emotion or transport, but as Saint Paul describes it, long suffering, kind, modest, unassuming, innocent, simple, orderly, disinterested, meek, pure hearted, sweet tempered, patient, enduring. Faith without charity is dry, harsh, and sapless; it has nothing sweet, engaging, winning, soothing; but it was charity which brought Christ down. Charity is but another name for the comforter. It is eternal charity which is the bond of all things in heaven and earth; it is the charity wherein the Father and the Son are one in unity with the Spirit; by which the angels, in heaven are one, by which the saints are one with God, by which the Church is one upon earth.

As love worships God within the shrine, faith discerns him in the world; and as love is the life of God in the solitary soul, faith is the guardian of love in our intercourse with men; and, while faith ministers to love, love is that which imparts to faith praise and excellence.

And thus it is that faith is to love as religion is to holiness; for religion is the divine law as coming to us from without, as holiness is the acquiescence in the same law as written within. Love then is meditative, tranquil, pure, gentle, abounding in all offices of goodness and truth; and faith is strenuous and energetic, formed for this world; combating it, training the mind towards love, fortifying in obedience, and overcoming sense and reason by representations more urgent than their own.

Christ takes you at your word, so to speak; he offers to make you different. He says, "I will take away from you the heart of stone, the love of this world and its pleasures, if you will submit to my discipline." Here a man draws back. No; he cannot bear to *lose* the love of the world, to part with his present desires and tastes; he cannot *consent* to be changed. After all, he is well satisfied at the bottom of his heart to remain as he is, only he wants his conscience taken out of the way. (Newman's emphasis)

What is meditating on Christ? It is simply this, thinking habitually and constantly on him and of his deeds and sufferings. It is to have him before our minds as one whom we may contemplate, worship, and address when we rise up, when we lie down, when we eat and drink, when we are at home and abroad, when we are working, or walking or at rest, when we are alone, and again when we are in company; this is meditating. And by this, and nothing short of this, will our hearts come to feel as they ought. We have stony hearts, hearts as hard as the highways; the history of Christ makes no impression upon them. And yet, if we would be saved, we must have tender, sensitive, living hearts; our hearts must be broken, must be broken up like ground, and dug and watered, and tended and cultivated, till they become as gardens, gardens of

Remember that your soul is a temple of the living God. "The kingdom of God is within you."

Night and day let your aim be to remain in simplicity and gentleness, calmness and serenity, and in freedom from created things, so that you will find your joy in the Lord Jesus.

Love silence and solitude, even when in the midst of a crowd or when caught up in your work. Physical solitude is a good thing, provided that it is backed up by prayer and a holy life, but far better than this is solitude of the heart, which is the interior desert in which your spirit can become totally immersed in God, and can hear and savor the words of eternal life.

With great purity of intention, aim in everything to do what pleases God. Always remain faithful to God and genuinely accept whatever he wishes.

SAINT PAUL OF THE CROSS

Saint Paul of the Cross († 1775) was an Italian priest, mystic, and the founder of the Passionists.

Prayer for the Evening

Let our prayer arise before God like incense,
the raising of our hands in prayer
like the evening sacrifice, alleluia!

Glory to the Father... Alleluia!

HYMN   Meter: 6 6 8 4 D

The God of Abraham praise,
Who reigns enthroned above;
Ancient of Everlasting Days,
And God of Love;
O Lord, the great I AM!
By earth and heaven confessed;
I bow and praise the sacred Name
Forever blessed.

COMMUNION ANTIPHON

We preach a Christ who was crucified; he is the power and the wisdom of God. (1 Cor 1: 23-24)

PRAYER AFTER COMMUNION

Lord,
in the life of Saint Paul
you helped us to understand the mystery of the cross.
May the sacrifice we have offered strengthen us,
keep us faithful to Christ,
and help us to work in the Church
for the salvation of all mankind.
We ask this in the name of Jesus the Lord.

MEDITATION OF THE DAY

How to Be Vigilant

The easiest way to keep your peace of heart is to accept everything as coming directly from the hands of the God who loves you. If you do this, any pain or persecution, anything which is difficult to accept will be transformed into a source of joy, happiness, and peace…

Silence and recollection are two very effective ways of bringing ourselves before the Lord and entering into the sanctuary of his love: "When peaceful silence lay over all, and night had run the half of her swift course, down from the heavens leapt your all-powerful word."

When a person comes to terms with his feelings, when he lives in God and walks by the light of faith, he has attained that stillness of the night which God is waiting for. It is then that the Word of God comes to birth in him in a way which is entirely of the spirit, entirely of God.

Remain within your deepest self, in the interior kingdom of your spirit.

Eden, acceptable to our God, gardens in which the Lord God may walk and dwell; filled, not with briars and thorns, but with all sweet-smelling and useful plants, with heavenly trees and flowers. The dry and barren waste must burst forth into springs of living water. This change must take place in our hearts if we would be saved; in a word, we must have what we have not by nature, faith and love; and how is this to be effected, under God's grace, but by godly and practical meditation through the day.

(*PPS* VI:4)

The Christian has a deep, silent, hidden peace, which the world sees not—like some well in a retired and shady place, difficult of access. He is the greater part of his time by himself, and when he is in solitude, that is his real state. What he is when he is left to himself and to his God, that is his true self. He can bear himself; he can (as it were) joy in himself, for it is the grace of God within him, it is the presence of the eternal comforter, in which he joys. He can bear, he finds it pleasant, to be with himself at all times—"never less alone when alone." He can lay his head on his pillow at night, and own in God's sight, with overflowing heart, that he wants nothing— and that he is "full and abounds"—that God has been all things to him, and that nothing is not his which God could give him. More thankfulness, more holiness, more of heaven he needs indeed, but the thought that he can have more is not a thought of trouble, but of joy. It does not interfere with his peace to know that he may grow nearer to God. Such is the Christian's peace, when, with a single heart and the cross in his eye, he addresses and commends himself to him with whom the night is as clear as the day. Saint Paul says the peace of God shall *keep* our hearts and our minds. By "keep" he means "guard" or "garrison" our hearts; so as to keep out our enemies. And he says "our hearts and minds" in contrast to what the world sees of us. Many hard things may be said of the Christian and done against him, but he has a secret preservative of charm and minds them not.

If we would have our minds composed, our desires subdued, and our tempers heavenly through the day, we must, before commencing the day's employment, stand still awhile to look into ourselves and commune with our hearts, by way of preparing ourselves for the trials and duties on which we are entering. A like reason may be assigned for evening prayer, viz. As affording us a time of looking back on the day past and summing up (as it were) that account, which, if *we* do not reckon, at least God has reckoned, and written down in that book which will be produced at the judgment; a time of confessing sin, and of praying for forgiveness, of giving thanks for what we have done well, and for mercies received, of making good resolutions in reliance on the help of God, and of sealing up and setting sure the day past, at least as stepping stone of good for the morrow. The precise times of private prayer are nowhere commanded us in Scripture; the most obvious are those I have mentioned morning and evening. In the texts just read you heard of praying three times a day (Dn 6:10) or seven times (Ps 119:164). All this depends of course on the opportunities of each individual. Some have not the leisure for this; but for morning and evening prayer all can and should *make* leisure.

(*PPS* I;19; Newman's emphasis)

The Lord's Prayer . . . consists of seven petitions: three have reference to Almighty God, four to the petitioners; and could any form of words be put together which so well could be called the Prayer of the Pilgrim? We often hear it said, that the true way of serving God is to serve man, as if religion consisted merely in acting well our part in life, not in direct faith, obedience, and worship: how different is the spirit of this prayer! Evil round about him, enemies and persecutors in his path, temptation in prospect, help for the day, sin to be expiated, God's will in his heart, God's name on his lips, God's kingdom in his hopes: this is the view it gives us of the Christian. What simplicity! What grandeur! And what definiteness! How one and the same, how consistent with all that we read of him elsewhere in Scripture!

You must *pray*; and this I say is very difficult, because our thoughts are so apt to wander. But even this is not all—you must, as you pray, really intend to *try to practice* what you pray for. When you say "lead us not into temptation" you must in good earnest mean to avoid in your daily conduct those temptations which you have already suffered from. When you say "deliver us from evil" you must mean to struggle against that evil in your hearts, which you are conscious of, and which you pray to be forgiven. This is difficult, but still more is behind. You must actually carry your good intentions into effect during the week, and in truth and in reality war against the world, the flesh and the devil. And any one here present who falls short of this, that is, who thinks it enough to come to church to *learn* God's will but does not bear in mind to do it in his daily conduct be he high or low, know he mysteries and all knowledge, or be he unlettered and busily occupied in his active life, he is a fool in his sight, who makes the wisdom of the world foolishness. Surely he is but a trifler, as substituting a formal outward service for the religion of the heart; and he reverses our Lord's words in the text, "because he knows these things, most unhappy is he, because he does them not" (Jn 13:17).

(*PPS* I:3; Newman's emphasis)

To love our brethren with a resolution which no obstacle can overcome, so as almost to consent to an anathema on ourselves, if so be we may save those who hate us—

To labor in God's cause against hope, and in the midst of sufferings—

To read the events of life, as they occur, by the interpretation which Scripture gives them and that, not as if the language were strange to us, but to do it promptly—

To perform all our relative daily duties most watchfully—

To check every evil thought and bring the whole mind into captivity to the law of Christ—

To be patient, cheerful, forgiving, meek, honest, and true—

To persevere in this good work until death, making fresh advances towards perfection—

And after all, in the end, to confess ourselves unprofitable servants, nay to feel, ourselves corrupt and sinful creatures, who (with all our proficiency) would still be lost unless God bestowed his mercy on us in Christ—

These are some of the difficult realities of religious obedience, which we must pursue, and which the apostles in high measure attained and which we may well bless God's holy name, if he enables us to make our own.

(PPS I:26)

He [Christ] has shown you the way; he gave up the home of his mother Mary to "be about his Father's business," and now he bids you take up after him his cross which he bore for you and "fill up what is wanting of his afflictions in your flesh."

Be not afraid—it is but a pang now and then, and a struggle; a covenant with your eyes, and a fasting in the wilderness, some calm habitual watchfulness, and the hearty effort to obey, and all will be well.

Be not afraid. He is most gracious, and will bring you on little by little. He does not show you whither he is leading you;

you might be frightened if you see the whole prospect at once. Sufficient for the day is its own evil. Follow his plan; look not on anxiously; look down at your present footing "lest it be turned out of the way" but speculate not about the future. I can well believe that you have hopes now, which you cannot give up, and even which you support in your present course. Be it so; whether they will be fulfilled, or not, is in his hand. He may be pleased to grant the desires of your heart; if so, thank him for his mercy; only be sure that all will be for your greatest good, and "as thy days, so shall your strength be. . . ." He knows no variableness, neither shadow of turning; and when we outgrow our childhood, we but approach, however feebly, to his likeness, who has no youth or age, who has no passions, no hopes or fears, but who loves truth, purity, and mercy, and who is supremely blessed because he is supremely holy.

(*PPS* I:26)

While we thus think of him [i.e. Christ], let us not forget to be up and doing. Let us beware of indulging a mere barren faith and love, which dreams instead of working and is fastidious when it should be hardy. This is only spiritual childhood in another form; for the Holy Ghost is the author of active good works, and leads us to the observance of all lowly deeds of ordinary obedience as the most pleasing sacrifice to God.

(*PPS* I:26)

To know God and Christ, in Scripture language, seems to mean to live under the conviction of his presence, who is to our bodily eyes, unseen. It is, in fact, to have faith but not faith as the heathen might have, but gospel faith. . . . The gospel is a *manifestation*, and therefore addressed to the eyes of our mind. Faith is the same principle as before , but with the opportunity of acting through a more certain and satisfactory sense. . . .

Hence it is, that the New Testament says so much on the subject of spiritual knowledge. For instance, Saint Paul prays that the Ephesians may receive "the spirit of wisdom and revelation in the knowledge of Christ, the eyes of their understanding being enlightened" (Eph 1:17). And he says that the Colossians had "put on the new man, which is renewed in knowledge, after the image of him that created him" (Col 3:10). Saint Peter, in like manner, addresses his brethren with the salutation of "Grace and peace, through the knowledge of God and of Jesus our Lord" (2 Pt 1:2); and according to the declaration of our Lord himself: "This is life eternal, to know thee, the only true God, and Jesus Christ whom thou has sent" (Jn 18:3).

(PPS II:14)

To know God is to know life eternal and to believe in the gospel manifestation of him is to know him; but how are we to "know that we know him?" How are we to be sure that we are not mistaking some dream of our own for the true and clear vision? How can we tell that we are not gazers upon a distant prospect through a misty atmosphere who mistake one object for another? The text [i.e. "Hereby do we know that we know him; if we keep his commandments" (1 Jn 2:3).] answers us clearly and intelligibly; though some Christians have recourse to other proofs of it, or will not have patience to ask themselves the question. They say they are quite certain that they have the true faith; for faith carries with it its own evidence, and admits of no mistaking, the true spiritual conviction being unlike all others. On the other hand, Saint John says "Hereby do we know that we know him, if we keep his commandments."

Obedience is the test of faith.

Thus the whole duty and work of a Christian is made up of these two parts. Faith and obedience; "looking unto Jesus," the divine object as well as author of our faith, and acting according to his will.

(PPS II:14)

The condescension of the blessed Spirit is as incomprehensible as that of the Son. He has ever been the secret presence of God within the creation: a source of life amid the chaos, bringing out into form and order what was at first shapeless and void, and the voice of truth in the hearts of all rational beings tuning them into harmony with the intimation of God's law, which were externally made to them. Hence he is especially called the "life giving" Spirit; being (as it were) the soul of universal nature, the strength of man and beast, the guide of faith, the witness against sin, the inward light of the patriarchs and prophets, the grace abiding in the Christian soul, and Lord and ruler of the Church. Therefore let us ever praise the Father Almighty, who is the first source of all perfection, in and together with his co-equal Son and Spirit, through whose gracious ministrations we have been given to see "what manner of love" it is where with the Father has loved us.

(PPS II:19)

He [i.e. the Holy Spirit] himself perchance in his mysterious nature, is the eternal love whereby the Father and Son have dwelt in each other, as ancient writers have believed; and what he is in heaven, that he is abundantly on earth. He lives in the Christian's heart, as the never failing fount of charity, which is the very sweetness of the living waters. For where he is, there is liberty from the tyranny of sin, from the dread which the natural man feels, of an offended, unreconciled creator. Doubt, gloom, impatience have been expelled; joy in the gospel has taken their place, the hope of heaven and the harmony of a pure heart, the triumph of self-mastery,

sober thoughts, and a contented mind. How can charity to all
men fail to follow, being the mere affectionateness of innocence and peace? Thus the Spirit of God creates in us the
simplicity and warmth of heart which children have, nay,
rather the perfections of his heavenly hosts, high and low
being joined togther in his mysterious work: for what are
implicit trust, ardent love, aiding purity, but the mind both of
little children and of the adoring Seraphim!

(PPS II:19)

What is faith? It is to feel in good earnest that we are creatures of God; it is a practical perception of the unseen world; it
is to understand that this world is not enough for our happiness, to look beyond it on toward God, to realize his presence,
to wait upon him, to endeavor to learn and to do his will and to
seek our good from him. It is not a mere strong act or impetuous feeling of the mind, an impression or a view coming
upon it, but it is a *habit*, a state of mind, lasting and consistent.
To have faith in God is to surrender one's self to God, humbly
to put one's interests, or to wish to be allowed to put them into
his hands who is the sovereign giver of all good.

Now, again, let me ask, what is obedience? It is the obvious
mode, suggested by nature, of a creature's conducting himself
in God's sight, who fears him as his maker, and knows that, as
a sinner, he has especial cause for fearing him. Under such
circumstances he "will do what he can" to please him, as the
woman whom our Lord commended. He will look every way
to see how it is possible to approve himself to him, and will
rejoice to find any service which may stand as a sort of proof
that he is in earnest. And he will find nothing better as an
offering or as an evidence, than obedience to that holy law
which conscience tells him has been given by God himself;
that is, he will be diligent in doing his duty as far as he knows
it and can do it. Thus, as is evident, the two states of mind are

altogether one and the same: it is quite indifferent whether we say a man seeks God in faith, or say he seeks him by obedience; and whereas God has graciously declared he will receive and bless all who seek him, it is quite indifferent we say, he seeks those who *believe* or those who *obey*. To believe is to look beyond this world to God and to obey is to look beyond this world to God; to believe is of the heart and to obey is of the heart; to believe is not a solitary act but a consistent habit of trust; and to obey is not a solitary act but a consistent habit of doing our duty in all things. I do not say that faith and obedience do not stand for separate ideas in our mind but they stand for nothing more; they are not divided one from the other in fact. They are but one thing viewed differently.

(*PPS* III:6)

If then faith be the essence of a Christian life, and if it be what I have described, it follows that our duty lies in risking upon Christ's word what we have, for what we have not, and doing so in a noble, generous way, not indeed rashly or lightly, still without knowing accurately what we are doing, not knowing either what we give up, nor again what we shall gain; uncertain about our reward, uncertain about our extent of sacrifice, in all respects leaning, waiting upon him, trusting in him, to fulfill his promise, trusting in him to enable us to fulfill our own vows, and so in all respects proceeding without carefulness or anxiety about the future.

(*PPS* IV:20)

What led our Lord to weep over the dead, who could at a word restore him, nay, had it in his purpose to do so? [See John 11:34–36 on the raising of Lazarus.]

First of all, as the context informs us, he wept from very sympathy with the grief of others. "When Jesus saw Mary weeping and the Jews also weeping which came with her, he groaned in the spirit and was troubled." It is the very nature of compassion and sympathy, as the word implies, to "rejoice with those who rejoice and weep with those who weep." We know it is so with men; and God tells us he is also compassionate, and full of tender mercy. Yet we do not know well what this means for how can God rejoice or grieve? By the very perfection of his nature almighty God cannot show sympathy, at least to the comprehension of beings of such limited minds as ours. He, indeed, is hid from us; but if we were allowed to see him, how could we discern in the eternal and unchangeable signs of sympathy? Words and works of sympathy he does display to us; but it is the very sight of sympathy in another that affects and comforts the sufferer more than the fruits of it. Now we cannot see God's sympathy, and the Son of God, though feeling for us as great compassion as his Father, did not show it to us while he remained in his Father's bosom. But when he took flesh and appeared on earth, he showed us the Godhead in a new manifestation. He invested himself with a new set of attributes, those of our flesh, taking into him a human's soul and body, in order that thoughts, feelings, affections, might be his which could respond to ours and certify to us his tender mercy. When, then, our Savior weeps from sympathy at Mary's tears, let us not say it is love of a man overcome by natural feeling. It is the love of God, the bowels of compassion, of the almighty and eternal, condescending to show us as we are capable of receiving it, in the form of human nature.

Jesus wept, therefore, not merely from the deep thoughts of his understanding, but from spontaneous tenderness; from the gentleness and mercy, the encompassing loving-kindness and exuberant fostering affection of the Son of God for his own work, the race of man. Their tears touched him at once, as their miseries had brought him down from heaven. His ear was open to them, and the sound of weeping went at once to his heart.

(*PPS* III:10)

How is our devotion to Christ shown? Ordinarily, not in great matters, not in giving up house and lands for his sake, but in making little sacrifices which the world would ridicule, if it knew of them; in abridging ourselves of comforts for the sake of the poor, in sacrificing our private likings to religious objects, in going to church at a personal inconvenience, in taking pleasure in the company of religious men, though not rich or noble or accomplished or gifted or entertaining; in matters, all of them, of little moment in themselves.

How is self-denial shown? Not in literally bearing Christ's cross and living on locusts and wild honey, but in such light abstinences that come in our way, in some poor effort at fasting and the like, in desiring to be poor rather than rich, solitary or lowly rather than well connected, in living within our income, in avoiding display, in being suspicious of comforts and luxuries; all of which are too trifling for the person observing them or thinking about, yet have their use in proving and improving his heart.

How is Christian valor shown? Not in resisting unto blood, but in withstanding mistaken kindness, in enduring importunity, in not shrinking from surprising and hurting those we love, in undergoing small losses, inconveniences, censures, slights, rather than betray what we believe to be God's truth, be it ever so small a portion of it.

As then Christian devotion, self-denial, courage, are tried in this day in little things, so is Christian faith also. In the apostles' age faith was shown in the great matter of joining either the Church or the pagan or Jewish multitude. It is shown in this day by taking this side or that side in the many questions of opinion and conduct which come before us, whether domestic or parochial or political or of whatever kind.

(*PPS* III:15)

He watches for Christ who has a sensitive, eager, apprehensive, mind: who is awake, alive, quick-witted, zealous in seeking and honoring him; who looks out for him in all that happens and who would not be surprised, who would not be over-agitated or overwhelmed, if he found out that he was coming at once. . . .

This, then, is to watch; to be detached from what is present, and to live in what is unseen; to live in the thought of Christ as he once came and as he will come again; to desire his second coming, from our affectionate and grateful remembrance of his first.

(*PPS* IV:22)

Whatever has been your past life, whether (blessed be God) you have never trusted aught but God's sacred light within you, or whether you have trusted the world and it has failed you, God's mercies in Christ are here offered to you in full abundance. Come to him for them; approach him in the way he has appointed and you will shall find him, as he has said, upon his holy hill of Zion. Let not your past sins keep you from him. Whatever they may be, they cannot interfere with his grace stored up for all who come to him for it. If you have in past years neglected him, perchance you will have to suffer it but fear not; he will give you grace and strength to bear such punishment as he may be pleased to inflict. Let not the thought of his just severity keep you at a distance. He can even make pain pleasant to you. Keeping from him is not to escape from his power, but only from his love. Surrender yourselves to him in faith and holy fear. He is all-merciful, though all-righteous; and though he is awful in his judgments, he is nevertheless more wonderfully pitiful, and of tender compassion above our largest expectations; and in the case of all who humbly seek him, he will in "wrath remember mercy."

(*PPS* IV:12)

I say that Christ, the sinless Son of God, might be living now in the world as our next door neighbor, and perhaps we do not find it out. And this is a thought which should be dwelled on. I do not mean to say that there are not a number of persons, who we could be sure were not Christ; of course, people who lead bad and irreligious lives. But there are a number of persons who are in no sense irreligious or open to serious blame, who are very much like each other at first sight, yet in God's eyes are very different. I mean the great mass of what are called respectable men, who vary very much; some are merely decent and outwardly correct persons and have no great sense of religion, do not deny themselves, have no ardent love for God, but love the world; and whereas their interests lie in being regular and orderly, or they have no strong passions, or have early got in the way of being regular, and their habits are formed accordingly, they are what they are, decent and correct, but very little more. But there are others who look to the world just the same, who are very different; they make no great show, they go on in the same quiet ordinary way as the others, but really they are training to be saints in heaven.

They do all they can to change themselves, to become like God, to obey God, to discipline themselves, to renounce the world; but they do it in secret, both because God tells them to do so and because they do not like it to be known. Moreover, there are a number of others between those two with more or less of worldliness and more or less of faith. Yet they all look about the same, to common eyes, because true religion is a hidden life of the heart; and though it cannot exist without deeds, yet these are for the most part, secret deeds, secret charities, secret prayers, secret self-denials, secret struggles, secret victories.

(*PPS* IV:16)

Faith is the first element of *religion*, and love, of *holiness*; and as holiness and religion are distinct, yet united, so are love and faith. Holiness can exist without religion; religion cannot exist without holiness. Baptized infants, before they come to years of understanding, are holy; they are not religious. Holiness is love of the divine law. When God regenerates an infant, he imparts to it the gifts of the Holy Spirit; and what is the Spirit thus imparted but the law written on its heart? Such was the promise "I will put my laws into their mind and write them in their hearts." And hence it is said "This is the love of God, that we keep his *commandments*" (1 Tm 1:5). God comes to us as a law, before he comes as a lawgiver; that is he sets up his throne within us, and enables us to obey him, before we have learned to reflect on our own sensations, and to know the voice of God. . . .

And thus our duty lies in faith working by love; love is the sacrifice we offer to God and faith is the sacrificer. Yet they are not distinct from each other except in our way of viewing them. . . .

And thus I answer the question concerning the connection of love and faith. Love is the condition of faith, and faith in turn is the cherisher and maturer of love; it brings love out into works, and therefore is called the root of *works* of love; the substance of the works is love, the outline and direction of them is faith.

(*PPS* IV:21; Newman's emphasis)

It is not an easy thing to learn that new language which Christ has brought us. He has interpreted all things for us in a new way. He has brought us a religion which sheds a new light on all that happens. Try to learn this language. Do not get it by rote or speak it as a thing of course. Try to understand what you say. Time is short; eternity is long; God is great, man is weak; he stands between heaven and hell; Christ is his Savior; Christ has suffered for him. The Holy Ghost sanctifies him; repentance purifies him; faith justifies; works save. These are solemn truths, which need not be actually spoken except in the way of creed or teaching; but which must be laid up in the heart. That a thing is true, is no reason that it should be said, but that it should be done; that it should be acted upon; that it should be made ours inwardly.

Let us avoid talking, of whatever kind; whether mere talking or censorious talking; or idle profession or descanting upon gospel doctrines, or the affectation of philosophy or the pretense of eloquence. Let us guard against frivolity, love of display, love of being talked about, love of singularity, love of seeming original. Let us aim at meaning what we say and saying what we mean; let us aim at knowing when we understand a truth and when we do not. When we do not, let us take it on truth, and let us profess to do so. Let us receive the truth in reverence and pray God to give us a good will, and divine light, and spiritual strength, that it may bear fruit within us.

(*PPS* V:3)

Let us then view God's providences to us more religiously than we have hitherto done. Let us gain a truer view of what we are and where we are in his kingdom. Let us humbly and reverently attempt to trace his guiding hand in the years we have hitherto lived. Let us thankfully commemorate the many mercies he has vouchsafed us in times past, the many sins he has not remembered, the many dangers he has averted, the many prayers he has answered, the many mistakes he has corrected, the many warnings, the many lessons, the much light, the abounding comfort, which he has from time to time given. Let us dwell upon times and seasons, times of troubles, times of joy, times of trial, times of refreshment. How did he cherish us as his children! How did he guide us in that dangerous time when the mind began to think for itself, and the heart was open to the world! How did he with his sweet discipline restrain our passions, mortify our hopes, calm our fears, enliven our heaviness, sweeten our desolateness, and strengthen our infirmities! How did he gently guide us towards the strait gate! How did he allure us along his everlasting way, in spite of its strictness, in spite of its loneliness, in spite of the dim twilight in which it lay! He has been all things to us.

(PPS V:7)

Let us never lose sight of this great and simple view, which the whole of Scripture sets before us: What was actually done by Christ in the flesh eighteen hundred years ago is in type and resemblance really wrought in us one by one even to the end of time. He was born of the Spirit, and we too are born of the Spirit. He was justified by the Spirit and so are we. He was pronounced the well beloved Son, when the Holy Ghost descended on him; and we too cry out Abba, Father, through the Spirit sent into our hearts. He was led into the desert by the Spirit; he did great works by the Spirit; he offered himself to death by the eternal Spirit; he was raised from the dead by the Spirit; he was declared to be the Son of God by the Spirit of holiness on his resurrection: we too are led by the Spirit into and through this world's temptations; we, too, do our works of obedience by the Spirit; we die to sin, we rise again through righteousness, through the Spirit; and we are declared to be

God's sons—through our resurrection unto holiness in the Spirit. . . .

He is formed in us, born in us, suffers in us, rises again in us, lives in us; and this not by a succession of events but all at once: for he comes to us as a Spirit, all dying, all rising again, all living. We are ever receiving our birth, our justification, our renewal, ever dying to sin, rising to righteousness. His whole economy in all its parts is ever in us all at once; and this divine presence constitutes the title of each of us in heaven; this is what he will acknowledge and accept on the last day. He will acknowledge himself—his image in us—as though we reflected him and he, on looking round about, discerned at once who were his; those, namely, who gave back to him his image. He impresses us with the seal of the Spirit , in order to vouch that we are his. As the king's images appropriate the coin to him, so the likeness of Christ in us separates us from the world and assigns us over to the kingdom of heaven.

(PPS V:10)

Let us think much, and make much, of the grace of God; let us beware of receiving it in vain; let us pray God to prosper it in our hearts, that we may bring forth much fruit. We see how grace wrought in Saint Paul: it made him labor, suffer, and work righteousness almost above man's nature. This was not his own doing; it was not through his own power. He says himself: "Yet not I but the grace of God which was within me." It was its triumph in him, that it made him quite another man from what he was before. May God's grace be efficacious in us also. Let us aim at doing nothing in a dead way; let us beware of dead works, dead forms, dead professions. Let us pray to be filled with the spirit of love. Let us come to church joyfully; let us partake Holy Communion adoringly; let us pray sincerely; let us work cheerfully; let us suffer thankfully; let us throw our hearts in all we think, say and do; and may it be with a spiritual heart! This is to be a new creature in Christ; this is to walk by faith.

(*PPS* V:12)

It is the death of the eternal Word of God made flesh, which is our great lesson how to think and how to speak of this world. His cross has put its due value upon everything which we see, upon all fortunes, all advantages, all ranks, all dignities, all pleasures, upon the lust of the flesh, and the lust of the eyes and the pride of life. It has set a price upon the excitements, the rivalries, the hopes, the fears, the desires, the efforts, the triumphs of moral men. It has given a meaning to the various, shifting, course, the trials, the temptations, the sufferings of this earthly state. It has brought together and made consistent all that seems discordant and aimless. It has taught us how to live, how to use the world, what to expect, what to desire, what to hope. It is the tone into which all the strains of this world's music are ultimately to be resolved.

Look around, and see what the world presents of high and low. Go to the courts of princes. See the treasure and skill of all nations brought together to honor a child of man. Observe the prostration of the many before the few. Consider the form and ceremonial, the pomp, the state, the circumstance; and the vainglory. Do you wish to know the worth of it all? Look at the cross of Christ!

Go to the political world: see nation jealous of nation; trade rivaling trade; armies and fleets marching against each other. Survey the various ranks of the community, its parties and their contests, the striving of the ambitious, the intrigues of the crafty. What is the end of all this turmoil? Grace. What is the measure? The cross.

Go, again, to the world of intellect and science: consider the wonderful discoveries which the human mind is making, the variety of the arts to which its discoveries give rise, the all but miracles by which it shows its power; and, next, the pride and confidence of reason, and the absorbing devotion of thought to transitory objects, which is the consequence. Would you form a right judgment of all this? Look at the cross.

Again, look at misery, look at poverty, and destitution, look at oppression and captivity; go where food is scanty and lodging unhealthy. Consider pain and suffering, diseases long or violent, all that is frightful and revolting. Would you know how to rate all these? Gaze upon the cross.

Thus, in the cross, and him who hung upon it, all things meet, all things subserve it, all things need it. It is their center and their interpretation. For he was lifted up upon it, that he might draw all men and all things unto him.

(*PPS* VI:7)

When we feel that Christ's mysteries are too severe for us, and occasion us to doubt, let us earnestly wait on him for the gift of humility and love. Those who love and who are humble will apprehend them—carnal minds do not seek them, and proud minds are offended at them—but while love desires them, humility sustains them. Let us pray him then to give us such a real and living insight into the blessed doctrine of the Incarnation of the Son of God, of his birth of a virgin, his atoning death and resurrection, that we may desire that Holy Communion may be the effectual type of that gracious economy. No one realizes the mystery of the Incarnation but must feel disposed towards that of Holy Communion. Let us pray him to give us an earnest longing after him—a thirst for his presence—an anxiety to find him—a joy on hearing that he is to be found, even now, under the veil of sensible things—and of good hope that *we* shall find him there. They have their reward *in* believing; they enjoy the contemplation of a mysterious blessing, which does not even enter into the thoughts of others; and while they are more blessed than others, in the gift vouchsafed to them, they have the additional privilege of knowing, that they are vouchsafed it.

(*PPS* VI:11)

Christ is already in that place of peace, which is all in all. He is on the right hand of God. He is hidden in the brightness of the radiance which issues from the everlasting throne. He is in the very abyss of peace, where there is no voice of tumult or distress, but a deep stillness—stillness, that greatest and most awful of all goods which we can fancy—that most perfect of joys, the utter, profound, ineffable tranquillity of the divine essence. He has entered into his rest.

(*PPS* VI:16)

Let us not seek for signs and wonders; for clear or strong or compact or original arguments; but let us *believe*; evidence will come after faith as its reward, better than before it as its groundwork. Faith soars aloft; it listens for the notes of heaven, the faint voices or echoes which scarcely reach the earth, and it thinks them worth all the louder sounds of cities or schools of men. It is foolishness in the eyes of the world; but it is a foolishness of God wiser than the world's wisdom. Let us embrace the sacred mystery of the Trinity in Unity, which, as the creed tells us, is the ground of the Catholic religion. Let us think it enough, let us think it far too great a privilege, for sinners such as we are, for a fallen people in a degenerate age, to inherit the faith once delivered to the saints; let us accept it thankfully; let us guard it watchfully; let us transmit it faithfully to those who come after us.

(*PPS* VI:23; Newman's emphasis)

God is the God of peace and in giving us peace he does but give himself, he does but manifest himself to us; for his presence is peace. Hence our Lord, in the same discourse in which he promised his disciples peace, promised also, that "He would come and manifest himself to them" and "He and his Father would come to them and make their abode with them" (Jn 14:21–23). Peace is his everlasting state; in this world of space and time he has wrought and acted; but from everlasting it was not so. For six days he wrought and then he rested according to the rest which was his eternal state; yet not so rested, as not in one sense to "work hitherto" in mercy and judgment, toward the world which he had created. And more especially, when he sent his only-begotten Son into the world, and that most gracious and all-pitiful Son, our Lord, condescended to come to us, both he and his Father wrought with a mighty hand; and they vouchsafed the Holy Ghost, the Comforter, and he also wrought wonderfully, and works hitherto. Certainly the whole economy of redemption is a series of great and continued works; but still they all tend to rest and peace, as at the first. They began out of rest and end in rest.

(*PPS* VI:25)

Let us pray God to give us *all* graces; and while, in the first place, we pray that he would make us holy, really holy, let us also pray him to give us the *beauty* of holiness, which consists in tender and eager affection towards our Lord and Savior; which is, in the case of the Christian what beauty is to the outward man, so that through God's mercy our souls may have, not strength and health only, but a sort of bloom and comeliness, and that as we grow older in body we may, year by year, grow more youthful in spirit.

(*PPS* VII:10)

What does nature teach us about ourselves, even before opening the bible? That we are creatures of the great God, the

maker of heaven and earth; and, as his creatures, we are
bound to serve him and give him our hearts; in a word, to be
religious beings. And next, what is religion but a habit? And
what is a habit but a state of mind which is always upon us, as
a sort of ordinary dress or inseparable garment of the soul? A
man cannot really be religious one hour and not religious the
next. We might as well say he could be in good health one
hour, and in bad health the next. A man who is religious, is
religious morning, noon, and night; his religion is a certain
character, a mould in which his thoughts, words, and actions
are cast, all forming parts of one and the same whole. He sees
God in all things; every course of action he directs towards
those spiritual objects which God has revealed to him; every
occurrence of the day, every event, every person met with, all
news which he hears, he measures by the standard of God's
will. And a person who does this may be said almost literally
to pray without ceasing; for, knowing himself to be in God's
presence, he is continually led to address him reverently,
whom he sets always before him, in the inward language of
prayer and praise, of humble confession and joyful trust.

(*PPS* VII:15)

It is one great peculiarity of the Christian character to be
dependent. Men of the world, indeed, in proportion as they
are active and enterprising, boast of their independence, and
are proud of having obligations to no one. But it is the Christian's excellence to be diligent and watchful, to work and
persevere, and yet to be in spirit *dependent*; to be willing to
serve, and to rejoice in the permission to do so; to be content to
view one's self in a subordinate place; to love to sit in the dust.
Though in the Church a son of God, he takes pleasure in
considering himself Christ's "servant" and "slave"; he feels
glad whenever he can put himself to shame. So it is the
natural bent of his mind freely and affectionately to visit and

trace the footsteps of the saints, to sound the praises of the great of old who have wrought wonders in the Church and whose words still live; being jealous of their honor and feeling it to be even too great a privilege for such as he is to be put in trust with the faith once delivered to them, and following them strictly in the narrow way, even as they have followed Christ. To the ears of such persons the words of the text are as sweet as music: "Thus saith the Lord, stand ye in the ways and see and ask for the old paths, where is the good way, and walk therein and ye shall find rest for your souls" (Jer 6:16).

(*PPS* VII:18)

So natural is the connection between a reverential spirit in worshiping God and faith in God, that the wonder only is, how anyone can for a moment imagine he has faith in God and yet allow himself to be irreverent towards him? To believe in God, is to believe the being and the presence of one who is all-holy and all-powerful and all-gracious; how can one believe thus of him and yet make free with him? It is almost a contradiction in terms. Hence even heathen religions have ever considered faith and reverence identical. To believe and not to revere, to worship familiarly, and at one's ease, is an anomaly and a prodigy unknown even to false religion, to say nothing of the true one. Not only the Jewish and the Christian religions, which are directly from God, inculcate the spirit of "reverence and godly fear" but those other religions which have existed and which exist whether in the East or in the South, inculcate the same.

(*PPS* VIII:1)

Let us seek the grace of a cheerful heart, an even temper, sweetness, gentleness, and brightness of mind, as walking in his light and by his grace. Let us pray him to give us the spirit of ever-abundant, ever-springing, love, which overpowers and sweeps away the vexations of life by its own richness and strength, and which above all things unites us to him who is the fountain and the center of all mercy, loving kindness, and joy.

(PPS VIII:17)

To consider the world in its length and breadth, its various history, the many races of man, their starts, their fortunes, their mutual alienation, their conflicts, and then their ways, their habits, governments, forms of worship; their enterprises, their aimless courses, their random achievements, and acquirements, their impotent conclusion of long-standing facts, the tokens so faint and broken of a superintending design, the blind evolution of what turns out to be great powers or truths, the progress of things, as if from unreasoning elements, not toward final causes, the greatness and littleness of man, his far-reaching aims, his sort duration, the curtain hung over his futurity, the disappointment of life, the defeat of good, the success of evil, physical pain, mental anguish, the prevalence and intensity of sin, the pervading idolatries, the corruptions, the dreary hopeless irreligion, that condition of the whole race, so fearfully yet exactly described in the Apostle's words "having no hope and without God in the world"—all this is a division to dizzy and appal; and inflicts upon the mind the sense of a profound mystery which is beyond human solution.

What shall be said to this heart piercing, reason bewildering, fact? I can only answer that either there is no creator or this living society of men is in a true sense discarded from his presence. Did I see a boy of good make and mind, with the tokens on him of a refined nature, cast upon the world without provision, unable to say whence he came, his birth-place or his family connections; I should conclude that there was some mystery connected with his history and that he was one, of whom, from one cause or another, his parents were ashamed. Thus only should I be able to account for the contrast between the promise and the condition of his being. And so I argue about the world—*if* there be a God, *since* there is a God, the human race is implicated in some terrible aboriginal calamity. It is out of joint with the purposes of its creator. This is a fact, a fact as true as the fact of its existence; and thus the doctrine of what is theologically called original sin becomes to me as certain as that the world exists, and as the existence of God.

(*Apologia Pro Vita Sua*; Newman's emphasis)

Little is told us in Scripture concerning the Blessed Virgin, but there is one grace of which the evangelist makes her the pattern, in a few simple sentences of faith. Zacharias questioned the angel's message, but "Mary said, 'Behold the handmaid of the Lord; be it done unto me according to thy word.'" Accordingly, Elizabeth, speaking with an evident allusion to the contrast thus exhibited between her own highly-favored husband, righteous Zacharias, and the still more favored Mary, said, on receiving her salutation, "Blessed art thou among women and blessed is the fruit of thy womb; blessed is she that believed for there shall be a performance of those things which were told her from the Lord."

But Mary's faith did not end in a mere acquiescence in divine providence and revelations; as the text informs us, she "pondered" them. When the shepherds came and told of the vision of angels which they had seen at the time of the nativity, and how one of them announced that the infant in her arms was "the Savior which is Christ the Lord" while others did but wonder, "Mary kept all these things and pondered them in her heart." Again, when her Son and Savior had come to the age of twelve years, and had left her for a while in his Father's service, and had been found, to her surprise, in the temple, amid the doctors, both hearing them and asking them questions, and had, on her addressing him, vouchsafed to justify his conduct, we are told "His mother kept all these things in her heart." And, accordingly, at the marriage feast at Cana, her faith anticipated his first miracle, and she said to the servants, "Whatsoever he says to you, do it."

Thus Saint Mary is our pattern of faith, both in the reception and in the study of divine truth. She does not think it enough to accept, she dwells on it; not enough to assent, she develops it; not enough to submit to reason; she reasons on it; not indeed reasoning first and believing afterwards, with Zacharias, yet first believing without reasoning, next from love and reverence, reasoning after believing. And thus she symbolizes to us, not only faith of the unlearned but of the doctors of the Church also, who have to investigate and weigh and define, as well as to profess the gospel; to draw the line between faith and heresy; to anticipate or remedy the various aberrations of wrong reason; to combat pride and recklessness with their own arms; and thus to triumph over the sophist and the innovator.

(Sermon XV from *University Sermons*)

Devotions to the Saints

On Saint Philip Neri

He lived in an age as traitorous to the interests of Catholicism as any that preceded it, or can follow it. He lived at a time when pride mounted high, and the senses rule; a time when kings and nobles never had more of state and homage, and never less of personal responsibility and peril; when medieval winter was receding and the summer sun of civilization was bringing into leaf and flower a thousand forms of luxurious enjoyment; when a new world of thought and beauty had opened upon the human mind, in the discovery of the treasures of classic literature and art. He saw the great and the gifted, dazzled by the enchantress, and drinking in the magic of her song; he saw the high and the wise, the student and the artist, painting and poetry and sculpture and music and architecture, drawn within her range, and circling round the abyss; he saw heathen forms mounting thence and forming in the thick air: all this, he saw, and he perceived that the mischief must be met, not with argument, not with science, not with protests and warnings, not by the recluse or the preacher, but by the great counter-fascination of purity and truth. He was raised up to do a work almost peculiar in the Church—not to be a Jerome, Savonarola, though Philip had a true devotion toward him and tender memory of his Florentine house; not to be a Saint Charles, though in his beaming countenance

Philip had recognized the aureole of a saint; not to be a Saint Ignatius, wrestling with the foe, though Philip was termed the Society's bell of call, so many subjects did he send to it; not to be a Saint Francis Xavier, though Philip had long to shed his blood for Christ in India with him; not to be a Saint Cajetan, or hunter of souls, for Philip preferred, as he expressed it, tranquilly to cast his net to gain them; he preferred to yield to the stream, and direct the current, which he could not stop, of science, literature, art and fashion, and to sweeten and sanctify what God had made very good and man had spoilt.

And so he contemplated as the idea of his mission, not the propagation of the faith, nor the exposition of doctrine, not the catechetical schools; whatever was exact and systematic pleased him not; he put from him monastic rule and authoritative speech, as David refused the armor of the king. No; he would be but an individual ordinary priest as others; and his weapons should be but unaffected humility and unpretending love. All he did was to be done by the light, and fervor, and convincing eloquence of his personal character and his easy conversation. He came to the eternal city and he sat down there and his home and his family gradually grew up around him, by the spontaneous accession of materials from without. He did not so much seek his own as drew them to him. He sat in his small room, and they in their gay worldly dresses, the rich and the wellborn, as well as the simple and the illiterate, crowded into it. It the mid-heats of summer, in the frosts of winter, still was he in that low and narrow cell at San Girolamo, reading the hearts of those who came to him and curing their souls' maladies by the very touch of his hand. It was a vision of the Magi worshiping the infant Savior, so pure and innocent, so sweet and beautiful was he; and so loyal and dear to the gracious Virgin Mother. And they who came remained gazing and listening, till at length, first one and then another threw off their bravery and took his poor cassock and girdle instead; or, if they kept it, it was to put haircloth under it or to take on them a rule of life, while to the world they looked as before.

In the words of his biographer, "He was all things. He suited himself to noble and ignoble, young and old, subjects and prelates, learned and ignorant; and received those who were strangers to him with singular benignity, and embraced them with as much love and charity as if he had been a long while expecting them. When called upon to be merry he was so; if there was a demand upon his sympathy he was equally ready. He gave the same welcome to all: caressing the poor equally with the rich and wearying himself to assist all to the utmost of his power. In consequence of his being so accessible and willing to receive all comers, many went to him every day and some continued for a space of thirty, nay, forty years to visit him both morning and evening, so that his room went by the agreeable nickname of the home of Christian mirth. Nay, people came to him not only from all parts of Italy, but from France, Spain, Germany, and Christendom, and even the infidels and Jews who had never any communication with him revered him as a holy man." [Bacci's *Life of St. Philp Neri*, translated by Frederick Faber.]

The first families of Rome, the Massimi, the Aldobrandini, the Colonnas, the Altieri, the Vitelleschi, were his friends and penitents. Nobles of Poland, Grandees of Spain, Knights of Malta, could not leave Rome without coming to him. Cardinals, archbishops, and bishops were his intimates; Federigo Borromeo haunted his room and got the name of "Father Philip's soul." The cardinal archbishops of Verona and Bologna wrote books in his honor; Pope Pius IV died in his arms. Lawyers, painters, musicians, physicians, it is the same too with them. Baronius, Zazzara, and Ricci left the law at his bidding and joined his congregation, to do its work, to write the annals of the Church, and to die in the odor of sanctity. Palestrina had Father Philip's ministrations in his last moments. Animuccia hung about him during life, sent him a message after death, and was conducted by him, through purgatory to heaven. And who was he, I say, all the whole, but a humble priest, a stranger in Rome, with no distinctions of family or letters, no claim of station or of office, great simply in the attraction with which a divine power had gifted him? And yet thus humble, thus unenobled, thus empty-handed, he has achieved the glorious title of Apostle of Rome.

(From Discourse IX in *The Idea of a University*)

A Prayer to Saint Philip

My dear and holy patron, Philip, I put myself into thy hands and for the love of Jesus, for that love's sake, which chose thee and made thee a saint, I implore thee to pray for me, that, as he has brought thee to heaven, so in due time he may take me to heaven also.

And I ask of thee especially to gain for me a true devotion such as you had to the Holy Ghost, the Third Person in the ever blessed Trinity; that, as he at Pentecost so miraculously filled thy heart with his grace, I too may in my measure have the gifts necessary for my salvation.

Therefore, I ask thee to gain for me those his seven great gifts, to dispose and excite my heart towards faith and virtue.

Beg for me the gift of wisdom, that I may prefer heaven to earth, and know truth from falsehood;

The gift of understanding by which I may have imprinted on my mind the mysteries of his Word;

The gift of counsel, that I may see my way in all perplexities;

The gift of fortitude, that with bravery and stubbornness I may battle with my foe;

The gift of knowledge, to enable me to direct all my doings with a pure intention to the glory of God;

The gift of religion, to make me devout and conscientious;

And the gift of holy fear to make me feel awe, reverence, and sobriety amid all my spiritual blessings.

Sweetest Father, flower of purity, martyr of charity . . . pray for me.

(One of four prayers composed for an unfinished
novena in honor of the saint)

From the Litany of Saint Philip

R/ Pray for us.

Saint Philip, *R/*
Vessel of the Holy Ghost, *R/*
Child of Mary, *R/*
Apostle of Rome, *R/*
Counselor of popes, *R/*
Voice of prophecy, *R/*
Man of primitive times, *R/*
Winning saint, *R/*
Hidden hero, *R/*
Sweetest of fathers, *R/*
Flower of purity, *R/*
Martyr of charity, *R/*
Heart of fire, *R/*
Discerner of spirits, *R/*
Choicest of priests, *R/*
Mirror of the divine life, *R/*
Pattern of humility, *R/*
Example of simplicity, *R/*
Light of holy joy, *R/*
Image of childhood, *R/*
Director of souls, *R/*
Gentle guide of youth, *R/*
Patron of thy own, *R/*
Who did observe chastity in thy youth, *R/*

Who did seek Rome by divine guidance, R/
Who did hide so long in the catacombs, R/
Who did receive the Holy Ghost in thy heart, R/
Who did experience such wonderful ecstasies, R/
Who did so lovingly serve the little ones, R/
Who did wash the feet of pilgrims, R/
Who did ardently thirst after martyrdom, R/
Who did distribute daily the word of God, R/
Who did turn so many hearts to God, R/
Who did converse so sweetly with Mary, R/
Who did raise the dead, R/
Who did set thy houses in all lands, R/

Let us pray.

O God, who has exalted blessed Philip, thy confessor, in the glory of thy saints, grant, that as we rejoice in his commemoration, so may we profit by the example of his virtues, through Christ our Lord. Amen.

Chronology

1801   Newman is born in London.

1817   He enters Oxford.

1822   Elected Fellow of Oriel College.

1824   He is ordained a deacon in the Church of England.

1825   He is ordained a priest in the Church of England.

1827   He is appointed a tutor at Oxford's Oriel College.

1828   He becomes vicar of Saint Mary's Church in Oxford with additional responsibility for the chaplaincy of the village of Littlemore.

1832   Neman is named select preacher to the university. The fifteen sermons he ends up preaching become the *University Sermons*.

Newman becomes ill while visiting Sicily. He becomes convinced that he will do important work for England. During his voyage home he writes, "Lead, Kindly Light."

1833–41 Newman becomes a central figure in the Oxford Movement.

1837   *Lectures on the Prophetical Office of the Church.*

1838   *Lectures on Justification.*

1841   *Tract 90.*

1842   Newman retires with a group of friends to Littlemore. They set up a quasi-monastic community.

1844   *An Essay on the Development of Christian Doctrine.*

1845   Newman is received into the Catholic Church on 9 October by Italian Passionist, missionary priest, Domenico Barberi.

1846   He is ordained a Catholic priest.

1847   He settles into and oratorian house outside Birmingham, England.

1851   Newman loses unfair libel suit brought by an ex-Domenican.

1852   Lectures in Dublin on the idea of a university.

1864   Writes the *Apologia Pro Vita Sua.*

1870   Writes *A Grammar of Assent.*

1875   *Letter to the Duke of Norfolk.*

1877   Newman is made an honorable fellow at Trinity College in Oxford.

1879   Newman is raised to the college of cardinals and given the name cardinal deacon of the Roman Church of San Giorgio in Velabro.

1890   Newman dies on 11 August at the Oratory near Birmingham.

1991   Newman is declared venerable, the first step in the canonization process.

Select Bibliography

The edition of Newman's works published early in the twentieth century is long out of print but many of the volumes have been reprinted in various editions since his work is now in the common domain. The books listed in the bibliography below are among those which have been consulted for this anthology. The University of Notre Dame Press, in conjunction with the Birmingham Oratorians, is attempting to reissue all of the works of Newman; to date four volumes have been published: *Lectures on the Present State of Catholics in England; Sermon Notes of John Henry Newman: 1849–1878; Rise and Progress of Universities and Benedictine Essays; The Arians of the Fourth Century.*

Blehl, Vincent, ed. *Cardinal Newman's Best Plain Sermons.* New York: Herder, 1967.

_____. *A Newman Reader.* New York: Mentor, 1958.

_____. *The White Stone: The Spiritual Theology of John Henry Newman.* Petersham: St. Bede, 1994.

_____. *Pilgrim Journey: John Henry Newman 1801–1845.* New York: Paulist Press, 2001.

Bouyer, Louis. *Newman: His Life and Spirituality.* New York: Kenedy, 1958.

Boyce, Philip, ed. *Mary: The Virgin Mary in the Life and Writings of John Henry Newman.* Grand Rapids: Eerdmans, 2002.

Chadwick, Owen. *Newman.* New York: Oxford University Press, 1983.

Dean, Kevin, ed. *Straight from the Heart: Thoughts of John Henry Newman.* Chicago: Thomas More Press, 1990.

Dessain, C. S. *John Henry Newman.* London: Nelson, 1966.

_____. *The Spirituality of John Henry Newman.* Minneapolis: Fortress, 1977.

Gilley, Sheridan. *Newman and His Age.* London: Darton, Longman and Todd, 1990.

Graef, Hilda. *God and Myself: The Spirituality of John Henry Newman.* New York: Hawthorne, 1968.

Honore, Jean. *The Spiritual Journey of Newman.* New York: Alba House, 1992.

Ker, Ian. *John Henry Newman: A Biography.* Oxford: Clarendon, 1988.

_____. *Newman on Being a Christian.* Notre Dame: University of Notre Dame Press, 1990.

_____. *The Achievement of John Henry Newman.* Notre Dame: University of Notre Dame Press, 1990.

_____, ed. *Newman the Theologian: A Reader.* Notre Dame: University of Notre Dame Press, 1990.

_____. *John Henry Newman: Selected Sermons.* New York: Paulist, 1994.

Martin, Brian. *John Henry Newman: His Life and Works.* New York: Paulist, 1990.

Middleton R. D. *Newman at Oxford: His Religious Development.* New York: Oxford University Press, 1950.

Newman, John H. *Apologia Pro Vita Sua.* Edited by David DeLaura. New York: Norton, 1968.

_____. *Fifteen Sermons Preached Before the University.* Notre Dame: University of Notre Dame Press, 1997.

_____. *Parochial and Plain Sermons.* San Francisco: Ignatius, 1997.

_____. *Prayers, Verses, and Devotions.* San Francisco: Ignatius, 2000.

_____. *The Idea of a University.* Notre Dame: University of Notre Dame Press, 1982.

Newsome, David. *The Convert Cardinals: John Henry Newman and Henry Edward Manning.* London: John Murray, 1993.

O'Connell, D., ed. *Heart to Heart: A Cardinal Newman Prayerbook.* New York: America, 1938. Reprinted by same press as *Kindly Light* in 1940.

O'Connell, Marvin. *The Oxford Conspirators:* 1833-1845 (New York: Macmillan, 1969)

Schmidt, Richard. *Glorious Companions: Five Centuries of Anglican Spirituality.* Grand Rapids: Eerdmans, 2002.

Stephen, Thomas. *Newman and Heresy.* New York: Cambridge University Press, 1991.

Thornton, John and S. Varenne, eds. *Selected Sermons, Prayers and Devotions of John Henry Newman.* New York: Vintage Spiritual Classics, 1990.

Strange, Roderick. *Newman and the Gospel of Christ.* New York: Oxford, 1981.

Trevor, Meriol. *Newman: Light in Winter.* Garden City: Doubleday, 1962.

_____. *Newman: The Pillar in the Cloud.* Garden City: Doubleday, 1962.

Van den Barselaar, Zeno. *Newman: His Inner Life.* San Francisco: Ignatius, 1987.

Ward, Maisie. *Young Mister Newman,* London and New York: Sheed & Ward, 1950.

Ward, Wilfred. *The Life of John Henry Cardinal Newman.* 2 vols. London: Longman, 1912.

Weathersby, Harold. *Cardinal Newman in His Age.* Nashville: Vanderbilt University Press, 1973.

Wilson, A. N. *John Henry Newman: Prayers-Poems-Meditations.* New York: Crossroad, 1990.

Withey, Donald. *John Henry Newman: The Liturgy and the Breviary.* Kansas City: Sheed & Ward, 1992.

University Sermons

"night prayer 56